I0867749

CAVALIERS and ECONOMISTS

SOUTHERN LITERARY STUDIES

Scott Romine, *Series Editor*

CAVALIERS and ECONOMISTS

Global Capitalism *and the* Development *of* Southern Literature, 1820–1860

Katharine A. Burnett

Louisiana State University Press Baton Rouge

Published by Louisiana State University Press
Copyright © 2019 by Louisiana State University Press
All rights reserved
Manufactured in the United States of America
First printing

Designer: Barbara Neely Bourgoyne
Typeface: Sentinel
Printer and binder: Sheridan Books

An earlier version of chapter 4 was first published in *College Literature* 42.4 (2015): 619–47. Copyright © Johns Hopkins University Press and West Chester University. Reprinted with permission of Johns Hopkins University Press. An earlier version of chapter 2 originally appeared in *PMLA* 131.1 (2016): 162–66, published by the Modern Language Association of America.

Library of Congress Cataloging-in-Publication Data
Names: Burnett, Katharine A., 1983– author.
Title: Cavaliers and economists : global capitalism and the development of southern literature, 1820–1860 / Katharine A. Burnett.
Other titles: Southern literary studies.
Description: Baton Rouge : Louisiana State University Press, [2019] | Series: Southern literary studies | Includes bibliographical references and index.
Identifiers: LCCN 2018050923 | ISBN 978-0-8071-6930-8 (cloth : alk. paper) | ISBN 978-0-8071-6931-5 (pdf) | ISBN 978-0-8071-7162-2 (epub)
Subjects: LCSH: American fiction—Southern States—19th century—History and criticism. | Slave narratives—Southern States—History and criticism.
Classification: LCC PS261 .B86 2019 | DDC 810.9/975—dc23
LC record available at https://lccn.loc.gov/2018050923

The paper in this book meets the guidelines for permanence and durability of the Committee on Production Guidelines for Book Longevity of the Council on Library Resources. ♾

In memory of Glenn and Corinne Burnett,
who would have read it cover to cover

and

To Mary, Buddy, and Patrick Burnett,
who were there for it all

and

To Todd,
always

CONTENTS

ACKNOWLEDGMENTS

The acknowledgments page is something that every writer thinks about while completing a project, yet when it comes time to compose it, the task seems impossible. However, I'll try my best.

First, I have to recognize two scholars whose help was essential. My good friend and colleague John Stromski read the entire manuscript multiple times, in multiple (often very rough) forms. I would not have been able to complete the manuscript without his feedback and insight or without our almost weekly meetings over the past few years. The book is better because of him. Matthew Raese read the manuscript in its nascent form, and without these early conversations and suggestions, the ideas for the eventual book would not have come to fruition.

I owe an enormous debt of gratitude to my professors and mentors in the English program at the University of Tennessee, Knoxville (UTK). Thomas Haddox helped guide my thinking about the work from the very earliest stages. His support, guidance, and willingness to challenge me have made me a better scholar. I also cannot come up with enough words to thank the professors and academic mentors who never hesitated to give their time and expertise. Bill Hardwig never flinched, no matter how many times I haunted his office door for advice and counsel, and Nancy Henry will always be a professional icon and friend. Working with Dawn Coleman, Martin Griffin, and Katy Chiles was formative to me as an instructor and a researcher, and I will always look to them as personal and professional models. I am also grateful for the support and guidance I received from Stephen V. Ash in the Department of History and Michael Lofaro in the Department of English. And finally, I received feedback and intellectual support from the scholarly community at UTK, including members of the Americanist and C19 Reading Groups, who read very early drafts of the manuscript: Kat Powell, Ben Lee, Gerard Cohen-Vrignaud, Misty Gale Anderson, Andrew Lallier, Amy Billone, Mary Papke, and Amy Elias.

The ideas for the book were first generated in my courses and graduate work in the University of Mississippi Department of English and the Center for the Study of Southern Culture. Many thanks to Katie McKee, Jay Watson, Jaime Harker, Ethel Young-Scurlock, and Anne Goodwyn-Jones for creating courses and conversations that made me want to be a scholar.

I also must acknowledge my friends and colleagues at Fisk University: Lean'tin Bracks, Holly Tipton Hamby, PC Fleming, Jessie Carney Smith, Princilla Evans Morris, Leslie Collins, Nancy Rasico, Ana Rueda-Garcia, Dani Smith, David Popkin, Reavis Mitchell, Linda Wynn, and James Quirin. Thank you for always providing insight and suggestions, and for encouraging my research. And I cannot say enough positive things about my students at Fisk. Whether they knew it or not, working with them made this project possible. I feel lucky to be part of the Fisk family.

There are many individuals who have lent their time and talent in less tangible ways over the years, whether it was in a classroom or on a conference panel or over dinner and a drink. So many thanks to Pip Gordon, Melanie Anderson, Neil Norman, Monica Miller, Todd Hagestette, John Miller, Amy King, Ellie Campbell, Jill Anderson, and Lisa Kammerud. I also have to extend a huge thank-you to my colleagues and students at Graceland University. And of course, so much love to friends and former roommates Kim Huinker and Jessica Kersey.

This project has been supported by an Andrew W. Mellon / American Council of Learned Societies Dissertation Completion Fellowship (2012–13), as well as a University of Tennessee, Knoxville, Humanities Center Fellowship (2012–13). The research would not have been possible without the resources and help of the special collections and libraries at Vanderbilt University; the University of Tennessee, Knoxville; the University of Mississippi; the American Antiquarian Society; and the University of Alabama.

The entire staff at Louisiana State University Press has made the process as painless as possible. Many thanks to James Long for his patience and thoroughness as an editor along every step of the way. Enormous thanks to the series editor, Scott Romine, and my reader, Coleman Hutchison, for their feedback on drafts and revisions. Their input elevated the manuscript, and I am grateful for it.

I must also thank my family—Mary, Buddy, and Patrick Burnett—who have always been supportive. Thank you for enduring the weirdness of academia and of a daughter and sister who launches into historical diatribes at the dinner table and can't seem to put down the book for two seconds to have a normal interaction. You never wavered in your encouragement and love, and for that I'm always thankful.

And most of all, I am grateful to Todd Ridley. I couldn't have done it without you.

CAVALIERS and ECONOMISTS

INTRODUCTION

Two Souths

To make the horrific acceptable: that was the primary motivation for early southern literature. Slavery was integral to the South before the Civil War, and the region relied on the exploitation of human beings for its existence and prosperity. The creative class in the South thus devoted itself to justifying the existence of slavery. How they did so—and how southern literature developed in conjunction with that impulse—is the central question of this book, which I will explore through the popular fiction of the era.

Fiction, and other forms of artistic representation, allowed upper-class white southerners to create an idea that slavery and the plantation system were not, at heart, completely immoral. It also allowed those who benefited from these systems to create a version of the South that portrayed itself as a progressive and dynamic part of a rapidly changing global society. An illustration dated around 1860, "Southern Planter and Scenes from the South," exemplifies these two interrelated ideas (fig. 1). It presents the iconography typically associated with the antebellum South: pastoral, agrarian images dominate the foreground, spearheaded by the representative figure of the "Old South," the gentleman planter dressed in dandified finery, leisurely sitting on a cotton bale to smoke a cigar. And not surprisingly, there are the flowering cotton bolls, the center of the early-nineteenth-century transatlantic economy, which dwarf almost everything else in the illustration.[1]

Fig. 1. "Southern Planter and Scenes from the South," ca. 1860. The Library Company of Philadelphia.

The background, however, represents a very different version of southern society. A steamboat is docked at a river port, waiting to load passengers and cargo, while a factory chugs in the background, smoke pouring out of its stacks. The images evoke the broader economic connections at work in the nineteenth-century South: interregional and international trade that emerged concurrently with growing industrialization in the northern United States and Europe, primarily Britain. This is the reason the gentleman planter is growing the cotton and the reason why the cotton bales exist: to be sold and transported throughout the United States and across the Atlantic.

But in the middle of it all are enslaved laborers working in the cotton fields, collecting smaller versions of the bolls in the foreground. In contrast to the cotton, gentleman planter, factory, and steamboat, they are tiny, almost nonexistent. As if far away, their bodies (notably well dressed and well covered) blend into the expanse of the cotton field. Their labor is the driving force of everything present in the illustration, yet they are eclipsed by the dominant images, erased by the formal elements that balance foreground with background.

"Southern Planter" is an example of how antebellum white southerners—the majority of whom were proslavery—attempted to represent the South in a way that reconciled a set of seemingly incompatible ideologies. By effecting a balance between pastoral and international, modern and antimodern, southerners diminished the actual violence of the society and economic system under a new, fictional version of the South that could account for the dual representations without having to acknowledge that southern society was built upon the deprivation of basic human rights to untold numbers of men, women, and children. In her analysis of popular representations of the South, Tara McPherson calls this reframing of the region a form of "lenticular logic," wherein two separate images shape a representation that, when viewed a certain way, "allows the viewer to see only one of the two views at a time" (25–26). When applied to representations of the South, lenticular logic enables the convenient forgetting or erasure of certain aspects of the region in favor of the more positive, easily marketable version.

A "lenticular" framework presupposes that although the two ideas of the South are contained in one image, they are nonetheless distinct and separate: if one view is visible, the other must be suppressed. Here it implies that, as Toni Morrison argues in *Playing in the Dark* (1992), slavery and race are always a "haunting" presence in American literature and U.S. literary history, a shadowy and violent entity hovering in the background. But what if slavery wasn't simply erased and suppressed in regional representations? What if, as Robert Levine puts it, slavery was "right there out in the open as a primary concern of nineteenth-century American literary culture?" (*Race, Transnationalism* 14). In the case of the antebellum South, the two views are always visible in a single representation. The region was connected to global trade and capitalist economic practices while at the same time being reliant on the structure of the plantation, the supposed agrarian pastoral, to maintain that economy. Southern authors—who often participated in these economies as slave owners, migrants to new territories, and businesspeople—evinced a clear awareness of that duality in their writings.

As a result, the logic of antebellum southern literature is not lenticular but bifocal, an attempt to balance and justify both visions at once through modern economic language, rather than to erase it or distract from it. That balance is attempted in "Southern Planter" through visual art, wherein the formal elements of the illustration allow for a composition that represents a multiplicity but comes together as a whole. The effort is evident much more consistently in fiction of the era. This blending of industrial and global features of the southern economy with rural and regional ones was the driving force behind most of the representations of the South at the time—especially the imaginative writing and fiction authored by southerners themselves.

This study is a history of southern literary development as it occurred in tandem with economic modernization—not in spite of it, as popular conception would have it. It is a common claim to say that southern literature began as a reactionary defense of slavery during the antebellum period. Yet when considering the region's primacy in the nineteenth-century global market, southern literature actually developed in response to shifts in an emerging capitalist system and used those shifts to rationalize slavery and southern society as it existed. Upholding the ideologies of modern capitalism gave southerners the perfect framework to create a society, through fiction, that was modern and progressive yet retained older social structures. In this way the obvious moral wrong and violence of slavery could be relegated to the middle ground in representations of the South, where it would remain for decades.

The antebellum South circulated in popular imagination, then, was always a constructed idea, whose end was self-preservation and perpetuating a system that benefited those in power. But how does literature contribute to and even create a set of cultural markers about a space and society? This question is particularly relevant in the formative moment of southern culture, one in which dramatic economic changes would force southerners to consider the region's role in the nineteenth-century global world and would define a social subset for decades thereafter. The emergence of southern literature as a distinct movement occurred in reaction to the global economy and the growing importance of U.S. slavery. In their works southern authors adapted modern economic theories to justify the continued existence of the slave system and create representations of the region in which liberal capitalism could coexist with the socially regressive sites of the antebellum plantation.

The Antebellum Southern Economy: "Capitalism with Its Clothes Off"

Capitalism, as it is usually defined, arose at the end of the eighteenth century in conjunction with the Industrial Revolution. "When we think of capitalism," Sven Beckert points out in *Empire of Cotton* (2014), "we think of wage workers, yet this prior phase of capitalism was based not on free labor but on slavery" (xvi). The U.S. South was at the forefront of this early phase of modern capitalism; the plantations that stretched across the southern United States were the key suppliers for cotton mills and factories in Europe and the North. In *The Black Atlantic* (1993), Paul Gilroy calls the structure of the plantation "capitalism with its clothes off," in which slavery becomes the most basic, unadulterated version of economic exploitation. Therefore, according to Beckert, "we associate industrial capitalism with contracts and markets, but early capitalism was based as often as not on violence and bodily coercion" (xvi).

Taking up this sort of characterization, historians Walter Johnson and Edward Baptist outline the integral role of the southern slave system to the growth of the U.S. economy more generally. In *River of Dark Dreams* (2013), Johnson argues that "the standard-issue milestones of nineteenth-century U.S. economic history locate the story of leading-sector development in the mills of Massachusetts" (6). "But," he continues, "if one sets aside the threadbare story of 'industrialization' for a moment," we find that the true economic innovations were taking place in the Mississippi Valley—on the river and the plantations that dotted its banks (Johnson 6). Baptist puts it very simply in *The Half Has Never Been Told* (2014): "Slavery's expansion shaped every crucial aspect of the economy and politics of the new nation" (xxi)—indeed, of the modernizing nineteenth-century world.

Southerners were keenly aware of the region's role in the global economy. A direct example of this intellectual trend—and a constant presence throughout this book—is the *Commercial Review of the South and West,* more commonly known as *De Bow's Review,* a periodical published and edited by southerner and journalist James D. B. De Bow. The journal ran from 1846 until 1880, and at the start of the Civil War the *Review* was circulated nationally.[2] De Bow, a supporter of slavery, was also an advocate for industrialization, global trade, and technological innovation. In articles that included topics such as "Commercial Jurisprudence" (January 1847); "The Progress of Southern Industry" (June 1850); "The Negro Race" (April 1855); and "Inalienability of Slaves" (August 1857), De Bow addresses all aspects of the southern economy—including its role as a modern, capitalist system and the importance of slavery to that system.

Recognizing the region's role in the modern economy was crucial to proslavery southerners' moral and rational justifications for slavery in their writings. Many southern intellectuals and authors, De Bow included, drew their philosophies from classical European economic theory of the eighteenth and early nineteenth centuries, including the work of Adam Smith, John Locke, and Thomas Malthus.[3] As such, De Bow and most white southerners upheld the basic principles of "liberal capitalism," or a system in which, theoretically, social and political freedom is inherently tied to economic freedom. In turn, liberal capitalist theories promote a form of laissez-faire economics driven by free markets and private property, as articulated by Adam Smith in *The Wealth of Nations* (1776). According to historian Laurence Shore, Smith's theories became "public grammar" by the nineteenth century, and "his book built the ideological foundation of political economy" (5).

Above all, in a liberal capitalist ideology, the free market is the governing force of economic and social change. Those who uphold these philosophies also adhere to a fundamental belief in the egalitarian nature of the market and the importance of the individual in it. Again, theoretically, if an individual can access the free market, then he or she—in the case of the antebellum South, it was almost always a man—can profit and thereby advance economically *and* socially, regardless of one's original standing. Liberal capitalism, in short, is the underlying philosophy at the heart of the American dream defined by self-sufficient socioeconomic mobility. In terms of the southern economy, the act of establishing a plantation required that the system and those participating in it be invested in individual opportunism in an open field of competition. If a man wanted to establish his own plantation and become wealthy in the southern United States, all he had to do was obtain some land and cultivate it through hard work. Once an individual capitalized on that industry, then he could sell his crops on a free market and make a profit from his labors.

In subscribing to this basic conception of then-modern economic philosophy, James De Bow represents a dominant trend in southern thought during the antebellum period, particularly on the part of those who supported the continuance of slavery (which was most white southerners). The articles published in *De Bow's Review* are a blend of reprinted works by British authors and economists as well as original essays by southern authors in which the tables of contents play out the transatlantic cross-currents of economic philosophy. The cover page of the journal itself manifests a similar awareness of industrial development and of the influence of British political philosophers and economists (fig. 2). As with the 1860 "Southern Planter" illustration, figures of slaves in the foreground blend with images of international commerce in the background, while the quotation from the British philosopher Thomas Carlyle, "Commerce is king!" indicates the journal's focus on global economic trends.

Yet the existence of slavery—and its essential role in the modern southern economy—raised an obvious moral and logical conflict with the liberal capitalist theories championed by southerners. Embracing the philosophies of liberal capitalism meant also embracing its fundamental tenets—individual freedom and free labor—which could not be universal in an economy reliant on the enslavement of a large portion of the population. It was the labor of slaves, not the labor of white, self-supporting individuals, that fueled a large, prosperous plantation. Dubbing the phenomenon the "Adam Smith problem," Laurence Shore writes: "Herein lay a vital point of danger to the South: the slaveholder could not be an ideal economic man. He would keep himself and his society wedded to a condition of economic and social backwardness" (8). The self-sufficient, upwardly mobile white plantation owner—who earned his socioeconomic success by dint of his own hard work and efforts—never existed and never would exist in the antebellum South conceived by proslavery advocates.

But proslavery southerners' ideological conflict went beyond economic philosophy and the Adam Smith problem—their espousal of liberal capitalist theories also revealed an inherent problem with the structure of southern society itself. That "problem" was slavery. If a society champions an economic system that purports to distribute wealth in an egalitarian manner in a free market and allows for socioeconomic mobility, how do its members justify the practice of enslaving individuals, robbing them of

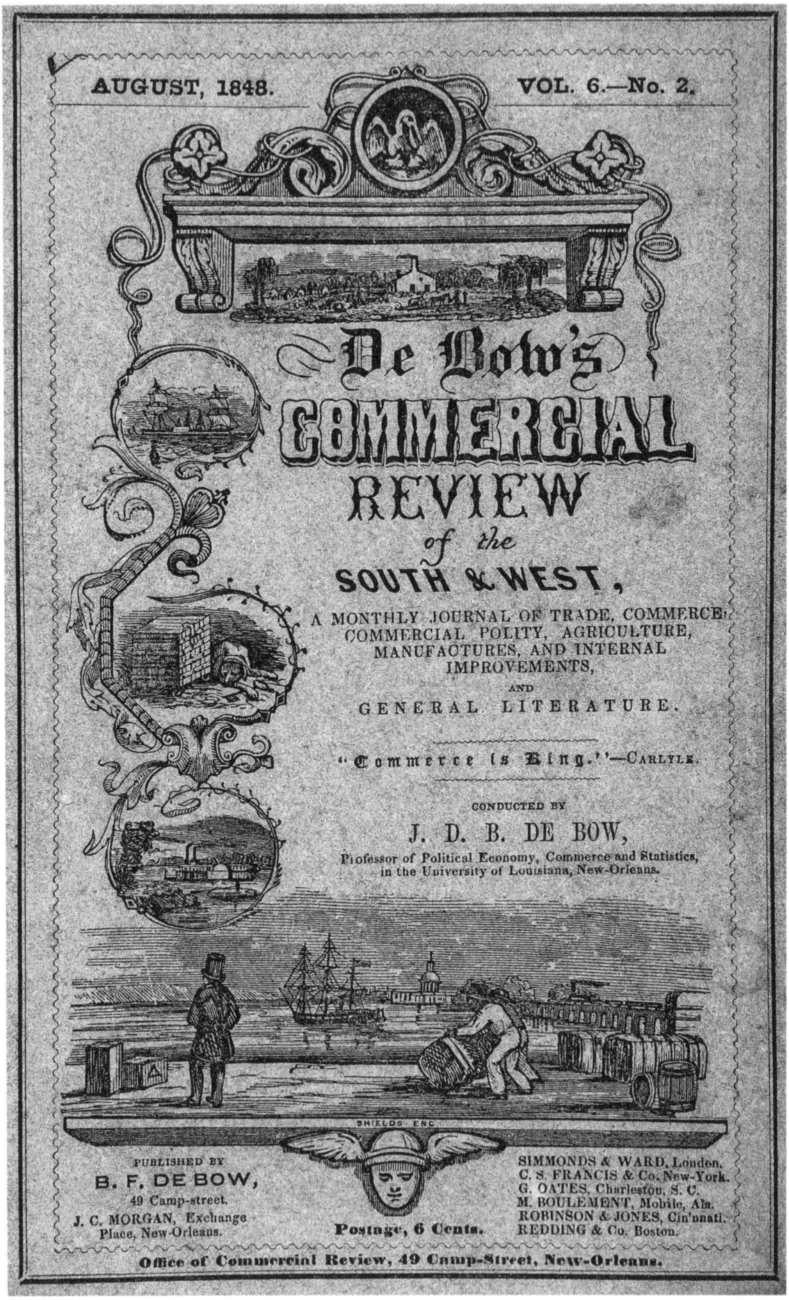
AUGUST, 1848.

VOL. 6.—No. 2.

De Bow's

COMMERCIAL

REVIEW

of the

SOUTH & WEST,

A MONTHLY JOURNAL OF TRADE, COMMERCE, COMMERCIAL POLITY, AGRICULTURE, MANUFACTURES, AND INTERNAL IMPROVEMENTS,

AND

GENERAL LITERATURE.

"Commerce is King."—CARLYLE.

CONDUCTED BY

J. D. B. DE BOW,

Professor of Political Economy, Commerce and Statistics, in the University of Louisiana, New-Orleans.

SHIELDS ENG

PUBLISHED BY

B. F. DE BOW,

49 Camp-street.

J. C. MORGAN, Exchange Place, New-Orleans.

Postage, 6 Cents.

SIMMONDS & WARD, London.
C. S. FRANCIS & Co. New-York.
G. OATES, Charleston, S. C.
M. BOULEMENT, Mobile, Ala.
ROBINSON & JONES, Cin'nnati.
REDDING & Co. Boston.

Office of Commercial Review, 49 Camp-Street, New-Orleans.

Fig. 2. Cover of *De Bow's Review,* Aug. 1848. Courtesy American Antiquarian Society.

their lives and labor, and then openly profiting from it—all without exerting any actual labor themselves? Even if enslaved laborers were not considered human beings, much less individuals, according to the prevailing biological theories on race—which most proslavery advocates espoused—southerners still had to contend with the regressive social and economic practices perpetuated by slavery that affected all levels of southern society.[4] As historian Eugene Genovese puts it, "In this case the tensions, ambiguities, and quarrels [in the antebellum South] had a special root and quality that derived from a need to reconcile slavery with both freedom and progress" (27).[5] On these terms, economic development and modernization promoted by liberal capitalism do not always translate into the form of liberalism that facilitates universal access to economic mobility and social progress, at least not in the slaveholding South.

The task for southerners representing and advocating for the interests of the region during this formative moment was to marry the ideologies of liberal capitalism and the global free market with the precapitalist, conservative social organization that defined the plantation system. Then, through that merger, it was imperative to integrate the existence of slavery in such a way that mitigated its violence and rationalized its central role in the antebellum South. In other words, representations of the South by proslavery southerners had to conceive of the "two" Souths as parts of an integrated whole and, in doing so, de-emphasize the clear human rights violations perpetrated in the slave system. For many southern authors who wished to uphold the South as it was, the language of economics allowed them to reframe mainstream representations of the region through popular literary forms and genres that proliferated in the early-nineteenth-century transatlantic literary culture.

Antebellum Southern Literature: "A Thing Apart"

Midway through *Uncle Tom's Cabin* (1852), Harriet Beecher Stowe features a series of extended debates between Augustine St. Clare, Tom's careless young master in Louisiana, and his northern cousin Ophelia St. Clare, or Miss Ophelia. One particular debate is prompted by proslavery advocates' religious justifications for slavery, which the southerner St.

Clare dismisses as false and hypocritical. Instead, he offers a much more straightforward reason: "We're in for it; we've got 'em, and mean to keep 'em,—it's for our convenience and our interest" (1:264). When his somewhat glib response draws questions from his cousin, who brings up biblical rationales for slavery that were popular at the time, he waves them off: "The whole frame-work of society, both in Europe and America, is made up of various things which will not stand the scrutiny of any very ideal standard of morality. It's pretty generally understood that men don't aspire after the absolute right, but only to do about as well as the rest of the world. Now, when any one speaks up, like a man, and says slavery is necessary to us, we can't get along without it, we should be beggared if we give it up, and, of course, we mean to hold on to it,—this is strong, clear, well-defined language; it has the respectability of truth to it; and, if we may judge by their practice, the majority of the world will bear us out in it" (1:265–66). In a novel that leans so heavily on religious and moral arguments to make its case against slavery, St. Clare's opinion is unusual in that it identifies very explicitly how economics was central to the conversation over slavery both in the U.S. South and beyond. It also reveals a literary representation of the self-interest that lay at the heart of perpetuating and promoting U.S. slavery.

The ideas articulated by St. Clare emerge in and shape the popular literature of the era by southerners and about the South in ways that have remained largely unexamined in critical scholarship. When nineteenth-century southern literature is discussed in critical works, it is treated as a distinct entity, separate from global intellectual networks and devoid of the economic motives identified in the St. Clare passage. The result is a general characterization of southern literature that evokes the foregrounded image of the southern planter in the 1860 illustration, a limited representation of a region defined by antimodern provincialism. In his massive study of the early southern literary field, *The South in American Literature, 1607–1900* (1954), Jay B. Hubbell identifies the critical blindness toward the literary history of the South in this regard, in which the tendency is to treat early southern literature "as a thing apart" (viii). Despite the fact that Hubbell's book was published in the mid-twentieth century, the same patterns he identifies have been replicated in literary studies in the latter half of the twentieth and the early twenty-first centuries. While there have been definite exceptions, literary scholarship on the nineteenth-century South—even in the field of U.S. southern studies—is often limited to individual chapters or readings of single authors and books.[6] With a few more exceptions, critics who have completed book-length studies of nineteenth-century southern literature tend to concentrate their efforts on postbellum texts by regional or local color authors.[7] And only a very few of these studies address the idea of an economically modern, self-interested South in the literature. As a result, the pre–Civil War South presented in this book, one driven by free market economic philosophies, is largely excluded from conversations on national and international literary development.

Considering the importance of U.S. slavery and the South to the nineteenth-century global economy, it would make sense that the literary productions of the region would hold equal importance. "The literature of the South," Hubbell argues, "cannot be understood and appraised if one neglects its many and complicated relations with the literature of the rest of the nation" (x). And indeed, the reverse is true: the United States and the nineteenth-century world cannot be understood without understanding the South and its self-fashioning through literary representation. The passages in *Uncle Tom's Cabin* reveal the centrality of the South and slavery to all aspects of modern nineteenth-century life—Stowe, a northern abolitionist whose novel sold millions of copies on both sides of the Atlantic, perceived the very economic self-interest that most southerners attempted to diminish with the language of liberal capitalism (or the religiously based moral relativism criticized by St. Clare). Southern novels were not unique for their time, and the attitudes they articulated were not expressed by social and cultural outliers. Nor were these works self-published blips in the nineteenth-century literary marketplace, gone and quickly forgotten in favor of the canonical authors that dominate nineteenth-century studies today (e.g., Hawthorne, Melville, and Whitman). In fact, many were best sellers, written by prominent, nationally and internationally recognized authors. Literature by southern proslavery advocates reveals how a society maintained an idea of itself that shaped a nation and a global economic system—until finally a war was required to dismantle it.

The idea of the antebellum South that drove the region's economic and social self-fashioning was just that, an idea, one that was constantly reshaped and repurposed through literature and cultural production. Yet most critical works assume fixity in regard to the South and its literature (again, with exceptions). Michael Kreyling writes in his revision of southern literary study, *Inventing Southern Literature* (1998), that for most of its existence as a field, southern studies scholars have presumed that "southern literature will always be recognizable by a formula as constant as the thing itself, for the South and its history are 'fact' and 'entities' that remain intact in and impervious to literary representation" (xi). In other words, "the South" is a given definition or a tangible object that the literature is simply describing. In the case of the antebellum South, that tangible object is usually the same isolated province characterized by the space of the plantation.

However, southern literature and the South as we know it today were created out of discursive processes, a pattern that has been identified in recent southern studies scholarship by critics such as Leigh Anne Duck, Martyn Bone, Michael Kreyling, Scott Romine, and Jon Smith.[8] These processes began during the antebellum period, the moment at which the racial and social politics associated with the South were solidified in the very literature contemporary readers often ignore. The terms *South* and *southern,* then, do not signify a distinct entity but refer to concepts that have been constantly re-created, reiterated, reshaped, and reaffirmed through artistic representation, specifically fictional narratives that constitute the story of the region and, by extension, the cultures and societies shaped by U.S. slavery (which was virtually every space on the globe). For the works featured in this study, slavery was the institution that dominated southern society and representations of it: defenses of slavery; accurate depictions of slavery; critiques of slavery; and most important for proslavery southerners, downplaying the realities of slavery in order to fit a liberal, progressive vision of the region. Reinterpreting the literature of the antebellum South opens up that process to modern readers and audiences and reveals the extent to which literature and artistic production do not merely describe a regional history but actively direct and shape later understandings of that history.

Recognizing the literary feedback loops that shape conceptions of the South and southern culture also means identifying the spheres of influence that molded the form of the literature itself. In this case, it was British writing and the transatlantic economy. If De Bow and other southern nonfiction authors borrowed from British traditions in their economic theories, then southern authors of fiction borrowed just as much from popular British fiction of the era to reimagine the South. The transatlantic connections in early American and nineteenth-century literature have been well examined in critical circles; however, most studies that highlight the Anglo-American literary sphere concentrate on New England and British writing cultures. Christopher Hanlon notes that these studies omit "a sense . . . in which U.S. sectionalism itself, the very circumstance for which reason we continue to term this period 'antebellum,' determined the ways U.S. thinkers understood the transatlantic constellation" (x). Outside of the influence of Sir Walter Scott or Edgar Allan Poe's transatlantic flair, there has been very little discussion of the interconnected nature of early southern fiction and British literary culture.[9]

Yet patterns in nineteenth-century studies are not the same thing as patterns in southern studies. Studies focused on the nineteenth century often discount the South, while southern studies often discounts pre–Civil War literature. The result is a constant negotiation of critical absences and gaps, which becomes a connecting thread throughout this book. So, while nineteenth-century transatlantic studies lacks an engagement with southern authors, many recent works in southern literary studies emphatically pull the *post*–Civil War South from its geographically delineated confines, the most notable being the "New Southern Studies" and "Global South" movements.[10] Barbara Ladd writes in a 2005 issue of *PMLA* that "the present horizon in United States southern studies is the question of how we are to reimagine the or a South or multiple Souths to take full measure of the significance of alternative memories, histories, and modes of cultural expression" (1633). And the title of Michael Bibler's introductory summary to a later collection of southern studies manifestos in *PMLA*—"Smash the Mason-Dixon!" (2016)—indicates that scholars continue to push conceptions of "southern" and region beyond typical spatial demarcations, at in least in regard to twentieth- and twenty-first-century literature.[11]

My study presupposes this geographic disintegration and approaches southern literature as a global artistic movement first. Critical studies in the past few decades have shown that nineteenth-century American literature—and particularly southern literature—was inherently transatlantic in nature, just as transatlantic as the economy and slavery itself. Leonard Tennenhouse observes in *The Importance of Feeling English* (2007) that "what we mean by American is most likely a reproduction of cultural practices that originated somewhere else" (9). The same can be said of "southern": what we usually assume to be a "thing itself," as Kreyling puts it, is actually a reproduction and refashioning of ideas and practices. Christopher Hanlon describes the interconnectivity and the geopolitical specificity of Anglo-American writing as "Atlantic sectionalism," in which cross-Atlantic exchanges must be understood along the regional and sectional lines that defined the antebellum period (x). Southern authors were notorious for their devotion to and replication of the "Scott novel" and other British corollaries—after the Civil War, Mark Twain famously and repeatedly castigated southern literature for its "Sir Walter disease."[12] Southern literary Anglophilia extended beyond the historical romance to other popular genres, including sketches, social problem novels, and adventure tales. Most often, however, those literary adaptations are eclipsed in critical studies by the texts' sectional politics, in which "sectionalism is *too* centrifugal a force . . . [or] external to the transatlantic frames of reference that have redefined the field over the past two decades" (Hanlon 10). Therefore, rather than participating in a multifarious transatlantic exchange of literary production, southern texts—especially proslavery works—are treated as a set of anachronistic objects in which the authors blatantly appropriate British forms but paradoxically isolate themselves from the global intellectual discourse of the nineteenth century.

Interpreting antebellum southern literature as a set of cultural relics from a sequestered province, however, ignores the very "literariness" of the texts themselves. In these readings, the works are viewed only in light of their historical significance or the ideologies they endorse—in other words, the novels are read as representative pieces, rather than as the stories and fictional narratives that they are. But if the South and southern culture is a set of discursive processes, we have to attend to the form of the writing itself, as novels and short stories produced in and about a space and culture. "Communities are to be distinguished," Benedict Anderson notes, "not by their falsity/genuineness, but by the *style* in which they are imagined" (6, my emphasis). Reading the fiction of the antebellum period discloses the process of a narrative construction of the South as it is happening. In the context of a society that was in the midst of navigating and unifying around a set of ideas and structures—as the region was molding itself around debates over slavery and the emergence of a modern global economy—*how* the story is told is just as important as its content. And narrative is key in creating shared cultural histories and memories, for narrative forms "'represent' the *kind* of community" in the process of forming (Anderson 25).[13] While there was plenty of southern poetry during the nineteenth century, fiction and narrative imagine the story of a place and people into being and subsequently influence the discourse surrounding that story.[14] Moreover, because the works discussed in this book were often best sellers and widely circulated, they could reach a broad audience, further disseminating the story of the region they present.

Taking up Hanlon's model of "Atlantic sectionalism," I identify early southern literary form as a performance of genre, specifically fictional genres that shape the narrative and re-transmission of the South. As Tennenhouse points out, the reliance of nineteenth-century American literature on British precedent does not diminish the formal or cultural distinctiveness of the literary works themselves. "America's brand of Englishness," he writes," is precisely what made it American" (Tennenhouse 12).[15] Likewise, classifying southern literature as simply derivative of the Scott historical romance belies the complexity of the authors' use of British traditions and the specificity of the representations that emerge from such practices. In his study of the "Anglophone literary field," Joseph Rezek argues that "Irish, Scottish, and American literatures were 'made' as material products of the book trade and cultural artifacts of the literary field" (9). Southern authors, in other words, did not take the formulas provided by various British genres and simply plug in southern settings and characters. A perfect example of this transatlantic "making" is the early southern book and periodical trade. In addition to frequent reprints and reviews of British texts in southern periodicals such as *De Bow's Review* and the *Southern Literary Messenger,* southern libraries and book purchases were dominated by British publications, to the extent that early southern bookshelves "probably resembled libraries in the farmhouses or small manor houses of rural England" (Davis, *Colonial Southern Bookshelf* 130).

Coming out of this transatlantic literary exchange, southern authors adopted popular British forms that were widely read at the time, then used those patterns in literary genre to shape their representations of the

South. In this interpretation, I take up Caroline Levine's redefinition of *form* as both "historical, emerging out of particular cultural and political circumstances" and "ahistorical, transcending the specifics of history" (2). And more important, forms are "portable" in that they can be "picked up and moved to new contexts" (7). Each of the following chapters interprets southern novels and short stories against the work of British authors who shape the core of the early nineteenth-century literary canon, well-known names such as Charles Dickens and Elizabeth Gaskell. These comparative readings reveal how southern authors reworked literary genre to represent the ideological pulls of free market capitalism and the precapitalist structures of the plantation that characterized the South and U.S. slavery at the time.[16] These reconceptualizations, in turn, were fed back into other representations of the region. The result is an oft-repeated, reconstituted South that cycles through audience, author, and literary work, building upon and altering itself each time.

To understand the cross-Atlantic connections, the readings of individual texts in each chapter of this book focus on form and incorporate a blend of biographical, historical, and rhetorical approaches that account for the multifaceted nature of literary production. Consistent in these interpretations, however, is the primacy of economic patterns and economic language in understanding imaginative writing. Drawing from works such as Pierre Bourdieu's *The Field of Cultural Production* (1993), Benedict Anderson's *Imagined Communities* (1983), or Ian Watt's *The Rise of the Novel* (1957), the following chapters demonstrate that the concurrent emergence of a capitalist economy and an identifiable, culturally specific literature is not coincidental. My readings are also indebted to work in the New Economic Criticism, a field of study in which critics read literature and literary production in light of how both are informed by economic practices.[17] By foregrounding the economic rationales for literary representation, my analysis of antebellum texts underscores how economics shaped southern literature into a discrete movement unto itself.

Following this line of thought, the intrinsic relationship between the development of the nineteenth-century global economy and the development of southern literature is a crucial point in this study. Rather than working against the rise of a capitalist economy, southern authors used the ideology of liberal capitalism as put forth by eighteenth-century political economists to represent a region seemingly pulled in two ideological directions. For the authors featured in this study, literary genre became a way of merging the impulses of modern capitalism (namely, laissez-faire principles and an investment in the free market) with the precapitalist structures that characterized southern social organization. In these representations, the South is at once a dynamic space of modern industrialization and economic expansion that also upholds a plantation system modeled on the fading aristocratic order of Europe—all while being reliant on the social and racial violence of slavery.

Ultimately, this book pulls the antebellum South—which has been viewed as an isolated province by most literary scholars—into the main currents of literary development. Fiction by southern authors is not "a thing apart" but is crucial to understanding the forms and popular literary genres that characterized the transatlantic print public. If read against the international connections maintained by the regional economy, literature of the antebellum South emerges as one shaped by modern economic forces and industrialization—*not* the product of an isolated backwater clinging to an outmoded agrarian economy and labor system—and southerners' literary justifications of slavery were central to the economic and intellectual developments of the era.

Proslavery Propagation and Panics

In terms of structure, this book follows two basic historical patterns. The first is the evolution of the literature's sectional tone. Although the U.S. South always relied on slavery for profit and was largely structured around the plantation system in its social organization, at the beginning of the nineteenth century, debates over slavery by southern whites were more ambivalent than defensive. As the century wore on, however, proslavery southerners closed ranks and were more overtly violent in their defense of the system. The shift was partly in reaction to the growing profitably of cotton; part of it was in response to the growth of the transatlantic abolitionist movement. The result was a deepening sectionalism in the United States that ultimately led to the Civil War. To account for this shift, the following chapters incorporate pairings or trios of texts that chart the development of proslavery ideology as it plays out in different literary genres. Beginning with texts published in the early decades of the century, primarily in the 1820s and 1830s, then ending with texts published closer to the Civil War, in the 1840s and 1850s, the book demonstrates how the somewhat conflicted support of slavery on the part of southern whites gradually hardened into an ardent, militant defense of a profitable, violent system.

But to again return to economics as one of the governing ideologies of the antebellum South, that change can be largely attributed to a significant (but seldom discussed) financial turning point in the nineteenth century: the Panic of 1837. The crisis was brought on by a series of complicated and coinciding events in the late 1830s, including the overissuance of currency and bad loans by state banks in the western territories, largely in reaction to rapid territorial expansion; the raising of interest rates by banks in England and the United States; the collapse of cotton prices; and rampant speculation in domestic and international markets. The financial panic would have consequences in the United States and abroad for years to come, but it hit southern plantation owners particularly hard. As a result, the moment of 1837 is the second historical element that structures this study, and the chapters adopt a "before and after" format in order to account for the reverberating effects of the economic crisis.[18]

To trace southern rationalizations and representations across the antebellum period, the book examines literary form, with each chapter devoted to a popular genre or trend.[19] I begin with what are considered the representative texts of the region and era: historical romances in the style of Sir Walter Scott. Chapter 1, "The Cavalier and the Economist: Southern Historical Romance," takes up two southern authors of the time who are most well-known to contemporary readers and critics. Novels such as John Pendleton Kennedy's *Horse Shoe Robinson* (1835) and William Gilmore Simms's *The Sword and the Distaff* (1852; later *Woodcraft* [1854]) use the genre to rewrite southern history within the context of nineteenth-century capitalism. By setting their novels during the Revolutionary Era and featuring characters who are practical, self-sufficient frontiersmen, Simms and Kennedy write a version of U.S. history that celebrates the modernizing global economy but still adheres to ideas of feudal honor and racial privilege represented by the single plantation community.

Chapter 2, "Sketching the 1830s Cotton Boom: Southwestern Humor," situates the genre of the sketch within the context of the 1830s international cotton trade and U.S. expansion into the Southwest territories. This chapter connects Charles Dickens's first book, *Sketches by Boz* (1836), to two Southwest humor collections set in Alabama and Mississippi: Johnson Jones Hooper's *Some Adventures of Captain Simon Suggs* (1845) and Joseph Glover Baldwin's *The Flush Times of Alabama and Mississippi* (1853). All three use the humorous sketch and the figure of the "confidence man" to represent the effects of cotton demand and industrialization in the United States and Britain. In these representations, the sketch form captures a unique moment in U.S. and regional history, when rapid territorial growth spurred the advent of a new economic paradigm that linked the frontier of the U.S. South with the urban spaces of Britain.

Chapter 3, "The Southern Imperial Dream: Novels of Adventure," discusses literature and the growth of the southern slaveholding economy in relation to the United States' expansion into Mexico, the far West, and eventually Cuba. I focus on three adventure novels that advocate for the appropriation of new territories, economic expansion, and ultimately a form of southern nationalism based on slavery. *The Texan Ranger* (1846) by Joseph Holt Ingraham, *Inez* (1855) by Augusta Jane Evans, and *The Free Flag of Cuba* (1854) by Lucy Holcombe Pickens are novels set during the Texas Revolution, the U.S.-Mexican War, and the attempted southern invasions of Cuba in the 1850s, respectively. With these historical backdrops, all three support the expansion of slavery into the far South. In doing so, these texts adapt the genre of the adventure novel in order to reframe the discussion of slavery and economic growth in terms of southern honor and free market individualism through the trope of the heroic, self-made man.

Chapter 4, "Narratives of Reform: The Proslavery Social Problem Novel," again highlights the transatlantic nature of the antebellum economy. This chapter addresses how southern authors drew from the genres of the eighteenth-century seduction novel and the industrial reform novel, made popular by British authors such as Samuel Richardson and Elizabeth Gaskell, to critique the southern economy and particularly the slave system. This chapter examines George Tucker's *The Valley of Shenandoah* (1824) and Maria J. McIntosh's *The Lofty and the Lowly* (1852). While both authors were proslavery apologists, each recognized that a plantation system reliant on slave labor was not economically sustainable. Their "proslavery social problem novels" utilize the vocabulary of social reform employed in British novels in order to criticize the inhumanity of plantation slavery and offer reforms to the system without proposing its outright abolition.

Chapter 5, "'Free Labor' and the Free Market: Slave Narratives," is a departure from the previous chapters and examines texts by authors who wrote *against* the attempts of white southerners to subsume regional culture under the racially defined hierarchies of the plantation system and the language of liberal capitalism. This chapter outlines how nineteenth-century slave narratives depict slavery in light of labor relations and economic exchange. The most frequent analysis of nineteenth-century texts by black authors is, naturally, to read them in light of critical race theory, as in Saidiya Hartman's *Scenes of Subjection* (1997) and Paul Gilroy's *Black Atlantic.* In many ways, however, this chapter takes its cue from Kenneth Warren's book *What Was African American Literature?* (2011) in thinking of African American literature published during the nineteenth century as less about the desire to forge a positive racial identity and more as a response to economic practices. In this light, I read the slave narratives of the 1840s and 1850s first as reflections on slavery as a structure of labor, then as a system of racial oppression. Drawing from abolitionist newspapers published in the United States and Chartist papers published in Britain, this chapter situates the work of authors such as Frederick Douglass, Henry Bibb, William Wells Brown, James W. C. Pennington, and Harriet Jacobs in the context of transatlantic debates over "wage slavery." In their narratives, former slaves take pains to present black labor in the South as part of the growing pool of skilled laborers in the developing global economy. In this way, former slaves harnessed the rhetoric of free labor in the mid-nineteenth century to create a narrative that countered the representations of slave labor in proslavery texts.

Finally, the epilogue, "How Did We Get Here?" moves beyond the antebellum period to discuss the lasting influence of slavery and capitalist economic models on representations of the South after the Civil War. Using George Washington Cable's novel *John March, Southerner* (1894–5) as a case study, the epilogue considers how the paradigms established in antebellum literature continue to circulate in representations of the South after slavery was abolished. Set during the Reconstruction and post-Reconstruction eras, Cable's novel presents a bleak portrait of the region's inevitable shift to an economic order based on industry and free market capitalism. Yet it does not hesitate to depict the long-term consequences of antebellum southerners' rationalizations of the slave system and the violence it perpetuated. By ending with literature written after the Civil War, this final section highlights the main objectives of *Cavaliers and Economists:* to delineate the connection between the development of literary form and economic shifts and to reveal the primary role played by representations of the U.S. South and slavery in global and national discussions of economic and social development.

The authors featured in the following chapters all actively participated in developing a southern literature founded on global free market capitalism. In doing so, they constantly renegotiated and re-justified the continued torture and exploitation of an entire group of Americans. Through this study of the major works of antebellum southern literature, my aim is to explore how that idea of the South—which is composed of ideologies so at odds with one another—continues to circulate in U.S. culture today.

1

THE CAVALIER AND THE ECONOMIST

Southern Historical Romance

In 1856, William Gilmore Simms embarked on a lecture tour in New York state. Although Simms was a nationally known novelist, poet, and essayist, in the decade leading up to the Civil War, the South Carolina native was called upon more frequently to defend the southern way of life. The lecture, "South Carolina in the Revolution," was prompted by an 1856 speech given in Congress by Senator Charles Sumner of Massachusetts. In "The Crime against Kansas," Sumner attacked the South for supporting slavery and its extension into the West and also implied that South Carolina's present degeneration could be traced to the Revolutionary War. He declared, "Were the whole history of South Carolina blotted out of existence . . . civilization might lose—I do not say how little; but surely less than it has already gained by the example of Kansas" (Sumner 29). In response, Simms decided to set the historical record straight.[1]

Simms first notes in the lecture that because the state engaged in active trade and did not compete with Britain in manufacturing—unlike the northern colonies—South Carolina had no economic incentive to separate during the Revolutionary War. Instead, the southern colony participated "for more sacred and national purposes" (527). In this representation, southerners were motivated by an investment in a community, honor, and a potential nation. Nevertheless, Simms carefully notes that the South Carolina revolutionaries were not independently wealthy plantation aristocrats or merchants of the upper class. Rather, they were "the *native* agricultural population; the *native* mechanics; the *native* lawyers and professions, mostly" (526). These men represented the socially mobile middle class, the artisans and laborers who would contribute to economic modernization and industrialization in the South. The defense of South Carolina's history in the lecture maintains the ideals represented by southern society (honor, communal values, tradition, slavery) and also situates the South in national economic development.

The lecture's narrative of the southern colonies during the Revolutionary era creates a lineage for the South that justifies the then current structures of southern society in the context of global capitalism. Such a position rebukes Sumner's characterization of the South but also refutes the idea that the region is backward or stagnant economically and socially. As Simms puts it, by denigrating South Carolina's history, critics of the South rob the region and the nation of the "monuments by which future generations are to be taught becoming lessons & examples" (523). Simms's 1856 speech represents a defense of the South in which conservative southerners upheld the ideals of self-sufficient agriculture articulated by early southern intellectuals such as Jefferson but then adapted those ideals to the modes of free market capitalism. That image of the South, then, is the one to be passed along to "future generations."[2]

Simms's 1856 lecture tour reveals a moment directly before the Civil War in which southern intellectuals' presentation of history becomes an act of self-definition. In speaking to primarily northern audiences on a topic of common American history, Simms situates the South in the larger narrative of the United States' development. For conservative southerners like Simms who viewed abolitionism as an attack on southern institutions, this was also a moment to defend what they saw as the "traditional" structures and values represented by the South: communal social organization; a chivalric code of honor; an emphasis on family; and most important, the institution of slavery. Many conservatives also wished for the South to maintain its viability as an economic and political power in the nineteenth-century global economy. This meant that in Simms's carefully structured histories of the region, the South could be both a space of traditional values and one that promoted industrialization and economic modernization in a free market.

In the context of 1850s sectional tension, and as the quarrel between Simms and Sumner reveals, how history was told became a way of defining and defending a place and people. This was never truer than in the popular genre for which Simms and most southern antebellum authors are best known: the historical romance. Although historical romances written by southerners during this period are typically dismissed in critical circles as reactionary defenses of the Old South—or simply "bad" literature—the novels evince the same complex engagement with the conflicting structures of the plantation economy represented by Simms's lecture. Rather than upholding a standard vision of plantation nostalgia, these novels "revise" southern history to correspond with the dual elements of the southern economy and create, through fiction, a long lasting lineage for the South that maintained the importance of plantation slavery but better suited the moral and ethical imperatives of a liberal capitalist economy.

This chapter traces the southern historical romance from its initial popularity in the 1830s up through later manifestations in the 1850s. During this time period, authors adapted the genre of the historical romance and reframed southern history to correspond with the complicated ideological pulls of the region's economy. In particular, *Horse Shoe Robinson; or, A Tale of the Tory Ascendency* (1835) by John Pendleton Kennedy, another premier author of the antebellum South, and Simms's 1854 novel, *Woodcraft; or, Hawks about the Dovecote,* reimagine a southern historical lineage from the moment of the Revolutionary War through their retelling and fictionalization of American history. These historical romances are attempts on the part of southern intellectuals to use literary genre as a method of resolving the ideological conflict between seemingly precapitalist visions of the antebellum South, a defense of slavery, and the drive toward relevance in the context of the mid-nineteenth-century global economy.

The Historical Romance Tradition and Southern Literary Criticism

> Critics may cavil and sophisticates may yawn, but the historical romance (in one form or another) goes on forever.
>
> —Alexander Cowie, introduction to the 1937 edition of Simms's *The Yemassee*

My choice to begin this book with a chapter on the historical romances of John Pendleton Kennedy and William Gilmore Simms is a pointed one. Though both are largely forgotten now outside of southern studies circles, Kennedy and Simms have become the representative figures for antebellum southern literature, singularities from a region that is often considered devoid of a literary culture.[3] These men were members of the intellectual class that aligned itself with wealthy plantation owners, businessmen, and politicians in the South. Kennedy and especially Simms also achieved more far-reaching acclaim as authors of fiction. Kennedy's first novel, *Swallow Barn* (1832), is one of the most frequently studied works of southern literature published before the Civil War and is often dubbed the "first plantation novel."[4] Up through the 1840s, William Gilmore Simms was known not just as a southern author but as one of the foremost American authors.

My focus on the historical romance genre also reflects the critical labeling of southern fiction of the era. Studies of antebellum literature often mimic the famous rant by Mark Twain: "But for the Sir Walter disease, the character of the Southerner—or Southron, according to Sir Walter's starchier way of phrasing it—would be wholly modern, in place of modern and mediaeval mixed, and the South would be fully a generation further advanced that it is" ("Enchantments and Enchanters," *Life on the Mississippi,* 284–5). As a result, the casual references in critical texts to southern fiction patterning itself after the "Sir Walter Scott novel," frequently eclipse a more thorough examination of what that term actually entails. As a result, the historical romances by Kennedy and Simms are often cited as the representative texts for the region and era, without an acknowledgment that other types of fiction were, indeed, written during the antebellum period.[5] The effect is to lump together all forms of antebellum regional fiction, then cast the pall of "romanticization" over the novels' representations of the South.[6]

Reducing an understanding of pre–Civil War southern literature to these terms discounts the cultural work the historical romance performed in American literary culture.[7] Southern authors (and their northern counterparts) admitted Scott as an obvious influence, but that influence did not mean that they followed a conventional formula. As Michael Davitt Bell demonstrates in *The Development of American Romance* (1980), American authors during the nineteenth century took pains to define the genre according to standards that were particular to the United States. They molded the romance to American topics and settings and also used the term to rethink the relationship between fiction, imagination, and reality. Bell notes, "Romance in America was less a genre than a set of attitudes or problems whose recurrence in the work of some of our best fiction writers before the Civil War constitutes something like a tradition—a tradition at once formal and intellectual" (148). Novelists such as Nathaniel Hawthorne, Herman Melville, and Edgar Allan Poe frequently wrote on the topic of romance and used their own fiction to examine the forms popularized by European authors. Limiting a description of antebellum fiction to the "Scott novel" oversimplifies—and undervalues—the history and cultural impact of the genre.

Labeling antebellum novels as plagued by the "Scott disease" also implies that the work of southern authors was dictated exclusively by popular literary taste and southern conservatism. The Scott novel in these discussions usually refers to an oft-repeated plot: a hero goes on adventures during a particular historical moment, encountering a love interest on the way, and the novel ends with their inevitable union.[8] The usual story circulated by critics holds that Hawthorne and Melville evolved in their adaptations of the British romance tradition, but southern authors obstinately refused to modify the formula provided by Scott.[9] According to these narrow interpretations, authors such as Kennedy and Simms were left behind to produce outmoded and uninteresting novels that touted the same conservative, proslavery party line through their tales of heroics and marriages among the planter class. For example, although he devotes an entire chapter to "the historical romance of the South" in his exhaustive study, *The American Historical Romance* (1987), George Dekker dismisses southern antebellum fiction as "clearly inferior to that of Cooper, Hawthorne, and Melville" (274). Instead, he bypasses nineteenth-century southern fiction altogether and begins his discussion of the southern historical romance with what is now the "gold standard" of southern writing: William Faulkner and Allen Tate.[10]

This critical trend accounts for the neglect of nineteenth-century southern texts in literary studies and would explain why few scholars and even fewer outside of academic circles read the novels. As Jane Tompkins points out in her recovery of popular and sentimental novels in *Sensational Designs* (1985), the value placed on literary texts in the academy often presumes intrinsic artistic merit, or qualities that transcend a particular time and place. Tompkins proposes, instead, that the value of literature can be reconceived to include texts that "offer powerful examples of the way a culture thinks about itself" and works that attempt "to redefine the social order" (xi). Despite the fact that Tompkins's study was published over thirty years ago, the critical treatment of southern historical romances repeats the same patterns of canonization and disregard that excluded sentimental and domestic fiction from the scholarly conversation for so long. Add in the fact that the romances by authors such as Kennedy and Simms overtly defend slavery, and we have a set of novels that quickly faded into popular and critical obscurity throughout the twentieth and twenty-first centuries.

Yet the southern historical romances are crucial to understanding the nineteenth-century world—they are an attempt to reconfigure a very specific and culturally dominant social order through fiction. Just as Hawthorne and Melville used the historical romance to raise questions about American identity and the function of fictional representation, the southern authors of conservative historical romances interrogated the structures of southern society and constantly reflected on the form. Although it is undeniable that Kennedy and Simms were much more conservative politically and socially than the New England authors, that did not necessarily translate into an unquestioning adoption of the literary formulas prescribed by European texts or an unwavering promotion of the southern aristocratic elite. Nor does it automatically relegate their writing to the "clearly inferior" status bestowed by Dekker. Like their northern counterparts, southern authors of historical romances took up nationalist themes and responded to the climate of antebellum economics and politics.[11] In the preface to his novel *The Yemassee* (1835), Simms makes a point of describing the text as a "Romance," not a "Novel." Further, he declares *The Yemassee* to be "an *American* romance. It is so styled as much of the material could have been furnished by no other country" (6). Kennedy, too, emphasized the particular characteristics of his historical fiction as both "romantic and picturesque" but also "American" (*Horse Shoe Robinson* iii, v).

Instead of assuming the authors are conservative holdovers from a previous generation, the genre of the southern historical romance can be read in the context of the region's economy before the Civil War. Not just derivative or defensive (because, let's face it, they are both of those things), these novels are representations of a southern history that accommodates the multiple ideological allegiances of the antebellum plantation economy and the centrality of slavery in southern culture. In this light, the authors' inability to move beyond the traditional formula for the historical romance is not an inherent literary stodginess but an attempt to use literature to maintain the ideological balance between southern society's investment in liberal capitalism, its adherence to slavery, and the social organization represented by the plantation. Put another way, the "clear inferiority" of the southern historical romance is a formal response to the demands of representing southern history and the development of antebellum southern society, not laziness or lack of literary talent. When read through this lens, the question of the novels' "quality" as literature becomes less important than understanding their function in representing the ideological drives that shaped the region.

The genre of the historical romance lends itself to a discussion of the interchange between economic structures and literary form in its balance of historical fact and imaginative representation.[12] In her book-length outline of the historical romance, Helen Hughes describes the "dual nature" of the genre: "Historical romance, with its links with both 'history' and the novel, is a genre in which two systems of myth operate: the archetypal episodes of romance . . . and the presentation of history" (13).[13] Indeed, in the 1832 preface to his romance of early New York, *The Pioneers* (1823), James Fenimore Cooper presents the novel as equal parts "literal fact" and "general picture" (6). Thus, for all of the genre's adherence to standard romance-driven patterns of plot and character development, the historical romance also insists on the veracity of its historical details and settings.[14]

The authors' claim to historical authenticity underscores the importance of the *way in which history is told* in the historical romance genre. The novels are not invented stories that happen to be set at historical moments or romanticized versions of a historical period. They are carefully plotted versions of history. That urge is what prompted Simms's reactionary lecture tour in 1856, which demanded a similar type of veracity. With both the lecture and the novels, how South Carolina's (and the South's) history is conveyed to contemporary audiences implies present-day social and political consequences.

Although the tradition represented by Scott's work undoubtedly carried cultural weight for southern authors, the historical romances formally diverge in important ways that transcend the limits of the Scott model. This is particularly true in how the narrative form plays a role in interpreting and conveying history. In *Metahistory: The Historical Imagination in Nineteenth-Century Europe* (1973), historian and critic Hayden White defines historical writing as a narrative of the past arranged and presented by the historian, rather than a set of immutable facts—much in the same way a novel is arranged and told by an author. The difference, according to White, is that the novel's basic stories are "invented" by the author (6).[15]

In turn, how the historian conveys past structures is just as important as how the novelist relates a tale in a historical romance. To describe the process of historical writing, White differentiates between what he calls a "chronicle" and a "story." A chronicle presents the basic facts of the past, while the story is the narrative of those facts. In the case of a historical romance, the chronicle is the setting and the basic outcome of the novels. Often the novels are set during moments of historical importance, such as wartimes and moments of rapid change within a nation or area. As a result, the settings are grounded in commonly accepted historical facts at the time the novels were published: which side won a particular war, which nation conquered a particular area, which people is now extinct, or which historical figures played a role in a particular event. Those details merely provide a realistic backdrop for the fictional plots and characters of the novels, the story.

The inherent duality of the historical romance patterns itself along this split between story and chronicle. In Sir Walter Scott's *Waverley* (1814)—the prototypical historical romance and the most frequently cited Scott novel in southern literary studies[16]—the 1745 Jacobite Revolution provides the basic historical framework for the novel, while the story tracks the life of its titular character in a quasi-Bildungsroman.[17] Or for a U.S. example, James Fenimore Cooper's Natty Bumppo novels follow what George Dekker calls the "*Waverley*-model" and are set during the European colonization of American territories and the creation of the United States. The stories themselves highlight the process of nation building and conquest.[18]

In contrast to *Waverley* and Cooper's romances, which emphasize individuals and nations, respectively, the southern historical romances use the framework of history to establish a lineage for southern institutions that fit within the growth of the nineteenth-century global economy. With a significant historical moment in U.S. history as the basic chronicle—in the case of the novels discussed here, the Revolutionary War—the romances construct a timeline of southern culture that is both "documented fact" and ideologically bound up with economic and political progress. The Revolutionary War, a formative moment in the national timeline, places the readers in familiar historical territory and aligns them with the southern characters through a commonly known and understood point of history.

The parameters of the chronicle then allow the authors of historical romances to employ the imagined plot and characters to different ends.[19] That shift into imaginative storytelling, like the historian's translation of chronicle into story, implies a particular ideological message on the author's part. White notes that the form taken by a historian's narrative automatically indicates its message, while the "formal coherence in the historical record brings with it theories . . . of historical knowledge itself which have ideological implications for attempts to understand 'the present,' however this 'present' is defined" (21). In other words, the way a story of history is narrated comments on the moment in which the story is assembled by the historian, not just the historical moment being recounted.

Therefore, a novel's adaptation of the historical romance form has clear implications for the social and political moment in which it is published. To again reference *Waverley* as a prime example, readers know the basic ending as having been determined by historical facts: the Jacobites lost, and the English government either killed the leaders or divested them of their property and titles. The "resolution" of the story at the end of the novel is not the vying of political or social factions during the Jacobite Revolution but a sustained character study of an individual's development in the midst of the emergent industrial economy of early-nineteenth-century Britain. Likewise, Cooper's American romances are concerned with the growth of a new nation, yet the most celebrated character in the novels is Natty Bumppo, who functions as a mediating figure between the white settlers and the Native American characters.[20] Thus, Cooper's American historical romances use their stories to interrogate the tension between U.S. national progress and the destruction of traditional cultures, a topic that would have been at the forefront of popular political consciousness in the 1820s and 1830s because of the debates leading up to the passage of the Indian Removal Act of 1830.

Through their adoption of and divergence from the form patterned by Scott or Cooper, the southern novels comment on the moment in which they were written by constructing an origin story of the antebellum South from the Revolutionary era. The novels follow the basic generic structure of the historical romance and culminate in a marriage (or marriages), usually between a hero and a lady from a wealthier or socially respected family. Those unions are a potential merging of social philosophies, in which the self-sufficient hero will take over the plantation system formerly governed by a titled aristocrat. Therefore, in the narrative created by the historical romances, the plantations strewn through the South in the 1830s, 1840s, and 1850s were owned and maintained by later generations of southerners descending from these self-made men of the Revolutionary era.[21]

In light of this reevaluation of the genre and its various manifestations, the southern historical romance is not merely a conservative and uninteresting holdover of a generic formula but a method of articulating a vision of the South that aligns itself with the ideologies of southern conservatives in the decades before the Civil War. Kennedy and Simms, like most of the authors of southern romances, espoused the values of the plantation elite. However, they were also cognizant of the capitalist systems that sustained the southern economy, including the increased reliance on the free market in the transatlantic economy. White notes that conservative historians "are inclined to imagine historical evolution as a progressive elaboration of the institutional structure that *currently* prevails" (25). The conflict between Simms and Sumner reveals that proslavery southerners such as Simms understood how history connected to contemporary understandings of a place or people and modified their stories accordingly. As fiction written by those invested in the southern plantation system and its accompanying way of life, the role of the southern historical romance was to reconcile the capitalist impulses of the southern economy with a need for the type of social order represented by slavery and individual plantations. The result is a story of southern history that aligns with a positive vision of the then-contemporary antebellum plantation South.

Throughout these fictional depictions, the presence of slavery is always accepted as a constant and integral part of southern and American life. Although Kennedy's *Horse Shoe Robinson* barely addresses slavery outside of a casual depiction of stock slave characters, it is nevertheless taken as a given. And Simms's *Woodcraft* posits the institution as fundamental to southern society and its economy. In both cases, slavery is automatically woven into the narrative of U.S. history. In these reconstructed timelines, racial privilege is as important to southern and American society as the ideal of economic autonomy in the free market.

The historical romance, the longtime emblem of antebellum southern fiction, therefore became one of the primary vehicles for authors' negotiation of the southern economy and the institutions it perpetuated. While other genres, such as Simms's lectures, assert particular regional ideologies, the romances allowed the authors to rewrite history and fashion a new lineage for the antebellum South that could embody those ideologies. *Horse Shoe Robinson* and *Woodcraft* incorporate the formal patterns of the romance genre to the ends of maintaining, through fiction, southern society's adherence to the structures of a liberal capitalist economy. However, they do so to slightly different ends. What was an uncertain representation of tensions between conservative aristocracy and socially and economically mobile democracy in novels of the 1830s would become an actual rewriting of southern history in Simms's 1854 romance according to the tenets of the free market.

Novels of the 1830s and Kennedy's *Horse Shoe Robinson*

John Pendleton Kennedy's first historical romance, *Horse Shoe Robinson; or, A Tale of the Tory Ascendency,* takes place in the Carolina and Virginia colonies during the Revolutionary War and features two main characters, Galbraith "Horse Shoe" Robinson and Arthur Butler, both officers in the colonial army. While Butler is a gentleman of South Carolina, whose family possessed extensive landholdings before the war, Robinson is a farmer on the Carolina frontier. The novel follows the two heroes through their various acts of bravery on the battlefield, reconnaissance missions, and interactions with civilians in the southern colonies.

Yet like any good nineteenth-century novel, the beginning of *Horse Shoe Robinson* delays the scenes of action in favor of a long rumination on the function of the historical romance and a description of the countryside that forms the novel's setting. Against the backdrop of the Revolutionary War, the preface establishes the focus of the narrative on the formation of the United States' national character and that of the southern region in particular: "The events narrated in the following pages, came to my knowledge in the progress of my researches into the personal history of some of the characters who figure in the story." Despite the insistence on historical record, the preface emphasizes the romantic tales extrapolated from that record "because they serve to illustrate the temper and character of the war of our revolution" (1:3). Or to take that assertion a step further, the temper and character of a forming society.

The first chapter then sets the tone for *Horse Shoe Robinson*'s depiction of the southern region amidst social and economic change. Titled "A Topographical Discourse," the chapter describes the Virginia and North Carolina countryside at the time the novel takes place, then considers the changes that have occurred up to the novel's composition in the 1830s. After delineating the natural merits of the area both during the Revolution and in the nineteenth century, Kennedy's narrator inserts what he dubs a brief "political reflection": "Since that period, well-a-day! the hand of the reaper has put in his sickle upon divided fields; crowded progenies have grown up under these paternal roof-trees; daughters have married and brought in strange names; the subsistence of one has been spread to the garner of ten; the villages have grown populous; the University has lifted up its didactic head; and every where over this abode of ancient wealth, the hum of industry is heard in the carol of the ploughman, the echo of the wagoner's whip, the rude song of the boatman, and in the clatter of the mill. Such are the mischievous interpolations of the republication system!" (1:16). The passage blends a fond reflection on the progress of a region with the crotchets of an unapologetic traditionalist. At times, it champions economic development, praising "the hum of industry heard in the carol of the ploughman." Yet the passage also bemoans the "strange names" brought in by intermarriage and the "divided fields" tended by individual farmers—rather than owners of large plantations—which disrupted the Revolutionary era social organization and hierarchies.[22]

The opening pages of *Horse Shoe Robinson* reveal a pattern that dominated southern intellectual thought and literature throughout the 1830s: namely, how to respond to the rapid changes that were occurring in the region and throughout the nation. The moment of the 1830s was a peculiar one, especially for the South. The transatlantic cotton trade flourished, leading many southern plantation owners to become wealthier, while middle-class individuals and families were climbing the social and economic ranks. Yet those changes came at a cost; for upper-class southerners of older families, that cost was the destruction of a plantation elite that dominated southern society in the post-Revolutionary, Jeffersonian era, giving way to the "strange names" making their way in the new social organization. The "mischievous interpolations" discussed in *Horse Shoe Robinson*'s opening pages indicate the overall tone of ambivalence that dominated the decade. Many upper-class southerners were caught up in the excitement surrounding the growth of the region, and definitely the excitement of profiting by that growth, yet many expressed reservations at the attendant changes.

Kennedy's first historical romance and other novels published in the 1830s by southerners such as William Gilmore Simms represent the South at a crucial moment in regional and national development. Despite the critical fixation on *Swallow Barn,* Kennedy's first novel, *Horse Shoe Robinson* represents the type of writing that occupied most southern authors during the early decades of the nineteenth century. In Kennedy's case, of his three completed novels, two are historical romances, and the duality represented by the genre mirrors the ambivalence of the 1830s and in his own life. Raised in Baltimore but the son of a prominent Virginia plantation family (the Pendletons), Kennedy's biography is emblematic of the antebellum South's multiple allegiances: to the commercial, industrializing forces of nineteenth-century capitalism that thrived in the port city of Baltimore; and to the rural, aristocratically inclined space of the Virginia elite. In this sense, Kennedy's biography was shaped by the same "mischievous interpolations" lamented in the opening pages of his novel.

This tension emerges, in part, from the novel's political context. *Horse Shoe Robinson* was written after Kennedy, like many prominent southerners of the time, became involved with the Whig political party.[23] The Whigs presented a platform that at once espoused modernization and capitalist enterprise but distrusted complete democracies governed by the masses. Many upper-class southerners of the early antebellum period aligned themselves with the party as a response to what they saw as changes occurring too rapidly and in an effort to distance themselves from Jacksonian Democrats.[24] More important for Kennedy, the party formed in the decades after the War of 1812 and in conjunction with the rise of what critic William R. Taylor has called the "New Man" of the South.[25] It was an ideal that the Whig Party, including Kennedy, would take up as one of its defining tenets: a man who was self-made and tapped into the forces of liberal, free market capitalism and republican values yet whose social and economic success was based on innate talents exemplified by the hereditary aristocracy of the plantation elite. According to this narrative, not everyone can take advantage of American social and economic systems; an individual must possess an intrinsic intelligence and ingenuity, or what Kennedy called a "singular genius."[26] Therefore, while some Americans may have access to and attain social and economic mobility in this new era of regional and national growth, they do so within certain constraints.[27]

Kennedy and the southern Whigs were not alone in their desire to control the emerging social order of the 1830s. Despite being a Jacksonian Democrat—the party that espoused total democratization (in theory)—William Gilmore Simms's writings in the 1830s also display trepidation toward a truly egalitarian approach to socioeconomic growth. One of the themes that ties together much of Simms's early social criticism and fiction is the concept of a nation's progress as it relates to the social and economic mobility of its middle-class citizens. Embracing a vision similar to that of the New Man concept—or what critic David Moltke-Hansen has called "ordered progress"[28]—in this conception of national growth, "progress" is facilitated by talented individuals who first secure the material foundations of a nation or society (i.e., wealth and landholdings), then cultivate its artistic and intellectual development.[29] Although Simms emphasized that only individuals with natural-born gifts of intelligence and talent could promote such development, he was a true Jacksonian Democrat in the sense that his version of social and economic progress would be generated by common men, the middle-class laborers who expand a nation's landholdings and its economy.[30] These principles of progress balance the impulse toward an entirely democratic version of social change with the need to retain some semblance of traditional order and social structures.

Simms's portrayal of American and southern history in the early portion of his career reveals his policies for controlled social and material progress that paralleled those of many upper-class southerners in the 1830s. In a review of British author Harriet Martineau's *Society in America* (1837)—based on her travels through the United States—Simms cautiously delineates the difference between "democracy" and what he calls "leveling": "Democracy . . . is, properly defined, the harmony of the *moral* world. . . . The definition of true liberty is, the undisturbed possession of *that place in society to which our moral and intellectual merits entitle us*" ("Miss Martineau" 653, my emphasis). Not everyone is "entitled" to the highest socioeconomic levels; attainment of such levels is dictated by "moral and intellectual merits." Instead, American society—according to Simms's representation—is created out of a balance between the structures of the free market and the intellectual hierarchies, or singular genius, promoted by Whigs such as Kennedy.[31]

The response of southern authors such as Kennedy and Simms to this overarching ambivalence was to imbue their novels with characters who could embody the pull between rapid growth and stability, tradition and the new. Using the chronicle of southern history as their framework, the historical romances of the 1830s conceive a story of the South and southerners that encompasses the vying cultural impulses that drove the region's growth during the early nineteenth century while still controlling the limits and terms of that growth. A perfect example emerges in Kennedy's second historical romance (and last novel), *Rob of the Bowl: A Legend of St. Inigoe's* (1838). At the beginning of the novel, the narrator introduces a character based on an actual historical figure, Captain Dauntrees, an officer in the Maryland military and an early settler in the province. Having moved to the Maryland colony to seek his fortune, the captain still retains his military bearing and sense of honor belonging to a gentleman. According to the narrator, his attire displays the finery of a high-ranked officer but also incorporates the style of a colonial plantation owner and businessman. The narrator concludes: "This combination of martinet and free companion exhibited in the dress of the Captain, was a pretty intelligible index to his character, which disclosed a compound . . . of the precisian and ruffler,—the cavalier and economist" (1:28). As the "cavalier and economist," the captain embodies the ever-present tension that made up southern society before the Civil War, extending back to the colonial era. He displays all of the trappings of a southern aristocrat and honorable military man, plus the qualities of a modern man in an emerging capitalist order, one who would seek prosperity in new territories and markets.

While Dauntrees may be representative of the early southern colonies, the narrator nevertheless takes care to insert his own view of that strange combination of cavalier and economist: "[Dauntrees] was worldly-wise, sagaciously provident, as an old soldier, of whatever advantages his condition might casually supply; in words, he was, indifferently, according to the occasion, a moralist or a hot-brained reveller—sometimes affecting the courtier along with the martialist, and mixing up the saws of peaceful thrift with the patter of the campaigns" (1:29). The rest of the novel displays Dauntrees's proficiency as a practical military man, yet this initial intervention on the part of the narrator limits the character's social mobility and power in the colony. His ludicrousness and waywardness prevent him from being anything more than "a hot-brained reveller." Thus, the narrative presents Dauntrees as a self-sufficient, practical man possessed of education and with aspirations of economic gain but limited by his innate lack of genius. Following a pattern that runs throughout the writings of southerners in the 1830s, Kennedy's historical romance allows the cavalier and economist figure to prosper, but not too much.[32]

The historical romances of the 1830s are populated by cavaliers and economists who illustrate the complicated relationship between a desire for progress and social mobility and a fear of unregulated free market enterprise and the destruction of social and economic regulations. Through the adventures of these heroes, the historical romances create a myth of the southern gentleman in the vein of the landed aristocrat of "good" stock; only good stock confers the innate genius possessed by New Men, cultivated through a form of ordered progress, and not necessarily determined by family lineage. As a result, the romances evince a "gatekeeper" mentality in terms of social and economic prominence, in which the conventions of the historical romance genre and the novels' presentation of the characters become methods of controlling who attains power in southern society.

The careful curation of the novels' heroes and characters—and the manner in which their exploits are continuously framed by narrative commentary such as that given in the opening passages of *Horse Shoe Robinson*—reveals the extent to which the form of the historical romance plays a gatekeeper role in refashioning southern history. This is not to say that Kennedy and Simms simply fictionalized southern history to their own ends; rather, like other authors of the time period, the genre of the historical romance presented possibilities for reenvisioning the interplay between fact and imagination to a particular ideological end. In the July and August 1860 issues of the *Atlantic Monthly,* for example, Kennedy published what comes closest to revealing his theory of historical fiction, particularly the historical romance. "A Legend of Maryland" details a story Kennedy discovered while researching the colonial history of Maryland for *Rob of the Bowl.* What follows is an account of the ways in which historical record and imaginative writing intertwine. While he concedes that archival materials and basic historical facts are necessary, he contends that fiction, fantasy, and romance could reveal the realities of history more fully to a reader than any supposedly straightforward chronicle, what he calls the "dry timbers of a vast old edifice": "But that which makes history the richest of philosophies and the most genial pursuit of humanity is the spirit that is breathed into it by the thoughts and feelings of former generations, interpreted in actions and incidents that disclose the passions, motives, and ambition of men, and open to us a view of the actual life of our forefathers. . . . History then becomes a world of living figures,—a theatre that presents to us a majestic drama, varied by alternate scenes of the grandest achievements and the most touching episodes of human existence" (29).[33]

"A Legend of Maryland" articulates the same conception of historical work and the translation of chronicle into story as outlined by Hayden White in *Metahistory.* Even though the climate of the nineteenth-century intellectual and literary world was fairly hostile to Scott-style romance as a form of "high" literature, Kennedy at least (and also Simms) recognized the genre's ability to reveal something about human experience in the midst of the "dry timbers" of historical fact—and to shape the presentation of that experience.

Throughout the romances of the 1830s, a clear narrative voice consistently inserts itself as a commentator, "breathing a spirit" into the historical details and shaping the ideological bent of the tale being told. "The phases of a time of errors and of wrongs," Simms writes in the preface to his 1835 novel, *The Partisan,* "it has been my aim to delineate, with all the rapidity of one, who, with the mystic lantern, runs his uncouth shapes and varying shadows along the gloomy wall, startling the imagination and enkindling the curiosity" (x). In holding up the "mystic lantern" to the past, the author casts light onto history, yet he also controls the direction of the lantern and, thus, what aspects of history are revealed to the reader and how.

Like the gatekeeper mentality that governs their economic and political views, this style of narration guides the reader through the historical records, events, and characters that form the basis of the tale. For instance, in *Horse Shoe Robinson,* the narrator will break frequently from the main plot to elaborate or comment: "I may pause here . . . to make an observation" (1:68). Or at the beginning of a chapter: "The thread which I have now to take up and weave into this history, requires that my narrative should go back some years" (1:91). This constant narrative framing creates distance from the tale being told and limits the characterization of the figure or event to the impressions conveyed by the narrative. Kennedy's narrator in *Horse Shoe Robinson,* in particular, steps back to comment on everything, from the presence or lack of historical archive on a topic or the personality of a character to his own narrative technique. The end results are novels that at once let the historical record speak for itself but also reassert and maintain narrative control. In doing so, the narrative voices in the earlier historical romances maintain the balance between economic growth and the fear of that growth shown in the representation of the heroes in the novels, particularly the socially and economically mobile characters who represent the antebellum period's cavaliers and economists. The reliance on historical record, the use of imaginative storytelling, and a strong narrative presence all converge to relay a particular story of southern history.

Simms's early novels pick up on these philosophies and follow many of the same patterns displayed by *Horse Shoe Robinson,* in which the form of the historical romance comments on modernization and defines the limits of social mobility for certain characters. Two of Simms's most popular (or most studied) early novels, both published in 1835, *The Yemassee. A Romance of Carolina* and *The Partisan: A Tale of the Revolution,* contain the same hero types featured in Kennedy's novel: the aristocratic gentleman planter and the middle-class frontier scout.[34] *The Yemassee* features conflicts between European settlers and native tribes during the early colonial period in South Carolina, and *The Partisan* is dominated by battles and skirmishes along the South Carolina frontier during the Revolutionary War. With their multiple heroes, the novels dodge through various cavalier and economist representations in their attempt to balance southern social traditions and economic growth.

The structure of the historical romance itself immediately sets the terms for socioeconomic mobility and progress in the novels and assigns those qualities only to particular individuals of so-called singular genius. The aristocratic heroes of *The Yemassee* and *The Partisan* maintain the primacy of the plantation aristocracy and traditional social orders through the marriage plots that conclude each. The heroes are paired with the noble women of the Carolina colonies and sustain the lineage of the planter elite. Yet these aristocratic figures are allowed to exhibit skills appropriate for the frontier setting and beyond the sphere of aristocracy in the novels. For much of *The Yemassee,* the aristocratic hero, Lord Craven, is disguised as Gabriel Harrison, a middle-class soldier; only later he is revealed to be the acting governor of the colony.[35] Similarly, the aristocrat in *The Partisan,* Major Robert Singleton, has lost his wealth and estate to the British soldiers and spends the entirety of the novel living and fighting in the swamps of South Carolina. Both unite with their corresponding love interests in the end—Craven marries Bess Matthews, the daughter of the local pastor,[36] and Singleton is engaged to Katherine Walton, the daughter of a landed aristocrat[37]—but they first prove their mettle as middle-class heroes by demonstrating their skills with practical matters and in battle. Thus, the primary heroes of Simms's 1830s historical romances occupy a liminal space: they can be members of a traditional southern elite while also demonstrating the skills valued in liberal capitalist philosophies.

Despite the limitations imposed by their adherence to generic form, both novels nonetheless allow their middle-class characters access to the qualities of a southern gentleman, if not the actual position, through their contact with aristocratic figures and their possession of natural abilities. In *The Partisan,* Lance Frampton, the youngest son of a middle-class farmer, becomes Singleton's protégé. Although his father and brother are uneducated farmers with little intellectual or personal grace, Lance is frequently described as "thoughtful and acute" as well as gentle of manner (2:123).[38] Lance's education as a gentleman becomes one of the incidental tasks for the novel's aristocratic figures, Singleton and Captain Porgy. The character of Hugh Grayson plays a similar role in *The Yemassee.* Also the son of a middle-class farmer, Grayson chafes under imposed class restrictions. On the topic of farming, he remonstrates to his older brother: "It will do for you, to take the mule's labour, who are so willing to be at the beck and call of every swaggering upstart; but I will not" (142). Like Lance Frampton, however, Grayson possesses abilities that would raise him beyond his current social and economic position. The narrator comments that "Hugh Grayson, with all his faults . . . was in reality a noble fellow. [He was] full of high ambition—a craving for the unknown and the vast, which spread itself vaguely and perhaps unattainably before his imagination" (336). Unlike his brother, and many of the other men in the colony, Hugh displays the ideal traits to succeed in a free market: ambition, intelligence, and drive in an open field of competition. To capitalize on these skills, Lord Craven tutors Grayson in military procedures.[39]

As part of the retelling of southern history, the middle-class characters of high intelligence and ingenuity in Simms's novels contain the promise of future generations—namely, those of the antebellum South in the 1830s. Yet as cavalier and economist figures, that promise is delimited by the plotting of the historical romance genre: neither of these men will marry the daughters of plantation aristocracy and produce future genteel southerners. In the same way that Simms's vision of democracy and economic modernization in his early nonfiction is always tempered by the presence of traditional social hierarchies, his early historical romances project the ideal of progress but only so far and only in a controlled, or "ordered," fashion.

In contrast to the ordered progress that colors the portrayal of Simms's middle-class characters, Kennedy's *Horse Shoe Robinson* foregrounds its nonaristocratic hero and offers the potential for more autonomy to a cavalier and economist. Horse Shoe Robinson is one of a pair of dual heroes and the titular character. Throughout much of the novel, neither he nor Arthur Butler, the aristocrat, takes precedence, and the plot shifts between the two as they encounter Loyalist troops and British forces, engage in rescue attempts and acts of espionage, and encounter civilians along the way. The characters also represent two distinct segments of southern society and modes of heroism: Arthur Butler is a member of the landed aristocracy, a gentleman cavalier who is an accomplished soldier and a well-educated landowner; Horse Shoe Robinson is a middle-class frontiersman who demonstrates military skill and the sort of self-motivated drive that spurs social and economic mobility. The plot of the novel maintains the efficacy of both men as heroes in its tale of southern social development, and that dual emphasis complicates the presentation of southern history and social institutions in a way that differentiates it from Simms's version of ordered progress.

Taken at face value, *Horse Shoe Robinson* seems to promote the practical, middle-class virtues represented by Robinson. The soldier is the most prominent figure in the novel and the main character through which much of the action is focalized. Throughout the novel's action, Robinson is a free agent in every sense of the word.[40] As a sergeant in the American army and an inhabitant of the southern colonies who is familiar with the area, he possesses the ability to move through enemy territories unscathed. The novel is peppered with scenes in which Robinson outwits and outfights British soldiers "with that acute insight which was concealed under a rude and uneducated exterior, but which was strongly marked in his actions" (1:227).

The novel also portrays Robinson as a man of practical foresight paired with a businesslike sense of organization. When making and executing decisions during battle or any military engagement, "his thoughts ran in no other current than to obey the order, and make the most *thrifty* and careful *provisions* for its safe execution" (2:235, my emphasis). The word choice here is significant: not only is Robinson a man of action; he is "thrifty," or economical, in those actions. That use of the word *thrifty* implies a mentality that takes into consideration future profits from a certain situation, not merely a facility with a gun or in combat. Robinson, through his acts on the battlefield, his wider knowledge of the frontier and its operations, and his implied success financially with his farming truly embodies the traits of a cavalier *and* an economist functioning in a liberal capitalist order.

In contrast, the other hero, Arthur Butler, spends much of the novel in British captivity and under the threat of execution for treason, while the other characters' rescue attempts occupy the rest of the plot. Butler is an aristocrat and cavalier in the purest sense of the word, whose features "denoted a gentle breeding predominating over a life of toil and privation" (1:18). Unlike Robinson, his character is entirely motivated by a sense of honor and duty to those he loves. In scenes of action, these qualities come to the forefront. During his captivity with the British forces, a commanding officer offers to free Butler if he renounces the cause of the Revolution and joins the Loyalist forces. Butler adamantly refuses, claiming: "Prisoner as I am, I will *avenge the insult* on the spot with the certainty of loss of life. The alternative you suggest, is to *dishonor* me and all who are dear to me by the foul opprobrium of treason to my country" (1:303, my emphasis). Butler's focus is on the perceived insult and resulting damage to his honor, not the simple act of living and fighting. The British officer observes the folly of this attitude: "I will not wound, by further converse, the exaggerated and delusive sense of honour which is too fatally predominant in your breast . . . and in the breast of many of your misguided countrymen" (1:303). Although the novel clearly presents Butler as an admirable figure, Robinson, as the other hero of the novel, is not hindered by such high-flown concerns of reputation. If Robinson is the emblem of frontier rebellion and progress, Butler represents the aristocratic, plantation-owning southern elite. As Robinson describes him, he is "Major Butler—a bold, warm gentleman—that's been used to tender life and good fortune" (1:257).

Butler is purportedly a man of action, yet he is thwarted continually by his own inexperience and inability to divest himself of a romantic view of the world. At the very beginning of the novel, the two men are introduced while riding through the North Carolina countryside. Robinson is focused on the ride and their scouting mission, but Butler is distracted by "the earnest emotions which this wild and beautiful scenery excited in his mind" (1:17). This mentality often fails him in moments of distress—Robinson evades capture, while Butler frequently fails to comprehend the tricks of the frontier scout, which results in his captivity throughout most of the novel.[41] Still, Butler is not some secondary character; the equal emphasis given to his and Robinson's exploits throughout the novel points to the tenuous balance between the divergent elements that lay at the core of antebellum southern culture and the ambivalence of the 1830s: southern economic modernization and southern aristocracy.

Yet through the form of the historical romance, the novel once again embodies the gatekeeper mentality evident in the representation of middle-class characters such as Lance Frampton and Hugh Grayson in Simms's novels. That perspective gestures toward the tenets of individual, free market enterprise evoked by liberal capitalism but nonetheless hedges away from complete democratization. Like Captain Dauntrees, Horse Shoe Robinson is equal parts cavalier and self-interested economist, a hero who cannot quite measure up to the standards of the New Man ideal. Therefore, despite the novel's seeming allegiance to the emblem of the cavalier and economist represented by Robinson, the conventions of the romance plot maintain the primacy of the plantation elite and its ideologies of racial and class hierarchies represented by Butler.

First, the presence of a large slave population is a given. There are few black characters depicted in *Horse Shoe Robinson,* and those who appear are always stock slave figures associated only with the wealthiest characters. Later in the novel, Kennedy introduces a young, pampered slave owned by Philip Lindsay, a wealthy plantation owner with British loyalties. The young boy is barely given a mention, and the description reduces him to a ridiculous accessory: he is a "fantastical little attendant . . . a diminutive negro boy, not above ten years of age, of a delicate figure, and now gaudily bedecked in a vest of scarlet cloth . . . . His business seemed to be at the present moment, to acquit himself of the responsible duty of holding an ivory-mounted riding-whip in readiness of the service of his mistress [Philip Lindsay's daughter]" (2:99–100). After that detailed and dismissive appraisal, the boy is never mentioned again. Middle-class characters such as Robinson, however, do not possess slaves. The novel's slave characters, like actual slaves during the antebellum period, become two-dimensional markers of wealth and privilege for the upper-class white characters, consistent and interchangeable background figures in the narrative of southern history.[42]

Second, and more important in terms of following the generic conventions of the historical romance, the marriage ending of the novel does not sustain the primacy of Robinson as a heroic character. The novel concludes with the union between Arthur Butler, the cavalier aristocrat, and Mildred Lindsay, Philip Lindsay's daughter. The marriage strengthens the bond between two prominent, landowning families in the southern colonies and also establishes a pedigree for the antebellum South at the time of the novel's publication. In one of the most significant narrative interventions, Kennedy's narrator comments on the fate of his characters in an epilogue.[43] Mildred and Butler, he notes, "lived long enough after the revolution to see grow up around them, a prosperous and estimable family" (2:297). According to Kennedy's version of southern history, families like the Butlers are the source of future generations of southerners that emerged from the Revolutionary War.

In promoting Butler's future prosperity and limiting Robinson's strength to frontier or martial settings, Kennedy's novel comments on the potential dangers of unrestrained growth and social mobility. Robinson may display proficiency in battle, but his role as a self-motivated free agent poses a threat to the established social order. In yet another narrative intervention, Kennedy's narrator describes Robinson's performance during an actual skirmish. Robinson is loyal to the American cause, but in the heat of battle, "he made no scruple of deserting his companions and trying his fortune on the field in such form of adventure as best suited his temper" (2:279). Here a sense of duty to a larger cause is momentarily overshadowed by the immediate benefits to Robinson himself, which violates the dictates of communal organization, honor, and singular genius represented by the New Man ideal.

Robinson can be the representative of future progress and social mobility for the South, yet the "economist" aspects of his character limit his ability to thrive in the context of Kennedy's novel. In the epilogue, the narrator encounters Robinson in the winter of 1818 as a bachelor on a small farm in North Carolina. He is still the practical problem solver (he sets a young boy's broken leg during the encounter) and a successful farmer, but he is not the progenitor of future generations like Butler—no wife, no children. He is simply an older version of the character described in the bulk of the novel: "It is sufficient to say that I saw the same man of mould in what was, to him, a green old age" (2:297). Just as the narrator intervenes to curtail the social mobility of Captain Dauntrees in *Rob of the Bowl*—or

Lance Frampton and Hugh Grayson in *The Partisan* and *The Yemassee*—the epilogue both advocates for yet limits the possibilities open to Robinson. The result is an ambivalent depiction of socioeconomic mobility within the increased dominance of a free market, slave-based economy.

In *Horse Shoe Robinson* and other novels of the 1830s, southern authors such as Kennedy and Simms use the historical romance genre to delimit the influence of the cavaliers and economists who were populating the South in the early decades of the century. Although many of the primary characters incline toward individual social and economic mobility, the narrative style and adoption of generic plot conventions assert the gatekeeper control over who and what defines southern society. These novels, as early southern historical romances, provide templates for the sort of balance sought by other southern authors later in the century. However, while the early romances display the social and political ambivalence of the New Man mentality, later novels, particularly those written by Simms in the 1850s, use the genre to *revise* southern history according to the antebellum narrative of upwardly mobile yet still aristocratic in nature plantation owners—the cavaliers and economists.

"Revising History": William Gilmore Simms

> The themes suggested by [Simms], viewed as he views them, would produce nothing but historical novels, cast in the same worn-out mould that had been in use these thirty years, and which it is time to break up and fling away.
>
> —Hawthorne, "Simms's *Views and Reviews,*" *Salem Advertiser,* 2 May 1846

> My novels aim at something more than the story. I am really, though indirectly, revising history.
>
> —Simms to John Reuben Thompson, 7 February 1856, *Letters*

In 1852, William Gilmore Simms wrote to John Pendleton Kennedy, "We differ in respect to party politics; but Whig and Dem. [Democrat] in the South are equally Conservative, & the demands of Conservatism, for Common Safety, require the Union of all our powers" (*Letters* 3:160). Although Simms was an avid Jacksonian Democrat throughout his life—a position that chafed against Kennedy's Whiggishness—he assumed that their common background as southerners was enough to unite them intellectually. Yet ideologically, Kennedy moved further away from the South during the growing sectional tension of the 1850s. Beginning in the 1830s, Kennedy either sold or freed what few slaves he owned, and when sectional tensions finally came to a head in 1860, he supported the Union (Bohner 169–71, 227–9).

Simms, in contrast, is probably best known for his conservative defenses of slavery, the plantation system, and the South, especially toward the end of his life.[44] The simplified trajectory of Simms's politics and writing adopted by most critics is the reverse of Kennedy: Simms has been characterized as having been an ardent nationalist at the beginning of his career, but a staunch southern sectionalist closer to the Civil War. According to this timeline, the historical romances published in the 1850s portray valorized images of South Carolina's history that uphold slavery and southern traditions in response to sectional debates.[45]

Simms's historical romances are consistent, however, in their representation of the South in a way not recognized in the common biographical narrative.[46] A proslavery position is always a constant in Simms's texts, but so is the representation of a particular type of economic philosophy. Chiefly through its promotion of Jacksonian democracy and the ideal of a self-sufficient, socially and economically mobile middle-class, Simms's fiction throughout his career adheres to a version of free market capitalism seemingly at odds with the conservative southern platform. Even his earlier novels—*The Yemassee* and *The Partisan,* for example—with their ambivalent representations of socioeconomic mobility, exhibit a ground-up mentality in regard to national economic progress, with growth being spurred by talented members of the middle class.

If his attitudes and political opinions did not change over time, what shifted is how the genre of the historical romance portrays a particular vision of the South in Simms's works.[47] While his romances of the 1830s parallel the New Man mentality of Whigs such as Kennedy in their response to the rapid economic growth of the era, Simms's historical romances of the 1850s establish a historical narrative for the antebellum South that advocates for future economic change in an emerging capitalist economy. In light of the economic fluctuations and sectional divisions of the 1830s and 1840s, especially the effects of the Bank Panic of 1837, Simms's later novels comment more on what the South and the nation could be versus voicing anxieties over the current state of southern society as it was.

Simms's 1854 novel, *Woodcraft; or, Hawks about the Dovecote,* "revises" the story of southern history to correspond to a vision of an aristocratic, slave-owning society that also advocates for economic development independent of plantation agriculture. This new story of the South retains the purportedly precapitalist properties of the region's plantation- and slave-based society yet nonetheless adheres to principles of democratic self-determinism and modernization in the context of the free market.[48] If Simms's 1856 lecture was a way of justifying the contemporary South through a rearticulation of its history, then the historical romance became a way of declaring an agenda for the South that projects both a progressive vision of economic self-sufficiency and a defense of social structures and slavery sustained by the plantation.[49]

Simms himself, as many of his biographers have pointed out, enacted the ideal form of social mobility envisioned in his early historical romances and fully realized in his later novels. Simms was born in Charleston, South Carolina, and his father was an Irish immigrant and tavern keeper who moved into the Southwest territories after his wife's death in 1808. Afterward Simms was raised by his grandmother in Charleston. This varied upbringing instilled a sense of respect for old Charleston society, along with a recognition of the opportunities for social mobility represented by his father's successful plantation in Mississippi (Guilds, *Simms* 9, 17–18). Although Simms would become a "gentleman planter" through his lucrative authorial career and his second marriage to the daughter of a wealthy Charleston family, an awareness of social class followed him throughout his life.[50] With his successful career as an author during the late 1830s, it would seem Simms achieved the social standing promised but never realized by the cavalier and economist figures of Lance Frampton and Hugh Grayson in his early historical romances.

The Panic of 1837 severely damaged Simms's finances, as it did for many Americans, and it hurt his writing prospects.[51] Longer two-volume novels such as *The Yemassee* and *The Partisan* were out of vogue due to the rising costs of publishing and printing. Simms observed in an 1838 letter: "I have been mightily worried—So much so as to have written little or nothing. Indeed, for that matter, to have written, would have been fruitless enough. There is no publishing, no selling, what one writes" (*Letters* 1:132). Following the Panic and throughout the 1840s, Simms devoted more of his energy to politics and writing nonfiction—though he still managed to write a few novels.

Publishing was not the only industry affected by the depression that followed the 1837 financial collapse. Crop prices, particularly cotton, fell, and hundreds of Americans who had invested their money in the markets or agricultural ventures were left destitute. The Panic led to a worldwide depression, but the South was hit particularly hard. A thriving triangular trade between Britain, the northern United States, and the South collapsed for a short period, leaving many southern farmers and planters with unsold harvests and debt, which then led to the failures of numerous cotton and agricultural firms.[52]

Although Simms had always advocated for southern industrialization and economic development as part of his theory of progress, his writing after the Panic places greater emphasis on the need for the South to be self-sufficient within the context of free market capitalism. Most critics who subscribe to the "nationalism to sectionalism" trajectory of Simms's career assume the shift reflected an intensified allegiance to the southern cause sparked by abolitionism.[53] In light of the concept of progress that emerges in his earlier fiction, however, Simms's writing on economic development indicates a growing awareness of the changing economic climate. The economy recovered after the 1837 Panic, but the South's continued dependence on global agricultural markets loomed as a constant threat for many upper-class southerners.[54]

In the context of the increased sectional tensions in the 1840s and 1850s, economic self-sufficiency became equated with cultural self-sufficiency, and southern conservatives advocated for industrialization as a way to attain greater regional autonomy. In an 1841 speech to the South Carolina Agricultural Convention, Simms's close friend and South Carolina politician James Henry Hammond posited that cotton cultivation would soon be a thing of the past: "But why . . . shall we confine ourselves strictly to Agricultural pursuits, possessing, as we do, so many other resources, inviting and rewarding as amply here as elsewhere enterprise and industry?" ("Anniversary Oration" 22). He then makes a case for southern manufacturing, noting, "[Manufacturies] add vastly to the nerve and sinew of the body politic. And when united in the same community with a class of industrious and enlightened agriculturalists, they mutually enrich and strengthen one another" (24). In the speech, Hammond amends Jefferson's vision in *Notes on the State of Virginia* (1787), which separates agriculture and industry by continents: "Carpenters, masons, smiths, are wanting in husbandry; but, for the general operations of manufacture, let our *workshops* remain in Europe" (166, my emphasis). Instead, Hammond presents the possibility of southern industrialization, modernization, and individual profit joining with the contemporary plantation-based agricultural system under a unified "body politic" (24).[55] According to this proposition, the South could maintain the institutions of slavery and the southern planter class while still allowing for economic mobility and industrialization.[56]

Simms takes up a similar call for the South to adapt economically in an 1850 article for the *Southern Quarterly Review,* "Summer Travel in the South." He first critiques the South's lack of economic development and general dependence on the North, which he claims is the result of an overreliance on plantation agriculture: "As a natural consequence, therefore, of the exclusive occupation of agriculture in the south, the profits of this culture, and the sparseness of our population, the Southern people left it to the Northern States to supply all their wants. . . . The Yankees furnished all our manufactures, or whatever kind, and adroitly contrived to make it appear to us that they were really our benefactors, at the very moment when they were sapping our substance, degrading our minds, and growing rich upon our raw material, and by the labour of our slaves" (31).

That dependence, Simms continues, is what prevents the South from becoming self-sufficient as a region: "To secure a high rank in society, as well as history, it is necessary that a people should do something more than provide a raw material. It is required of them to provide the genius also, which shall work the material up into forms and fabrics equally beautiful and valuable" (32). Again, the term *genius* appears: it is not enough to provide "raw material" (i.e., cotton) or even to implement manufacturing in the region. Those involved must also possess the innate skills and talent to make both industries thrive. The dynamic recycles the same theories of social hierarchy seen in Simms's earlier writings and in Kennedy's conceptions of the New Man. And as with Hammond's earlier proposals, Simms's observations adapt Jefferson's ideals so that the region progresses with a modernizing and industrializing economy. Therefore, in order "to secure a high rank in history," southerners must have the best of both worlds: a South that descends from the honorable and intelligent cavaliers represented by the plantation elite yet one that still fits within the economic modernization occurring on a global level.[57]

This impulse toward self-sufficiency and progress was not limited to southern intellectuals. Numerous authors of the era proposed a similar form of national autonomy, particularly in regard to literature and art. Ralph Waldo Emerson—with whom Simms would have been connected through his correspondence with Nathaniel Hawthorne in the "Young America" circle in the 1840s[58]—declared a similar goal of *national* autonomy in regard to art and learning in his 1837 speech, "The American Scholar." Advocating for American intellectuals to use their life experiences and talents as the basis for creativity, his language is virtually identical to that of Simms more than a decade later: "[Experience] is the *raw material* out of which the intellect moulds her splendid products. A strange process too, this, by which experience is converted into thought, as a mulberry leaf is converted into satin. The *manufacture* goes forward at all hours" (98, my emphasis). For Emerson, a sense of unity and autonomy derived from the daily experiences of all Americans was the avenue to a distinct national art, an American renaissance. "We have listened too long to the courtly muses of Europe," he concludes (107). Simms, instead, translates that impulse into *regional* capital and cultural self-sufficiency, to create a new, regionally based economic system.

For Simms, the historical romance was the ideal form to achieve this economic and social autonomy, as fiction's ultimate goal was to create a story of the national timeline and revise history according to the impulses of economic development and progress. "The true and most valuable inspiration of the poet," Simms writes in his essay collection *Views and Reviews in American Literature, History, and Fiction* (1845), "will be found either in the illustration of the national history, or in the development of national characteristics" (53–4).[59] If the work of the poet or author is to outline the dimensions of a nation and national history, Simms's later historical romances of the Revolutionary era modify that historical development through fictional representation. Simms declares in *Views and Reviews:* "It is the artist only who is the true historian. It is he who gives shape to the unhewn fact, who yields relation to the scattered fragments,—who unites the parts in a coherent dependency, and endows, with life and action, the otherwise motionless automata of history. It is by such artists that nations live. It is the soul of art . . . [that ensures] the possessions of the past, and to transmit, with the most happy confidence in fame, his own possessions to the future" (36).

This passage again echoes Hayden White's interpretation of historical writing, Kennedy's philosophy of history articulated in "A Legend of Maryland," as well as Simms's own charge in the preface to *The Partisan* to "hold a lantern" to history. The language also mirrors that of Emerson in his essay "The Poet" (1844), when he asserts: "The sign and credentials of the poet are, that he announces that which no man foretold. He is the true and only doctor; he knows and tells; he is the only teller of news. . . . He is the beholder of ideas" (205). Yet Simms takes the function of art, or historical fiction, a step further to uphold its continued importance for defining future generations. While *The Yemassee* and *The Partisan* projected visions of progress through the gradual attainment of social mobility and economic development, they use the form of the romance to limit their cavalier and economist characters. The later novels, written during economic and sectional crises, focus on revising history according to Simms's vision of a future South through those same generic conventions of the historical romance. What to Hawthorne was a tired repetition of the "worn-out mould" of the British romance tradition—a trite deference to the "courtly muses of Europe"—was, in fact, a way of laying the foundation for a southern renaissance.[60]

Simms's novel, *Woodcraft; or, Hawks about the Dovecote,* performs this work of historical revision as his only Revolutionary novel set after the war. *Woodcraft* is the novel most discussed by critics, which makes it useful for discussing Simms's representations of the southern economy. But as a historical romance set after the war, it is also about rebuilding a community and society and, in the process, sorting through which important social values to keep and which to disregard. More than many of the other Revolutionary novels, *Woodcraft* draws from the impulse of the historical romance to "illustrate national characteristics," as Simms articulates it in *Views and Reviews.* In this case, the "nation" described is the South, the region that Simms and so many other conservative southerners wished to become economically self-sufficient and eventually independent.

Published originally in 1852 as *The Sword and the Distaff; or, Fair, Fat, and Forty, Woodcraft* tells the story of South Carolina at the end of the Revolutionary War through the experiences of Captain Porgy, a once-wealthy plantation owner and soldier.[61] Porgy is first introduced in *The Partisan* as a fat "gourmand," but the later novel reveals more nuances to his character. After the British withdraw from South Carolina, Porgy returns to his plantation, Glen-Eberley, to find it ravaged by British soldiers. Most of the slaves have been run off, the plantation house and his possessions have been stolen or destroyed, and the fields are fallow. The plantation has also been mortgaged to a Scottish businessman, McKewn.

According to this configuration, Porgy could be the typical hero of a historical romance. But rather than a military foe, his enemy is a businessman who represents the debts and financial losses Porgy incurred during the war. Despite its frequent scenes of adventure and battle, the novel is primarily about securing property and wealth in the aftermath of war—in other words, achieving the economic and material self-sufficiency advocated by southern conservatives in the 1840s and 1850s. *Woodcraft* begins with a description of the state of affairs in Charleston after the Revolution, emphasizing the financial state of the Americans: "Peace was agreed upon; the British army was about to evacuate the city; the Americans were crowding about their outposts, eager to come in. Meanwhile commissioners from both were in the city, preparing for a peaceable restoration of prisoners, chattels, and soil. . . . The American commissioners were particularly solicitous in respect to this matter. South Carolina had already lost twenty-five thousand slaves, which British philanthropy had transferred from the rice-fields of Carolina, to the sugar estates of the West India Islands; and there were yet other thousands waiting to be similarly transported" (5–6). From the beginning, the novel stresses the importance of property, specifically slaves, in rebuilding South Carolina after the war. The rest of the novel then revolves around the financial revitalization of the area as told through Porgy's attempts to recover his slaves, pay the mortgage on his plantation, and begin the process of planting and harvesting.

Porgy, however, defies the blueprint for the aristocratic hero present in the earlier novels. At a basic level, he represents the virtues of a gentleman demonstrated by figures such as Arthur Butler in *Horse Shoe Robinson,* Robert Singleton in *The Partisan,* and Lord Craven in *The Yemassee.* He inherited his plantation as the only son of a wealthy South Carolina family; he is educated; and he possesses a sense of honor demonstrated by any good cavalier in the romantic tradition. However, he also displays all of the failings of the southern plantation elite. Brought up in prosperity, Porgy "had never been taught the pains of acquisition. Left to himself—his own dangerous keeping—when a mere boy, he had too soon and fatally learned the pleasures of dissipation" (101). As Porgy admits of himself, "I was always one of that large class of planters who reap thistles from their planting. I sowed wheat only to reap tares" (189). Despite the blame he places on luck, Porgy recognizes that his laziness and lack of experience in earning his own way are constant barriers to his own material security.

As a result, the novel is peppered with scenes of Porgy's follies, most of which stem from his inability to live within his means or run the plantation.[62] Because he always left the management of the farm and his finances to others—in the true style of the plantation aristocrat—the decimation of his estate after the war leaves Porgy completely adrift. He eats and drinks away his troubles, finding consolation in the pleasures of life he can no longer afford and "temporary relief in usury" and bad loans, which only exacerbate the money problems (101–2). These problems are compounded by Porgy's misplaced sense of honor and duty; in one scene, Porgy gives a sum of money, a large portion of his remaining funds, to the young daughter of a neighboring family struggling to survive. The action, though charitable, reflects a "philosophy a little too strained for common use," as one character observes (232). Whatever improvements to his finances occur by the end of the novel are due to the help of his middle-class, wartime compatriots, who take over the planting, rebuilding, and reorganization of the estate while Porgy looks on.

The nonaristocratic characters are, in fact, the ones who adopt the roles of the more practical heroes according to *Woodcraft's* narrative of economic improvement. Porgy returns from the war accompanied by several of the men with whom he served; all plan to live on Glen-Eberley and help the captain rebuild his fortune. One of them is Lance Frampton from *The Partisan,* who is now a few years older and engaged to the daughter of Porgy's neighbor Mrs. Griffin. Lance still retains the intelligence and gentleness of nature that mark him in the earlier novel, but he is more skilled in farm management than Porgy. When the group returns to the plantation, he pitches in with the rest to rebuild the farm, which Porgy seems incapable of doing. He is also more familiar with the basic functioning of the legal system. The condition of Porgy's finances means that his estate is perpetually subject to repossession by the sheriff (acting under McKewn's direction). Porgy's solution is to fight and defend his honor, in the style of a cavalier. Frampton, however, points out the folly of this approach, based on his own experiences. "You're a man of learning," he remarks to Porgy, "and can tell much better than me; but I'm rather dubious. When I was a boy, old Humphries . . . sent the sheriff after my father, and took him, and took all the property besides. . . . Now, won't they take you, captain, if you can't pay?" (112). The "man of learning" comment, though meant earnestly by the speaker, is ironic in this case. Porgy's education and breeding are what keep him from functioning in the environment of the post–Revolutionary War South, while Lance's real-life (and tragic) experiences enable him to prosper.

The other character even more adept at negotiating the uncertainties of life after wartime is Fordham, the overseer of a neighboring plantation owned by Mrs. Eveleigh, a gentlewoman of the South Carolina elite. In most criticism of the novel, Fordham is virtually ignored and rarely identified by name. Yet he is afforded a long description in the opening chapters. Although "he was evidently a backwoodsman, in humble life," Fordham's features tell of his higher intellectual qualities: "His great blue eye was expressive of much benevolence, but mixed with a decisive and earnest manliness" (23). At the moment of his introduction, Mrs. Eveleigh is in the process of recovering her property (i.e., slaves), and "in this business [Fordham] was much more efficient than any of the more eminent friends of Mrs. Eveleigh could have been" (24). While Porgy and other Carolina aristocrats are at a loss in recovering financially after the war, Fordham thrives with his practical knowledge.

Fordham's talents are further demonstrated in an extended battle scene that occupies a large portion of the novel's first half. After recovering her slaves, Mrs. Eveleigh travels with her young son, Arthur, and Fordham back to her plantation. The party is attacked on the road by agents of McKewn (who had stolen her slaves in the first place). Porgy eventually comes to their rescue at the end of the skirmish, but Fordham takes the lead during most of the fight by utilizing the titular "woodcraft," or knowledge of the forest and skill at avoiding detection. The battle scene follows the patterns of Simms's earlier romances set during the Revolution but replaces the aristocratic figure adept at frontier fighting with the nonaristocratic figure adept both at battle and negotiating matters related to finance and property. In a chapter appropriately titled "Lessons in Woodcraft," Fordham instructs young Arthur Eveleigh, the budding aristocrat, in the nuances of frontier fighting as the pair ambushes a bandit in the forest. The scenes reverse the dynamic of the earlier novels. Instead of the aristocrats instructing the promising middle-class figures, the frontiersman, with "quick, sagacious experience," instructs the young aristocrat. The main characters escape the skirmish in large part due to the "perfect success by the practiced woodsman," with "Arthur Eveleigh following promptly in his track, and emulating his circumspection" (73–4). Simms uses the scene of battle to associate the young aristocrat with practical knowledge and valorize the skills of the frontiersman.

Another nonaristocratic figure who distinguishes himself in *Woodcraft* is Sergeant Millhouse, also one of Porgy's compatriots from the war. Like Fordham, Millhouse's talents are in battle and practical matters, particularly in running a plantation. He and Porgy have an extended argument over the uses of "utilitarianism" midway through the novel.[63] Throughout the dialogue, Millhouse points out—and Porgy freely admits—the captain's complete lack of practical knowledge: "You see your ixperence is jest none at all in the way of business. You don't know what's useful in the world. You only know what's pleasant, and amusing, and ridikulous, and what belongs to music, and poetry, and the soul; and not about the wisdom that makes crops grow, and drives a keen bargain, and swells the money-box, and keeps the kiver down" (290). Millhouse's condemnation echoes Simms's criticism of the South in "Summer Travel": that the South, especially the aristocratic planter class, has neglected to cultivate its own material self-sufficiency. The result is that southerners have contented themselves with cultural and economic stagnation.

The debate makes a clear case for economic self-sufficiency, but it also makes clear that such self-sufficiency should work within the confines of the social structures and racial hierarchies of the southern plantation system already in place. Frequently, particularly when he discusses business or farming matters, Millhouse will identify himself or others as "white men" or "free white men." Early in the novel, for example, Porgy expresses a desire to go shooting, and Millhouse chastises him: "When a man's wanting flesh for the pot, and meal for the hoe-cake, its not reasonable that he should be a sportsman and a gentleman. That's a sort of extravagance that's not becoming to a *free white man,* when he's under bonds to a sheriff" (191). Later, when he pleads for Porgy to adopt more practical methods in running his plantation, Millhouse remarks, "And ef there was any other sensible *white man,* of *business,* you might listen to him too" (289, first emphasis mine).

Not only do these passages indicate the primacy of financial concerns in the novel; they demonstrate the constant presence of slavery and racial privilege that characterizes all of Simms's writing. The common critical assumption is that *Woodcraft* was a response to *Uncle Tom's Cabin*—mainly based on a letter Simms wrote to James Henry Hammond after its publication.[64] The scene used to support this assertion is an interaction between Porgy and his servant, Tom, toward the end of the novel. Porgy offers to free Tom, who promptly rejects the gesture, declaring, "Ef *I* doesn't b'long to *you, you* b'longs to *me!*" (509).[65] The exchange replicates the standard proslavery argument that slavery is, in fact, beneficial to those enslaved and that owning another human being is a symbiotic exchange.

If the novel is a narrative of the economic foundations of a region, however, Millhouse's position in *Woodcraft* indicates how Simms writes racial privilege and the institution of slavery into economic revitalization. "Free white men" have access to the opportunities for social and economic mobility as Simms presents them in the novel—not black men and women. And as with all of Simms's novels and writing, slavery is a given. Tom is a constant presence yet still a minor character, and none of the white characters enter into overt debates over slavery as they would in other proslavery texts. The slaves on Porgy's plantation are not even present for most of the novel; during the war they fled to the swamps to escape capture by British soldiers and only emerge midway through the novel. Therefore, despite *Woodcraft's* repeated advocacy for social mobility and criticism of the plantation elite, the novel presumes the importance of plantation aristocracy and social order, especially when it comes to maintaining racial hierarchies and the institution of slavery.[66]

A natural question for any reader of *Woodcraft* would be: why validate an aristocratic figure who is so ridiculous? In light of Simms's writings on national literature, his ideas of ordered progress, and his defense of South Carolina history in his 1856 northern lecture tour, the depiction of Porgy makes sense. For Simms and many other southerners at the time, justifying certain southern cultural markers was just as important as advocating for the region's economic modernization. Although Simms pushes his depictions of southern history further than Kennedy and his own earlier novels, entirely doing away with aristocratic characters like Porgy would also mean a total denial of a region that was on the decline and on the defensive, economically, politically, and socially.

The marriage plot ultimately cements Simms's revision of history by adapting the conventions of the historical romance. The ending fashions an image of the South that can progress according to the tenets of a free market economy but still retain the defining social structures of the region represented by slavery and Porgy the aristocrat. Of course, the novel ends with a marriage. Yet Simms does not follow the conventions of the standard romance of his earlier novels, in which the two aristocratic characters, Porgy and Mrs. Eveleigh, would unite. Porgy proposes to the widow, but she refuses, claiming her desire to remain independent.

Instead, Simms realigns the bride and groom to "transmit," as he puts it in *Views and Reviews,* his vision of an economically viable South to future generations. After Mrs. Eveleigh rejects his offer, Porgy then turns his attentions to Mrs. Griffin, a middle-class widow and the owner of a small but prosperous farm near Glen-Eberley. When he arrives at her home at the end of the novel, however, he discovers he is too late: "There, in the piazza, stood the fair Griffin, clasped close in the arms of the overseer, Fordham, and that audacious personage was actually engaged in tasting of her lips, as a sort of dessert after dinner" (516). Other than being told from the perspective of Porgy himself—thus accounting for the humorous description—the scene is nearly identical to the conclusions of Simms's earlier romances or those of Kennedy and Scott. Yet as in the earlier battle scene, Fordham, the overseer, supplants the traditional aristocratic hero. If the ending of *Horse Shoe Robinson* indicates that Arthur Butler fosters future generations of southerners, the ending of *Woodcraft* revises southern history to create a lineage for the antebellum South that corresponds to economic and social mobility in a competitive free market while still maintaining the structures of genteel aristocracy in the form of Mrs. Eveleigh and her young son.[67]

The record of the novel's publication further indicates this revision of history through the romance. The first title, *The Sword and the Distaff; or, Fair, Fat, and Forty,* highlights the novel's theme of domestic recovery after wartime. The title also places emphasis on the two upper-class characters: Porgy, the sword; and Mrs. Eveleigh, the distaff, or spindle. In addition, Mrs. Eveleigh is described in the novel as "fair, fat, and forty," and the subtitle maintains the focus on her character (370). In contrast, the second title, *Woodcraft; or, Hawks about the Dovecote*—the one by which the novel is usually known—shifts the emphasis to the middle-class characters, particularly Fordham, and their talents. In the image that accompanies the 1854 publication of *Woodcraft,* the featured scene is taken from the extended battle at the beginning of the novel in which the overseer assumes the heroic position (fig. 3).

Thus, *Woodcraft* begins with the financial and physical desolation of war but ends with the promise of future economic growth at the hands of the novel's nonaristocratic characters. By setting the novel after the war, Simms lays the groundwork for a revision of history that coincides with the version of the South articulated by him and his fellow southern conservatives in their nonfiction. In the end, the "worn-out" genre of the historical romance balances those ideologies while still achieving a form of resolution: the South can continue to rely on slavery and aristocratic social tenets while modernizing according to the principles of nineteenth-century liberal capitalism. Ultimately, what emerges is a united vision of the South sought by southern conservatives of the 1850s through its cavalier and economist figures that incorporate future southern economic progress into the social structures of the southern past.

Fig. 3. From William Gilmore Simms, *Woodcraft,* 1854.
Vanderbilt University Special Collections and University Archives.

In 1852, Simms wrote to Kennedy that in order to produce truly important work, an author's time should be devoted to "writing & *working wholly for yourself*" (*Letters* 3:175). For Kennedy, in his historical romances, this meant reflecting on the past in the present moment and imbuing it with imaginative life. For Simms, this meant that an author's role was to shape the history of a place and its people for future generations through literary form. In employing the historical romance to represent southern history, both writers navigated the complicated relationship between southern institutions and the changing social and economic world of the nineteenth century. While Kennedy's novels and the works of the 1830s open up the field to the cavaliers and economists of the early nineteenth century, Simms's novels in many ways more successfully adapt genre and integrate those figures into the future of southern cultural development. This impulse to modernize economically yet remain the same socially was a constant for southern authors throughout the antebellum period.

2

SKETCHING THE 1830s COTTON BOOM

Southwestern Humor

In 1836, Edgar Allan Poe reviewed a new book for the *Southern Literary Messenger* by a then unknown author. *Sketches by Boz* was Charles Dickens's first major publication and features a collection of stories, impressions, and character descriptions of London life that Dickens composed while working as a journalist in the city.[1] In his evaluation of the book, Poe identifies a critical trend to read sketches in a collection as "detached passages, without reference to the work as a whole—or without reference to any general design." He points out that Dickens's *Sketches,* in contrast, collects various impressions to create what Poe dubs a "unity of effect," in which the reader is left with a single impression of 1830s London (205). Using the metaphor of visual art to make his point,[2] Poe writes, "To the illustration of this one end all the *groupings* and *fillings in* of the painting are rendered subservient—and when our eyes are taken from the canvass, we remember the personages of the sketch not at all as independent existences, but as essentials of the one subject we have witnessed" (206). Therefore, according to Poe, the sketches "are all exceedingly well managed, and never fail to *tell* as the author intended" (205). In this case, the sketches in Dickens's collection tell of the rapidly changing space of London and the varied social classes that made up life in urban England in the mid-nineteenth century.

Poe's evaluation of *Sketches* reveals how the sketch form during the 1830s and 1840s could serve the ends of conveying a particular impression of a place or society. During this time, the sketch became more commonplace and more popular in conjunction with the boom in print journalism and growing urbanization on both sides of the Atlantic. In contrast to the novel, Poe argues in his review, the sketch has the ability to create a "unity of effect" that nonetheless pulls from a varied set of subjects and themes. While the novel's unity is assumed, the sketch collection creates that unity through its diverse and brief representations.

At the same time that Poe wrote his review of *Sketches,* the center of growth for the southern American region was shifting from the East Coast—where Poe, Simms, Kennedy, and the *Southern Literary Messenger* were all based—to the West. As a result of the growing demand for cotton in factories in the North and England—and motivated by the promise of plentiful land in the growing territories of Georgia, Alabama, Mississippi, and Arkansas—thousands of settlers poured into the South, and plantations sprang up throughout what was then known as the "Southwest." The growing and diversifying 1830s London featured in Dickens's *Sketches* was one node in the transatlantic economy that connected the southern American region to the rest of the globe.

In turn, fiction written about the South increasingly shifted from the historical romances to sketches of the Southwest. The same economic downturn that led to longer novels becoming passé in the 1840s gave rise to the popularity of the sketch throughout the United States. Beginning in the 1820s and lasting up through the Civil War, American newspapers published humorous stories and sketches set in the expanding territories of the West, particularly the Southwest.[3] Two collections of such stories, Johnson Jones Hooper's *Some Adventures of Captain Simon Suggs* (1845) and Joseph Glover Baldwin's *The Flush Times of Alabama and Mississippi* (1853), are both set during the boom of the 1830s, when immigrants flooded into the southwestern region and individuals became wealthy through land speculation. All of this would culminate in the 1837 Panic that drastically changed the fortunes of most white southerners (and northerners, for that matter).

Just as London and the Southwest were connected by trading patterns during the nineteenth century, sketches representing these areas depict spaces that were quickly changing due to the Industrial Revolution and transatlantic trade. The collections by Hooper and Baldwin emerge from the economic moment that united the British metropolis with the southwestern frontier through global trade and industrial development. The mid-nineteenth-century sketch form, particularly as it was employed in southern literature, focused more on representing a temporal change and cultural shifts than a particular location. The sketch collections, with their ability to create "unity" from heterogeneity (to paraphrase Poe), present the ideal literary form to represent spaces in economic and social flux.

But rapid change also entailed an upending of previously stable mores and social structures, a problem that the early-nineteenth-century sketch also addressed. As a result, the collections discussed in this chapter employ the confidence man trope as a way of negotiating the pull between older economic and social systems and the emerging transatlantic economy. In settings that were shaped by an increasingly dominant free market economy, the financially savvy but untrustworthy man was king, and these figures are central characters in the Southwest humor sketches. Their role is to embody the potential for socioeconomic mobility in a free market but also to represent the potential dangers.

Southern authors used the sketch form to negotiate rapid change occurring in the region throughout the antebellum period. Dickens's *Sketches* provides a model for understanding the way in which southern authors would approach representations of the 1830s "flush times" and the attendant changes to the southern economy and social order. The sketch collections by Hooper and Baldwin trace the emergence of a new economic standard through the confidence man figure. With the sketch form as a framework for understanding the economic patterns represented in Southwest humor collections, a new social order develops at the beginning of the nineteenth century through a literary paradigm, in which older, precapitalist economic structures give way to the dominance of free market capitalism. Yet that shift was not without ambivalence on the part of the participants, and the sketch authors utilized their representations to balance the advent of the new—and sometimes treacherous—economic context with the desire to maintain elements of older, more traditional social structures.

Little Pictures of Visible and Violent Transition

In 1835, Nathaniel Parker Willis wrote: "America is much farther off from England than England from America. You in New York read the periodicals of this country, and know every thing that is done or written here, as if you lived within the sound of Bow-bell. The English, however, just know of our existence, and if they get a general idea twice a year of our progress in politics, they are comparatively well informed. Our periodical literature is never even heard of" (369). In the passage Willis highlights a constellation of economic, social, and literary networks that defined transatlantic culture during the 1830s. Taken from a sketch of London that was republished in the *Southern Literary Messenger*—the South's premier literary magazine before the Civil War—and written by one of the most famous American journalists of the day, this small passage traverses large distances, both geographically and conceptually.[4] Despite his assertions of the English ignorance of American culture, Willis's passage inadvertently draws attention to a triangle of connection that structured British-American transatlantic relations from the colonial period up through the Civil War.

The publication date alone is significant: 1835, just at the moment that the southwestern territorial boom was reaching its peak. In the years leading up to the Panic of 1837, what was then known as the American Southwest—primarily the states of Georgia, Alabama, Mississippi, and Arkansas—experienced an influx of new settlers hoping to capitalize on "open" territories and the thriving transatlantic cotton market. A higher demand for cotton required a larger portion of land on which to grow it, and the southern states as they were (namely, Maryland, Virginia, Tennessee, and the Carolinas) could not logistically meet that demand, both in terms of space and also the conditions needed to grow a large amount of cotton. The Old Southwest stretching from the Carolinas to Arkansas, however, could fill that need with its varying soil composition and space on which to organize larger-scale plantations. Through the movement of raw cotton from these plantations and cotton manufactures interregionally in the United States and then across the Atlantic, England and America formed a global network that influenced the economic structures of each region and nation and eventually shaped the cultural production of those spaces.

Therefore, however "far off" America was from England, the U.S. South was crucial to the British economy and transatlantic trade in the 1830s and afterward. The period from 1800 to 1840 in England witnessed massive industrial and economic changes, particularly in the area of cotton manufacturing. As English novelist Edward Bulwer-Lytton would remark in his 1833 history, *England and the English,* it was "a time of visible and violent transition" (2:68). Due to numerous technological innovations in cotton processing as well as transportation and manufacturing, England evolved from an agriculturally based economic and social system to a social and economic structure that emphasized more urban industrial centers.[5] More factories meant more jobs, and those who farmed or worked as laborers in rural areas migrated to cities for better job opportunities. As a result, early-nineteenth-century England was marked by an increased urban population that corresponded with the population influx in the more rural southwestern territories in the United States.

Willis's passage also reveals that despite the urge to distinguish the urban, cosmopolitan space of 1830s London as distinct from the rural, regional space of the Southwest—and by extension, the territorial expansion of southern slavery—they *have* to be understood as functioning in tandem. The context of the passage highlights the interdependency of British and southern culture and, in turn, the interdependency of urban and regional culture across the Atlantic. Most of Willis's sketch revolves around stories of the dynamic London social life, the aristocracy, and brief physical descriptions of the city (all carefully focused on its charms or beauty). Yet the vibrant, cosmopolitan community that Willis observes existed primarily because of the ever-more-profitable cotton trade between the southern United States and England. Likewise, the growth of the U.S. southern economy—the profits that made the continued existence of regional publications such as the *Southern Literary Messenger* possible—relied on that very same trade.

The unifier of these two seemingly disparate areas, whose economies nonetheless relied on one another, is literature—specifically, the sketch. The very American periodicals that Willis claims were "never heard of" in England published texts that paralleled the work of popular British authors of the time. Although the sketch had achieved popularity during the eighteenth century,[6] the form gained prominence during the early part of the nineteenth century in such a way that coincided with the increased urbanization of the transatlantic world and the simultaneous growth of transatlantic trade. Further, the changing dynamic of print culture and the rise and diversification of print journalism led to a greater emphasis on shorter, impressionistic pieces that would appear in newspapers and then later be collected in full-length book form.[7]

As a result, the sketch became a popular way for authors witnessing rapid change to translate their experiences. Both Hooper and Baldwin grew up on the East Coast—Hooper in North Carolina and Baldwin in Virginia—and both moved to the southwestern territories during the land boom of the 1830s due to their families' financial problems. Eventually, the men turned to the law to earn their livings, an easy feat in the Southwest, where simply hanging out a sign and posting an advertisement in the local paper meant one was, officially, a lawyer. Similarly, on the other side of the Atlantic, Dickens's family was beset by financial difficulties throughout his childhood, and he eventually took advantage of London's active literary marketplace to work as a journalist and later, of course, a novelist.[8] The genre of the sketch, its basic structure, lends itself to representing these spaces and the experiences of the authors. By limiting its representation to a single moment, snapshot, or impression, the sketch captures the fleeting temporal quality of a space that will not remain the same for much longer. And when those sketches are collected into a single body, their whole, or—to return again to Poe's phrase—their unity, assembles a representation of a space and culture that is diverse and mutable but also cohesive. As Amanpal Garcha observes, "Literary sketches present time at once as fragmented, ever-changing, and thus best represented by static images and plotless analysis" (5).

The sketch, then, allows the readers to comprehend rapid change through two-dimensional and even simplified characters and plots. The complicated process of modernity is thereby rendered intelligible in a brief and uncomplicated literary representation. In his preface to the first edition of *Sketches by Boz,* for example, Dickens asserts: "[The author's] object has been to present little pictures of life and manners as they really are" (7). Ranging from scenes depicting city streets and neighborhoods to short character descriptions of London inhabitants, Dickens's sketches represent the varied society developing in conjunction with the effects of the Industrial Revolution and the transatlantic economy of the 1830s.[9]

In the same turn, *Sketches* draws from the particularities of London life to comment on the larger social and economic changes arising out of the increasingly commercial and international nature of England's central city.[10] The collection contains a diverse range of short fictional works that piece together the detailed and varied space of the city. Here the "little pictures of life and manners" align to create a single image—or the unity that Poe praised in his review—of London's rapidly changing social and cultural life.[11]

However, because of the authors' roles as observers and the collections' "unifying" quality, many critics assume that the sketches—both the Southwest humor tales and Dickens's *Boz* pieces—serve an ameliorating or distancing function for their largely middle-class, white readers. To return again to Bulwer-Lytton's characterization of the period: the shifts manifested during the early part of the nineteenth century were both visible and violent. The violence of that change represents an overturning of established social structures and conventions that had defined British and American societies. As such, the open nature of the southwestern frontier and the new urbanized Britain was not all prosperity and legitimate financial gain. In the Southwest, those not interested in running a plantation could also enter into other "fields"; the Southwest was overpopulated by lawyers and land speculators seeking to profit from the abundant and cheap land available after American Indian tribes were forced out of the region. Many self-appointed "lawyers" also profited from the numerous legal disputes that arose from land claims and the chaotic nature of the still-forming legal system in the West. Further, the issuance of credit by local banks led many migrants to take financial risks in land speculation and investment. In all, the nebulous nature of the social, legal, and economic structures in London and the Southwest created an atmosphere that was at once highly democratic and also rife with deception and manipulation.

The typical critical approach is to read the sketches as reassuring counterpoints to those cultural and economic changes. In sketches featuring urban areas, for example, critics frequently cite Walter Benjamin's definition of the flaneur, or the strolling gentleman of leisure, in order to identify the narrative voice, in which the authorial observer is removed from the often dirty and bawdy scenes described.[12] Indeed, many of the sketches in Hooper and Baldwin's collections employ a framing device in which an unnamed narrator, often of a higher class than the figures being described, enters into a situation anonymously and details the experience for the presumably middle-class reader. In reference to the Southwest humor stories in particular, Kenneth Lynn describes the framing as a "cordon sanitaire": "By containing their stories within a frame, the humorists also assured their conservative readers of something they had to believe in before they could find such humor amusing, namely, that the Gentleman was as completely in control of the situation he described as he was of himself" (64).

Yet the British and southern sketch authors occupied an uncomfortable position in regard to the spaces they represented, a role that is not entirely accounted for by interpreting the sketches as starchy, immutable counterpoints to change. While it is easy to read Hooper and Baldwin—and by extension Dickens—as gentlemen observers, brief overviews of their biographies reveal that they were anything but. All three authors were embedded in the very changes featured in their sketches—and profited from them. The result is that sketches set in the 1830s evince a dual ideological allegiance. As participants in the changes occurring in the spaces represented, nineteenth-century sketch authors negotiated the pull between the possibilities represented by the emerging economic systems and a desire to retain older social orders through the sketch form.[13]

In Dickens's *Sketches,* for example, the varied minutiae of London life reflect the tension between the possibilities represented by the new social and economic order and the threat posed by those changes. Throughout the collection, Dickens moves from bleak depictions of lower-class Londoners who are morally corrupt and almost animalistic to representations that emphasize London as a freer space of social and economic mutability. One sketch, "A Visit to Newgate," describes the conditions of London's debtors' prison and reveals the sort of social commentary for which Dickens would be known in his later novels. Yet the collection also features "Seven Dials," which details alcoholism and debauchery in a lower-class London neighborhood (fig. 4). By constantly shifting between subjects and limiting his representations to brief snippets, the sketches allow Dickens to simultaneously advocate for and criticize modern industrialization and urbanization, without having to present a sustained or consistent position.

Fig. 4. "Seven Dials," by George Cruikshank. From Charles Dickens, *Sketches by Boz,* 1837. Special Collections, Patricia Cornwell Collection, University of Tennessee, Knoxville—Libraries.

The primary way in which the sketches set during the 1830s navigate the tension between old and new economic systems is by incorporating the trope of the confidence man figure. In one sense, the confidence man parallels the ideal of socioeconomic mobility that could potentially exist in spaces structured around the free market. Through a talent for adapting to new social and economic conditions as well as operating independently of entrenched social restrictions, the confidence man upholds the values of free market capitalism within a new industrialized transatlantic economy, whether it is in London or the southern United States. However, the confidence man also embodies the potential moral and ethical pitfalls that accompany the abandonment of older social mores—at least from the perspective of the nineteenth-century sketch authors. As trickster figures, they represent the hazy conception of trust in a free market and highlight the problems inherent in a system based on individual profit.

To draw again from the example of the British sketches, the confidence men that populate *Sketches by Boz* deepen the duality already inherent in Dickens's representation of 1830s London life. The character type emerges repeatedly throughout the sketches in the form of brokers, dancing instructors, shop owners, and even beadles, all of whom frequently cheat or swindle unsuspecting Londoners who cross their paths. Yet the two most prominent confidence men in *Sketches* are the omnibus cads and the hackney cabdrivers.[14] An earlier sketch in the collection, "The Last Cab-Driver, and the First Omnibus Cad," takes on a mock-heroic tone and begins with the story of "the driver of the red cab." The driver (according to the sketch) was a mythic figure when hackney cabs were the main mode of public transport. However, while the driver of the red cab earns money by serving the public, he usually does so on his own terms: "The driver of the red cab, confident in the strength of his own moral principles, like many other philosophers, was wont to set the feelings and opinions of society at complete defiance. Generally speaking, perhaps, he would as soon carry a fare safely to his destination, as he would upset him—sooner, perhaps, because in that case he not only got the money, but had the additional amusement of running a longer heat against some smart rival. But society made war on him in the shape of penalties, and he must make war upon society in his own way. This was the reasoning of the red-cab-driver" (173).

The driver, in the sketch's ironic way, is a defiant figure of the antiestablishment, a sort of noble thief in the vein of German gothic tales or Robin Hood. By the end of the passage, he is not merely a mock "philosopher" but his own entity, "*the* red-cab-driver," and one who defies both the dictates of "society" and the economic system that defines his identity. Read another way, he is an independent contractor, participating in the free market economy on his own terms.

In a changing economy, however, the red-cab-driver must give way to new modes of transportation, in this case the omnibus, which operated in much the same way a public bus system functions today. The first man to capitalize on the innovation and become an omnibus cad in the sketch, Mr. Barker, observes the opportunities afforded by the new public transport and profits by them: "The genius of Mr. Barker at once perceived the whole extent of the injury that would be eventually inflicted on cab and coach stands, and, by consequence, on watermen also, by the progress of the system of which the first omnibus was a part. He saw, too, the necessity of adopting some more profitable profession; and his *active* mind at once perceived how much might be done in the way of enticing the youthful and unwary, and shoving the old and helpless, into the wrong buss, and carrying them off, until, reduced to despair, they ransomed themselves by the payment of sixpence a-head, or, to adopt his own figurative expression in all its native beauty, 'till they was rig'larly done over, and forked out the stumpy'" (178–9, my emphasis). Mr. Barker also acts independently to create a situation for himself by which he can earn money and employment in a space of rapid change. Here, his *active* industry corresponds to the values of the free market that drove the economic development of 1830s London. Like any participant in the free market that sustained the cotton trade and promoted the growth of London—and also the American Southwest—both he and the red-cab-driver are able to observe economic opportunities and act on them outside of the parameters of social acceptability, primarily because they are not hindered by a sense of ethics.

That lack of ethical code necessitates the sketches' humorous or ironic tone. Though these men may master the system, that mastery also entails dismantling the supposedly stable ethical and moral codes that (again, supposedly) characterized British society before the advent of capitalism and industrialization. The London defined by the global free market of the 1830s, in contrast, presents an ethically ambiguous space. Taken together, the sketches perform the work of representing rapid change in such a way that highlights that the consequences of that change are both positive and negative. As a result, neither the cad nor the red-cab-driver are heroes; they are only mock heroes. Nor does either achieve what anyone would call a "happy" and prosperous end: the red-cab-driver ends up in prison, and Mr. Barker simply works the "buss."

Fig. 5. "The Last Cab-Driver," by George Cruikshank. From Charles Dickens, *Sketches by Boz,* 1839. Special Collections, Patricia Cornwell Collection, University of Tennessee, Knoxville—Libraries.

The illustration that accompanies the sketches highlights the pull between the potential for economic mobility and the dubious morality associated with the free market (fig. 5).[15] The cabdriver, presumably the red-cab-driver, is in the foreground, sitting alone in his cab. The first omnibus cad stands in the background next to his bus with a woman inside plaintively wailing (probably wondering where she will be dropped off). Both men are dressed neatly, projecting (somewhat) an air of competence.

And unlike the rest of the illustrations in which the characters are walking, sitting, standing in groups, or with other characters (see fig. 4, p. 70), each man is featured with the vehicle by which he earns his living. That isolation gives the presumption of both physical and economic mobility as well as independence. Still, the illustration does not make either man trustworthy: the cabdriver's eyes are shaded, and the cad is slouched against the bus, glaring sinisterly. Once again, they are the confidence men of London's new economic space: they actively take advantage of technological change and new economic practices, but their ability to do so is accompanied by a sense of questionable moral standards and abandonment of ethics.

The figures of the drivers and cads as confidence men are emblems of the changing London, a space defined by commercial exchange and free markets. They exist in and profit by the changes occurring in technology while also being integrated into the new image of London as the center of a growing empire. Although the collection partially mourns the passing of the older order, through the figures of the cads and drivers, it also embraces the possibilities of the new, which entails an uneasy moral balance and an ill-defined (or entirely absent) ethical code.[16] Within a single character type, Dickens can both champion and critique the new economic order.

Likewise, nineteenth-century southern authors' treatment of the confidence men in their sketch collections reveals an effected balance between old and new economic systems, in the same way that Simms and Kennedy attempt to represent southern history in their historical romances. Through humor and satire, plus the impermanent quality of the sketches themselves, Hooper and Baldwin can use the confidence men to champion the economic shifts of the 1830s while also cautioning against them. However, that humorous treatment of the figure alters as the century wears on, eventually culminating in the dominance of new economic paradigms. With publications such as Dickens's *Sketches* as the distant models, the confidence man shifts from being an object of mild satire in Hooper's *Some Adventures of Simon Suggs* to being the figure employing the satire in Baldwin's *Flush Times of Alabama and Mississippi*. As such, the nineteenth-century sketch collection featuring the Southwest, a space of rapid economic change, interprets the rise of transatlantic free market capitalism in a region dictated by the structures of the plantation economy.

"Whiggish Gentlemen"

When Johnson Jones Hooper's *Some Adventures of Simon Suggs* and Joseph Glover Baldwin's *The Flush Times of Alabama and Mississippi* were first published, the southwestern land grab of the 1830s was almost a decade in the past. Although the Southwest humor tales represent the same tension between older and newer economic systems, they extend the trend established in the earlier British sketches to present the developing economy of the southern frontier as a burgeoning area of financial possibility and social mobility. The stories' settings in new territories—and the collections' publication dates after the boom occurred—changes how the authors employ the literary form of the sketch to represent the space. Earlier sketches such as Dickens's developed concurrently with the shift, while the southern humorists had the benefit of some hindsight. Therefore, the sketch collections published by Hooper and Baldwin reflect back on the changes that have already occurred and attempt to reinterpret the lasting effects of the era on the region. Rather than the characters maneuvering through a social or economic system that is changing, they are the forerunners in creating a new system formed out of international trade and free market capitalism.

Still, the authors who wrote about the Southwest evince some reservations regarding the economic models that made such growth possible. The Old Southwest lent itself to the economic opportunism seen with the cads and cabdrivers in Dickens, perhaps to the extent of enabling even more economic and social mobility. Yet that growth also opened up greater possibilities for fraud and cheating; in a territory with at most a loosely defined legal system, there was very little to prevent anyone from taking advantage of more naive immigrants to the area, which many of the characters in Hooper and Baldwin's stories indeed do. The paradox inherent in the expanding space of the Old Southwest then leaves the primary characters of the stories in a contradictory moral position: they are at once the embodiment of the changing economic model that exists in conjunction with the extension of the frontier and also representations of the moral corruption that comes with a new economic order.

The term *confidence man* perfectly encapsulates the characters' roles in the stories. The word *confidence,* like the men themselves, takes on a dual meaning in the realm of the Old Southwest. Taking into account later novels such as Melville's *The Confidence Man* (1857) or the duke and the dauphin in Twain's *The Adventures of Huckleberry Finn* (1885), confidence men are frequently symbols of a chaotic modern order. "The American confidence man embodies forces of disorder, transition, and unrest," William E. Lenz writes, and he relies "on the fluid nature of society in the New World with its unique opportunities of self-government, self-promotion, self-posturing, and self-creation" (1).[17]

However, the word *confidence* itself is far less sinister in definition. "Confidence" implies "trust" or "faith," in this case faith in a system that will ultimately provide those who invest in it with far greater wealth than that with which they began. Otherwise, why bother taking the risk in the first place? In this definition, the "swindles" and "seductions" of the confidence man are nothing out of the ordinary; they are simply more neatly packaged and presented by someone who knows the business, so to speak.

The ethical ambiguity that characterizes the space of the Old Southwest and the confidence men of the stories is, as with Dickens's *Sketches,* manifested generically. They are, after all, usually referred to as Old Southwest humor stories, and that humor, as many critics have pointed out, is a method of presenting the southwestern frontier and its inhabitants in a palatable fashion for middle-class, "civilized" readers.[18] In all of these interpretations, humor functions as a way of diverting readers from the morally compromised qualities the Old Southwest represented, just as the ironic and humorous tone describing the London cads and cabdrivers in *Sketches by Boz* makes the seedy quality of their practices more amusing than threatening.

This line of thinking follows the critical assertion that many of the humorists, Hooper and Baldwin especially, were morally ambivalent about the characters and events they depicted in their fiction. The forerunner of such an argument is Kenneth Lynn and his book, *Mark Twain and Southwestern Humor* (1959). Forming what would become the defining interpretation of southwestern humor for the next fifty years, Lynn sets forth the political affiliations of the authors as being the defining characteristic of their fiction. They were southern Whigs who, according to his arguments, feared the growth of Jacksonian democracy in the 1820s and 1830s and valued more conservative social structures represented by the southern planter class. These "Whiggish gentlemen" carried the beliefs to their fiction, using a framing technique in their narratives by which a gentleman narrator observes and interacts with the "locals," the cordon sanitaire that effectively contained the uncontrolled impulses of the new economic and social system on the Southwest frontier.[19]

But as mentioned earlier, dismissing the authors' narrative stances in their writings as crotchety reactions to rapid change completely ignores the sketches' much more complicated approach to the spaces represented —a complication represented by the confidence men characters that dominate their stories. As James H. Justus points out, "The humor does not emphasize skepticism, violence, and cheerful anarchism because such subjects served the program of Whig moralists, but because the authors lived in and made their way in that kind of society. The evidence shows that they rather enjoyed it" (74). That assessment of "they rather enjoyed it" is particularly true in the case of Hooper and Baldwin, for their personal experiences with the southwestern frontier indicated that they were far more sympathetic to the changes taking place in the Southwest than the cordon sanitaire interpretation allows.

And while both men can be characterized as "southern Whigs," the term itself is not as monochromatic as many critics have implied. Usually, southern Whigs become synonymous in literary criticism with southern conservatives in the context of increased sectionalism in the 1830s through the 1850s. As with John Pendleton Kennedy, Whigs—and particularly those in the South during the mid-nineteenth century such as Hooper and Baldwin—presented a strange blend of socially conservative yet economically and politically pragmatic ideologies.[20] Like most southern Whigs, Hooper and Baldwin both saw the need for national expansion through an investment in economic modernization. In 1854, for example, Hooper argued in an editorial for the *Montgomery (AL) Daily Mail* that the state should invest in the development of railroads, stating that new methods of transport would facilitate commerce and travel while improving communication between regions and countries ("Railroads"). On these terms, Hooper and Baldwin were Whigs who were also firm advocates of a laissez-faire system.[21] In his 1855 study of early American politicians, *Party Leaders,* Baldwin writes: "The man free, and stimulated to activity, finds a thousand avenues of business and enterprise, that invite his talents. Instead of a few men thinking for all, each man is thinking for himself. From *passive* recipiency, his mind is awakened to energetic and independent *action*" (84, my emphasis). Baldwin's individual does not lead a passive existence but adapts and uses his talents to benefit himself and, ideally, stimulate those around him. In this sense, the Whig individual is the London cabdriver of the American scene, a confidence man of the modern order—in sum, the "New Man" on the southwestern frontier.

The emphasis on individual freedom that led Hooper and Baldwin to embrace economic expansion and modernization as a form of national progress also drove their respective critiques of older traditions and social systems. From the perspective of both men, a society stagnates when it holds onto traditional forms of social hierarchies based on family and inheritance, in which neither social merit nor wealth is based on individual talent or effort.[22] In their nonfiction, Hooper and Baldwin unite progress and modernization with newer economic models that followed the patterns of the free market and international commerce represented by the cotton trade. Hooper decries the American social practice of universally favoring the wealthy or well-born in a 1854 editorial called "The Morality of the Country," and in *Party Leaders,* Baldwin draws a comparison between "Conservativism" and "Progression," identifying conservatism with a stultifying adherence to older norms: "The principle of stability [versus] the principle of change; the principle which is more solicitous of keeping, than of hazarding what it has to the chance of getting more, and the principle which considers what it has as mainly valuable as *capital* for future acquisitions. The one principle owns prudence for its parent; the other enterprise. The one looks to the past; the other to the future. . . . Progress delights in achievement; preferring the turbulence and dangers of agitation to the calm which rusts the genius, and dulls intellect, and invites despotism" (71). Here not only does Baldwin make the case for progress, but he aligns that progress with capitalism. On these terms, everything is situated as "capital," a means of creating more—either more landholdings or more money.

Both Hooper and Baldwin, however, expressed reservations about economic development under an emerging capitalist system. While they saw the individual as the driving force of progress, individuals also had the ability to taint that progress. The freedom for individuals to exert their own talents and abilities independent of aristocratic traditions also left them open to moral corruption. Hooper expresses his doubt in an 1855 *Daily Mail* editorial in which he complains of what he calls the "cow heel aristocracy," or a form of pretend gentility that was based only on wealth ("Cow Heel Aristocracy"). In his estimation, what can earn a man wealth will not necessarily earn him moral decency and respect. In a similar fashion, although Baldwin expressed a belief in the ability of individuals to adapt and flourish in new circumstances, he hoped that ability would inspire, as Adam Tate puts it, "individual responsibility, not license" (*Party Leaders* 83–4; Tate 288). As evidenced by the speculation and fraud rampant in the Old Southwest, individual responsibility could often disappear in the face of accumulating wealth.

Despite their reservations, Hooper and Baldwin were more advocates than critics of frontier expansion and the economic systems that fostered that expansion. Their brand of "Whiggery" was not of the kind to adopt blindly the cause of economic conservatism, especially for two men who took advantage of the opportunities for economic mobility afforded by the Southwest territories. As attorneys and politicians, Hooper and Baldwin participated in the space that bred the figure of the confidence man, and though perhaps only indirectly, they were part of the morally nebulous space that was the Old Southwest's legal and economic system. They were definitely not of the planter class by origin, and their political affiliations and beliefs reflect that.

In turn, neither Hooper nor Baldwin's representations of the confidence men who dominate their sketches nor their use of humor can be read as a consistent whitewashing of the realities of life on the southwestern frontier. As with Dickens's *Sketches,* their brand of comic sketch writing can be seen more as a technique of literary realism than generic diversion. Both *Some Adventures* and *Flush Times* represent the heterogeneity of the Southwest by using the short sketch form to shift between subjects and situations. And both authors also utilize humor to depict morally ambiguous but situationally adept characters who deviate from older, more traditional social and economic systems.

But rather than a method of distancing readers from the subjects and settings of the stories, the humor functions as a form of realism, a way of presenting the Old Southwest that does not deny the less-than-savory qualities. For Hooper and Baldwin, this meant presenting an image of the frontier that recognized it as a space of economic progress as well as of potential corruption. Unlike Dickens, the shifting quality of their sketches and the humorous treatment of the confidence men do not convey ambivalence over the moral and ethical implications of economic and social change. Ultimately, the duality of their confidence man figures comes down in favor of the new economic systems that spawned the growth of the Southwest.

Shiftiness: Simon Suggs

Of the two southwestern humorists discussed in this chapter, Johnson Jones Hooper was by far the most extreme in his loyalty to the U.S. South and the culture it represented. Though he wrote for and edited several Whig papers, when the sectionalism and animosity between North and South increased in the decade before the Civil War, his brand of Whiggery became less about national progress and more about states' and southern rights.[23] Related to this extreme sectional loyalty, Hooper evinced a distrust of larger institutional structures, particularly the federal government, that correlates to the evils of traditional economic models. On these terms, Hooper saw modern society as shaped by the effort of individuals and individual merit. Yet he also believed that individuals could not be trusted to regulate their own inclinations, an opinion that was perhaps based on his own problems with gambling and drinking. "For Hooper," writes Adam Tate, "a society based solely on self-interest was anarchic. Unless human nature could be contained or directed in some way, modern freedom degenerated into license" (273).

As a tenuous balance of his worldview, Hooper eventually came to espouse "wit" as the means for distinguishing individuals. Wit, intellect, or simply being clever utilizes the talent of individuals without relying on their "baser" passions, hopefully bringing a certain amount of control to otherwise chaotic human nature. Employing his concept of wit in his sketches allowed Hooper to advocate more clearly for economic change by positing a philosophy that aligns with the tenets of the free market but nonetheless recognizes the failings of the system.

The idea of individual wit as the means of surviving and thriving in the Southwest runs throughout Hooper's first collection, *Some Adventures of Captain Simon Suggs,* and particularly his first fictional sketch published in the LaFayette *East Alabamian* in 1843.[24] "Taking the Census in Alabama. By a Chicken Man of 1840" features a fictionalized version of Hooper as the "chicken man," or federal census taker, in Alabama.[25] Though published before the Suggs stories, "Taking the Census" was featured at the end of the first edition of *Some Adventures.* The story follows the chicken man as he visits various homesteads and farms in rural Alabama, and the early pages are a series of humiliations for the narrator: one woman sets her dogs on him, while a man, Sol Todd, tricks him into fording the deepest part of a river as he rides between homesteads.

However, the census taker quickly learns the tricks of the country; after the dunking in the river, he informs Sol that he lost twenty-five dollars "in hard money" while submerged. Convinced that he can pocket the money himself, Sol proceeds to dive into the icy river repeatedly, never knowing, as the narrator confesses, that "this, of course, was a regular old-fashioned lie, as we had not seen the amount of cash mentioned as lost in a 'coon's age'" (155). The chicken man eventually leaves Sol "diving for the pouch [of money] industriously" and goes on to have better luck in his encounters with the residents of Tallapoosa County, Alabama (157). Through the experiences of the federal census taker and his ability to adapt to frontier society, Hooper re-creates the Alabama countryside as an open space in which traditional institutions can be manipulated beyond their original intent and wit alone aids in the success of an individual. In examining the story, Adam Tate observes, "Hooper presents the frontier as an equalizer that marked sharply the differences between those who possessed the wit and self-restraint necessary to succeed in the modern order and those who could not cope with modern freedom" (325).

Simon Suggs, however, is the centerpiece of *Some Adventures.* The sketches are framed as a political biography of Suggs, and like any good biographical work, the frontispiece is a portrait of the man in question (fig. 6).[26] This initial framing structure serves the same function as the

Fig. 6. "Captain Simon Suggs," by F. O. C. Darley. Frontispiece, Johnson Jones Hooper, *Some Adventures of Captain Simon Suggs,* 1845. University of Alabama Libraries Special Collections.

mock-heroic humor of "The Last Cab-Driver." As the frontispiece makes clear, the subject who merits such a biography is not a bastion of clear-cut ethics and moral uprightness. In the illustration, Suggs is on his horse, in a shabby dark coat and hat, and his face is craggy and lean, almost wolfish in appearance. Indeed, in the initial sketch of the collection, which is a general overview of the man and his character, he is described as "lithe, long, and sinewy" (7). As with the cabdriver and cad in the Cruikshank illustration for *Sketches,* Suggs is alone, and also like the autonomous figures in Dickens, he is mobile. The later stories in the collection demonstrate that this mobility enables him to maintain his standard of living, such as it is; he escapes many of his swindles by riding off on his horse. In all, the image portrays a sort of scavenger, a man of nomadic inclinations who forages for a living—in essence, the prototypical confidence man.

The initial biographical sketch highlights the ambiguity evident in the frontispiece through its humorous characterization of Suggs's "talents." After presenting the reader with a physical image of Suggs, the sketch then outlines his character, which can be summed up by his motto: "It is good to be shifty in a new country." And if nothing else, Suggs demonstrates throughout the sketches just how well his talent for "shiftiness" has been developed in the frontier space of Alabama. The sketch elaborates: "The shifty Captain Suggs is a miracle of shrewdness. He possesses, in an eminent degree, that tact which enables man to detect the *soft spots* in his fellow, and to assimilate himself to whatever company he may fall in with. Besides he has a quick, ready wit, which has extricated him from many an unpleasant predicament, and which makes him whenever he chooses to be so—and that is always—very companionable. In short, nature gave the Captain the precise intellectual outfit most to be desired by a man of his propensities" (8–9). While Suggs may have a tendency to cheat his fellow man, the passage implies that this is the very talent that enables him to survive in the southwestern territories. In fact, it is a particular skill to feel out the "soft spots in his fellow." He is, in short, "a miracle." But the irony that runs throughout the description, like the humorous characterization of the cads and drivers of London, and the collection's ironic framing device as a political biography balances the representation of Suggs as both a "miracle" of modern progress and a threat to its moral stability. Suggs is a figure of modernization advocated by Hooper in his political views, able to adapt and assimilate, but that modernization comes at the price of ethical ambiguity and shiftiness.

Whatever ambivalence may be present in the characterization of Suggs's ethics, Hooper's sketches nonetheless position him as an improvement on previous modes of economic and social interaction that is far less ambivalent than the conflict between social orders in Dickens's *Sketches*. The general introduction that comprises the first sketch transitions into a story from Suggs's childhood in which he and a young African American boy (presumably a slave), Bill, are gambling. They are soon caught by

Simon's father, a supremely ignorant yet avowedly devout minister who frequently punishes Simon for his "devilish" ways. Wishing to avoid the violent thrashing his father administers to Bill, Simon convinces his father to play cards, appealing to his ego by claiming that a local neighbor can make money easily from gambling.[27] Eager to prove himself just as smart as "Bob Smith," Simon's father agrees to play one hand. They bet that if Simon wins, he can take the family pony and leave, but if his father wins, Simon receives his punishment. Simon, of course, wins (by cheating), and the next story begins with him riding off from the family farm.

Aside from further proof of Suggs's shiftiness at an early age, this scene also highlights the abandonment of traditional social and economic structures in favor of the free market models that dominated the early Southwest. At the beginning of the sketch, Simon and Bill are playing cards in the middle of a field that is being plowed by Simon's older brother Ben. Yet it is Simon, the nonlaborer, who is successful in the context of the sketches. When confronted with his card playing, which his father calls "devilment," Simon stoutly responds: "I'd win more money in a week than you can make in a year. There ain't nobody round here kin make seed corn off o' me at cards. I'm rale smart" (17). And indeed he can and is, for unlike his father or his brother, Simon has modern wit, and further, he is entirely devoid of the social pretensions that cause his father (also ironically called the "Reverend Jedediah") to sermonize and preach a form of false morality.

The scene's critique of traditional structures is also evident in the representation of Jedediah, who is a hypocrite in contrast to his son, for Simon makes no effort to conceal his shiftiness. While the two play at cards, Jedediah pulls out all of the "picter ones," or so he thinks. But he still loses, for Simon knows how the swindling game is played. He uses his wit to the end of individual capital gain, a talent that follows him throughout the stories in the rest of the collection. Though Jedediah is just as morally corrupt, he lacks the wit and intellectual capacity to adapt and participate in a free market, represented by the small-time gambling. Ultimately, the collection does not mourn the loss of traditional institutions; instead, it uses the humorous portrayal of Jedediah to present them as simply not viable in a space that expanded entirely due to international commerce and the free market.

The next sketch further illustrates the particular economic system that governed the frontier through an anecdote of land speculation. "Simon Speculates" begins with Simon riding off on his own, then picks up the timeline of his life when he is an adult. It is set at the time Alabama grew rapidly due to the release (e.g., outright stealing) of Native American lands in the 1830s and an influx of migrants who sought to profit from land speculation. The sketch emphasizes the peculiar nature of the Southwest's financial sphere early on, elaborating on how a man like Suggs "without a dollar should be a land speculator." But as the narrator explains: "We admit that there is a seeming incongruity in the idea; but have those in whose minds speculation and capital are inseparably connected, ever heard of a process by which lands were sold, deeds executed, and all that sort of thing completely arranged, and all without once troubling the owner of the soil for an opinion even, in regard to the matter? Yet such occurrences were frequent some years since, in this country, and they illustrated *one* mode of speculation requiring little, if any, cash capital" (31).

While the passage represents speculation in the Southwest region as a morally dubious practice, it is nonetheless a realistic portrayal of the nature of real estate and capital in an area that was expanding in accordance with the demand for more land in the southern region. If Dickens's sketches function as a way to connect the particularities of place with larger, even global trends, this sketch featuring Simon Suggs uses the particular space of 1830s Alabama to comment on larger trends in the nineteenth-century U.S. (and global) economy, whether good or bad. Suggs, in turn, becomes the fictional emblem of the sort of character bred in this space, the perfect model of the southwestern man. As the sketch's narrator comments, "To buy, to sell, to make profits, without a cent in one's pocket," as Suggs does, requires "in short, genius!" (31).

In the context of rampant land speculation, Suggs's first foray into the practice occurs almost by accident. One night, while stopping at a roadside inn, Suggs overhears two men discussing a particular tract of land that one wishes to purchase. Suggs decides to take advantage of the information he has acquired and pursues the man on the road the next morning. When they meet, Suggs gives the impression that he will put in an offer on the same tract of land; the man pays him a substantial amount of money not to do so. When the transaction is over and both have ridden off, Suggs reflects: "Now some fellers . . . would milk the cow dry, by . . . enterin' that land in somebody else's name before Jones [the swindled man] gits thar! But honesty's the best policy. Honesty's the bright spot in *any* man's character!. . . . What's a man without his integrity?" (36–7).

As this humorous exchange reveals, within a space in which land speculation, trade, and credit are all foundational to the economic system, "honesty" comes to mean something beyond merely "telling the truth" as a set of facts. Rather, the confidence man must adhere to the facts as he has presented them. For that is the basis of investment and credit: to have confidence in what is being presented as fact. Otherwise, the investment and the system fail. In the story, Suggs has presented himself to Jones as intent on placing a bid; he accepted money not to do so; he does not do so; and thus further business transactions may proceed without complication. This is how the emerging economic system of the Old Southwest continues to function, through a warped form of honesty. And while, once again, the humor in the passage recognizes the moral complications inherent in this sort of reasoning, through Suggs it also recognizes that reasoning as the foundation of the southwestern social and economic system.

The humorous representation of Suggs as the confidence man figure allows the sketch to celebrate a changing space that was at once open for individual opportunity but also subject to the moral complications posed by emerging nineteenth-century capitalist systems. Although Dickens's representation of the cabdrivers and cads may uphold their role as "active" members of the London economy, Hooper's representation of Suggs in his various dealings throughout the Southwest is far less ambiguous in its praise. Through wit and its correlation with the functioning of the free market, Hooper's sketches present a version of the Southwest that encompasses all of its varied elements and, further, stakes a claim for what would become the overriding economic structure for the nineteenth-century transatlantic economy.

A New Order: Simon Suggs Jr.

When Joseph Glover Baldwin traveled with his family to California in 1854, the Southwest had long been settled and developed. Plantations were established all throughout the "cotton kingdom" of Alabama and Mississippi. At this point, according to historian Martin Crawford, cotton "constituted between 60 and 82 percent of the total value of American imports into Britain and upon which an estimated 20 percent of the British population directly or indirectly depended for its livelihood" (458). Further, the southern region was solidifying ideologically as the nation became more embroiled in the controversy over slavery and states' rights that eventually led to the Civil War. In the midst of all this change, California was the next space of economic opportunity. The end of the U.S.-Mexican War in 1848 opened up the far West to a wave of settlers from the East, an influx that was further spurred by gold and silver discoveries. Like the Old Southwest, California quickly became a space in which any individual could capitalize on the fuzziness of the legal system and the natural resources abundant in the area.

Yet the flush times of the 1830s, despite any similarities to the far West in the 1840s, remained a unique space and time. On first moving to the far West, Baldwin wrote *The Flush Times of California,* a book that remained unpublished in his lifetime.[28] In it, he observes that the nation had moved beyond a moment when the frontier space was unique in valuing the individual wit that came with the free market. He begins with an observation that "the times of 1836 in Mississippi were quiet, dull, tame, insipid, flat, stale, unprofitable—to what they are here now" (13). Taken at face value, the meaning derived from the comparison seems pretty obvious. However, as with Baldwin's fiction, most of *Flush Times in California* is ironic in tone. In that light, the characterization of the 1830s Southwest in relation to California is much more ambiguous. Take, for instance, a later passage in which Baldwin describes the nature of California society: "Society is kept together on a principle of *universal distrust.* Nobody has confidence in any body else. Hence no one being trusted, no one is deceived: and therefore, no one has any right to complain of being taken in. It is a great mistake to suppose that confidence keeps society together: it is the very thing that keeps men apart. Nothing so harmonizes a community as a modest and well grounded diffidence in each other's integrity" (18, my emphasis). Unlike the Simon Suggs stories, confidence no longer implies a contract between individuals or the careful presentation of facts. In turn, wit is no longer a singular virtue but a trait possessed by anyone living in California, which is not a good thing. For a Whig who believed in the abilities of the individual and that modern progress rested on those abilities, Baldwin's presentation of a confidence-free society is necessarily ironic. Throughout *Flush Times of California,* Baldwin emphasizes the pervasiveness of the very qualities located in a few individual figures in the earlier Southwest humor sketches.[29]

By 1853, when the collection *The Flush Times of Alabama and Mississippi* was published, the traits that made the Old Southwest unique economically and socially were no longer the traits of a burgeoning frontier society. Rather, the sort of self-interested, free market participation demonstrated by fictional characters such as Simon Suggs had pervaded American culture to become the defining mode of economic exchange. The collection is set during the flush times of 1836 in Alabama and Mississippi, and the characters are not scruffy frontiersmen in the manner of Suggs. They are lawyers.[30] In this sense, Americans, at least as Baldwin presents them, *were* confidence men. Like Hooper and Dickens before him, Baldwin's sketches represent this idea in both its positive and negative lights and, further, demonstrate the transition from the confidence man as an outlying figure to one who is integral to the makeup of American society. From Dickens to Hooper to Baldwin, as the temporal distance between the sketch collections' publication and the moment of the 1830s grows, the ambivalence of their representation of the free market mentality decreases.

To reimagine a place and time in which free market capitalism took root in nineteenth-century American society, *Flush Times*'s various sketches use the confidence man figure to establish the basic tenets of the new economy prevalent in the Southwest. These tenets include adhering to rules of confidence and honesty that form the basis of credit (seen in "Simon Speculates") but also moving beyond traditional institutional structures. The collection begins with a sketch of a character who adapts to the changing times to the extent that he actually disrupts the balance between moral ambiguity and economic progress maintained by the humor in Dickens's and Hooper's sketches.[31] "Ovid Bolus, Esq.," like Suggs, is a devious liar yet a strangely likable figure, a lawyer whose lies are counterbalanced by his charm. As the sketch puts it, Bolus's lying is more in the realm of "fine arts"; as the narrator elaborates, "Some men are liars from interest; not because they have no regard for truth, but because they have less regard for it than for gain." Bolus, however, "was a natural liar, just as some horses are natural pacers" (2). Like Suggs, he is the "genius" of the Southwest, a mock hero of the free market.

Yet Bolus's form of lying, unlike that of Suggs, is not limited to confidence tricks or swindling for individual profit—he lies simply for the sake of lying, which undermines the confidence system that forms the basis of the southwestern economy. While the sketch adopts a mock-heroic tone, much in the same manner as "The Last Cab-Driver" and *Some Adventures,* the description breaks to describe one instance of Bolus's lying that the narrator "can never forgive." In need of money, as usual, Bolus convinces a friend, Ben, to sign a bill of exchange to cover a series of debts. In contrast to Bolus, Ben owns "a fine tract of land," and his name is "unfortunately good." When Bolus, naturally, defaults on his debts, Ben is left with nothing. The lie was to the benefit of no one, not even Bolus, who does not profit by it; in essence, the sketch observes, deceiving Ben is tantamount to "crude larceny" (8).

Bolus's penchant for unprofitable lying exposes the moral problems inherent in the nineteenth-century free market system through the example of a southwestern community. The sketch makes clear that if an individual cannot practice the version of honesty foundational to a capitalist mode of existence, then the system falls apart. Eventually, Bolus is pushed out of the area by those who treat lying as a business: "Bolus not having confined his art to political matters, sounded, at last, the depths, and explored the limits of popular credulity." In a space in which confidence forms the basis of a somewhat functional society and economy, even simple gossip comes to stand for a version of credit. Using the small southwestern society to illustrate modern modes of credit, the sketch narrates Bolus's eventual exile: "The credit system, common before as pump-water, adhering, like the elective franchise to every voter, began to take the worldly wisdom of Falstaff's' mercer, and ask security; and security liked something more substantial than [Bolus's] plausible promises" (13). Bolus's form of lying, in other words, threatens the economic and social system upon which the Southwest is built. In the end, he leaves for the far West, which as we know from Baldwin's later descriptions, is rife with the sort of lying that permeates every aspect of society.

If Bolus is a poor example of honesty and the practice of confidence, then those who do not adapt to newer economic models at all are equally at fault in the sketches. Like Dickens and Hooper before him, Baldwin's sketches and stories present an imperative to leave behind older economic and social institutions in order to embrace more modern and, in turn, more capitalist-oriented practices. "My First Case at the Bar," the story immediately following "Ovid Bolus," uses a somewhat allegorical tale to illustrate the contrast between older and newer social practices, in which the older ways come off as ridiculous and simply outdated. As the title implies, the sketch recounts the narrator's (ostensibly Baldwin's) first experience as an attorney in an Alabama courtroom. Unfortunately, the lawyer for the opposing side is the older and more experienced Mr. Caesar Kasm (a tongue-in-cheek play on *sar-casm*).

The trial proceeds, and the narrator does well—that is, until the closing statements. Feeling overly confident, the narrator launches into an overblown rhetorical style, quoting poetry and Shakespeare and generally making an ass out of himself. Kasm tears him apart during his own closing argument, stating, "I find it difficult, gentlemen, to reply to any part of the young man's effort, except his argument, which is the smallest part in compass, and, next to his pathos, the most amusing" (26). This practitioner of "vituperation," though given to rhetorical theatrics himself, recognizes that to adopt the style of a high-flown orator of the old order gets one nowhere in the Alabama courts. Poetry has no place in the Southwest; "facts" are the order of the day. To emphasize his point, Kasm produces a newspaper clipping that features a love poem the narrator had written for a lady's album—a common practice among members of the upper class in the nineteenth century—then was subsequently published. After reading a few lines that describe the narrator's "bosom's anguish" and the "venomous worm" piercing his heart, Kasm dryly comments: "Now, if he (Kasm) might presume to give the young gentleman advice, he would recommend Swain's Patent Vermifuge. He had no doubt that it would effectually cure him of his malady" (31–2). Needless to say, Kasm wins the trial.

The narrator's humiliation illustrates the move from older economic and social forms to the more modern structures that made up the Southwest. Establishing a line of thought that he would continue in *Party Leaders* with his contrast between Conservativism and Progression, Baldwin represents the traditions of the southern aristocracy (the gentility represented by poetry writing) as ineffectual in a space driven by modern economic networks. After the trial, the narrator moves to Natchez, Mississippi, where he begins a new law practice. Rather than putting on pretensions to "gentlemanly" manners and arts, he thereafter employs practicality; he "associated only with skinflints, brokers and married men, and discussed investments and stocks; [and] soon got into business." Although there is a certain amount of irony to the narrator's description of his new mode of conducting business, the story implies that it is nonetheless successful: "Thus, by this course of things, [I] am able to write from *my sugar plantation,* this memorable history of the fall of *genius* and the rise of solemn humbug!" (33).

A later sketch in the collection, "How the Times Served the Virginians," bolsters the image of conservativism inherent in more traditional social modes. The sketch describes the transition from a South defined by the states along the East Coast to a region that was increasingly defined by its westward expansion. Here the older, more traditional social structures are represented by Virginians and old Virginian families who move west to reestablish themselves. These are the "old guard" of the South, the First Families of Virginia (FFVs) that Mark Twain would later describe, and they represent the South's version of landed aristocracy.[32] But just as the young lawyer's attempts at poetry fail at the Alabama bar, these Virginians, with their adherence to more traditional practices, are ill-suited to life in the Southwest: "Certainly the Virginia character has been less distinguished for its practical than its ornamental traits, and for its business qualities than for its speculative temper" (57). *Business* in this passage means a conservative version of business—operating on good name, slowly saving, and avoiding financial risks. None of these are qualities that serve to profit individuals in the southwestern states. Thus, the story takes on the tone evinced more often in Dickens's sketches: it balances a mix of nostalgia, bemoaning the passing of the older generation and its values while at the same time criticizing those who do not adapt to the new economic modes of the southwestern states. "How the Times Served the Virginians" again marks the passing of the old into the new.

And the new is represented by the frontispiece of the collection, a portrait of Simon Suggs Jr. (fig. 7).[33] Though the story featuring Suggs Jr. is just one in the collection, his image is the masthead. Further, it is an obvious continuation of Hooper's conceit. Suggs embodies the proto-

Fig. 7. "Simon Suggs, Jr.," by John McLenan. Frontispiece, Joseph Glover Baldwin, *Flush Times of Alabama and Mississippi,* 1853. Vanderbilt University Special Collections and University Archives.

typical characters that populate all of Baldwin's stories in the collection: cunning lawyers who manipulate a fledgling legal and economic system to their own advantage. Yet unlike his father, Suggs Jr. is solidly successful and wealthy, and what's more, he is actually integrated into the economic expansion of the Southwest territories as one of the authors of that expansion—he is a lawyer and established land speculator. As with the cabdrivers and Suggs Sr., in the illustration, Suggs Jr. is featured alone and looks somewhat devious: his eyes are shaded, and he is casually smoking a cigarette. Yet he is dressed respectably in a vest and top hat and wears a watch chain. In this sense, he is more of a "gentleman con man" in the style of Caesar Kasm; he has left behind the shabby exterior, but he is just as much of an opportunist.

The sketch featuring Suggs, "Simon Suggs, Jr. Esq.; A Legal Biography," extends this characterization of the man to American institutions as a whole, implying that swindling or cheating is not limited to the actions of single individuals but also is undertaken by larger organizational practices. The sketch's frame is an exchange of letters between Suggs and a literary editor who solicits him for his biography. The conversation is obviously meant to be comical: the staid editor quotes poetry and flatters Suggs's ego with pompous, overblown language; Suggs replies with a somewhat literate acceptance that, despite spelling errors and the use of dialect, comes off as more practical and direct. However, when the editor mentions that Suggs would have to pay a hundred and fifty dollars to have his biography published, Suggs politely refuses.

While it is tempting to read the exchange as mocking Suggs himself, the satire is directed at the "shifty" quality of the literary field.[34] The editor may claim to be a purveyor of culture and history, but ultimately, he is just as much of a swindler as Suggs. First, the letters from the editor are dated from the northern city of "Got-Him," obviously a reference to "Gotham" and a play on the practice of swindling. Second, the editor's tone and style reveal a man who is used to manipulation: his flattery; overusing, and sometimes misusing, seemingly educated language; and the technique of slipping the subject of payment into his postscript rather than in the main body of the letter. Suggs, being a master of the con himself, immediately catches on and points out, "Your p.s. . . . seems to be the creem of your correspondents" (88).

That frame provides the backdrop for an ironic political biography of Suggs as the gentleman con man, in which the less-than-moral nature of the economic and legal exchanges are not just practiced by Suggs but integrated into the social structure of the Southwest itself, and by extension, the national economy. The sketch reveals the pecuniary motives of the literary profession in the North, then almost all of the institutions in 1830s Alabama and Mississippi are depicted in the rest of the collection as financially motivated or spurred by the advancement of individual interests. Thus, Baldwin's sketches feature a shift from peripheral figures on the frontier to those who are part of the general structure of American social and economic institutions.

This move is shown through Suggs's biography, which follows a character through life whose "genius," as Baldwin proclaims, "was eminently commercial" (90). Like Hooper's earlier collection, Baldwin's short narrative of Suggs's life begins with his childhood and follows him up through the present day. In one scene, when Suggs Jr. is still a young man, he and his father are playing cards. At one point, Suggs Jr. places a snuffbox on the table, knowing that his father will take a pinch. Unbeknownst to Suggs Sr., the snuff is mixed with pepper. While he sneezes, Suggs Jr. produces a hidden jack and wins the hand.

It is a strange example of an adolescent reaching manhood, but it also demonstrates the effects over a generation of economic growth on the frontier. The "talent" of "shykeenry," as Suggs Sr. calls it, is being passed on, but it takes a much more socially integrated form in his son. That transition is illustrated in the image that accompanies the sketch, "Turning the Jack" (fig. 8). In the illustration, father and son face off over a table on which a hand of cards has been laid out. The contrast is striking—Suggs Sr. looks much as he did in the frontispiece to Hooper's collection, with his scruffy clothes and lean wolf features. Suggs Jr., on the other hand, is verging on a Tammany Hall caricature from later in the century: he still sports the top hat, vest, and chain, but his face is fuller, more well fed than that of his father. Unlike Suggs Sr., Suggs Jr. has used his talent to integrate himself into general American society in a more socially acceptable way, becoming a sanctioned confidence man like Caesar Kasm and other lawyers in the Southwest. Thus, the sketch depicts a second passing of the torch: from "Reverend" Jedediah to his son Simon Suggs and, finally, to Suggs Jr.

But as evidenced by Baldwin's political position in his nonfiction and the humor that dominates the sketches, this shift to an all-pervasive characterization of Americans as confidence men is not necessarily a positive development. Though Baldwin advocated for national economic progress driven by westward expansion, *Flush Times of Alabama and Mississippi* reveals that progress often comes at the cost of "universal distrust" described in *Flush Times of California.* While the scene between father and son Suggs is comic in its tale of a swindler being swindled, it reveals, at a very basic level, the extent to which confidence games taint even familial

Fig. 8. "Turning the Jack," by John McLenan.
From Joseph Glover Baldwin, *Flush Times of Alabama and Mississippi,* 1853.
Vanderbilt University Special Collections and University Archives.

relationships. If all Americans participate in the free market for individual profit, how will communities and interpersonal connections remain intact?

Baldwin's answer to this problem, in the context of his fictional sketches, seems to be incredibly cynical: in the cause of national expansion, certain morals and communal structures will inevitably disintegrate. But as with all of the sketch collections that feature the expanding spaces of the 1830s international cotton trade, the use of humor mitigates the realistic representations of the inherent moral ambiguities. The rest of the short biography follows Suggs through his early years as a con man in the vein of his father, then as an attorney in Arkansas, then as a state's attorney, and finally, as a government agent in charge of handling the land claims of Native American tribes. In each case, not only does Suggs exploit his position to benefit himself financially, but he also eventually acts on behalf of the federal government, a career path that mirrors the increasing geographic growth of the United States and the growth of the American economy. Suggs's role as an ethically suspect agent for the federal government in matters of Native American tribal relations is summed up in the same ironically heroic tone that dominates *Sketches by Boz, Some Adventures,* and the rest of *Flush Times:* "May his shadow never grow less; and may the Indians live to get their dividends of the arrears paid to their agent [Suggs]" (103).

The southern sketches set in the 1830s reveal that economic models based on free market economic philosophies were gradually integrated into the very nature of transatlantic society through expansion into the southwestern territories and the development of British cotton manufacturing. The three collections discussed here map out—and through their representations, shape—the growth of a new social order at the beginning of the nineteenth century, one governed by individual opportunism and a larger network of economic development, in which a particular region was always necessarily connected to a global network of trade, commerce, and modernization. Yet those who represented the moment at which the United States and Britain expanded their economies via the southwestern territories also used their fiction to depict that change in all its particularities, including the morally questionable elements. While *Sketches by Boz, Some Adventures,* and *Flush Times of Alabama and Mississippi* all seem to advocate economic development and modernization, the ever-present confidence man figure demonstrates the moral pitfalls inherent in such change. Just as the historical romances rewrite the region's historical lineage, Hooper's and Baldwin's sketch collections, taken as a whole, guide the idea of the expanding southern states as that expansion occurred. The tension that arose as a result of the moral ambiguity attendant with rapid change is navigated through the sketch form, in which the collections of the varied sketch scenes and characters create the unity of effect that Poe praises so highly.

In many ways, that conflict between a desire for economic progress and the ethical complications demanded by such progress reflects the general tension present in capitalism and the southern plantation economy itself. In this sense, the Old Southwest humor stories, though they do not explicitly depict the space of the plantation, nonetheless take up the issues of a plantation economy that was progressive in its economic philosophy but nonetheless advocated for the morally and ethically regressive practices used to propagate that philosophy. Further, as the generic overlaps between the three collections discussed here reveal, the ostensibly localized space of the Old Southwest reflects a broader nineteenth-century mindset. For both the Southwest humor writers and Dickens, the expansion of the global free market economy was not merely a new and frightening trend but the foundation of nineteenth-century society as a whole. That foundation would ultimately drive the desire on the part of proslavery southerners to create a southern empire that extended beyond the geographic limits of the region and, ultimately, farther south into Mexico and the Caribbean.

3

THE SOUTHERN IMPERIAL DREAM

Novels of Adventure

In 1855, Augusta Jane Evans published her first novel, *Inez: A Tale of the Alamo.* Set during the Texas Revolution in 1836, Evans claimed to have written the novel while living in San Antonio with her family at the end of the U.S.-Mexican War. Unlike her subsequent works, which are mostly domestic tales set in the South, *Inez* is an adventure novel full of battle scenes, intrigue, thrilling moments of betrayal, and hidden identities. The novel begins with a dedication page, which reads: "To the *Texan* Patriots . . . who wrenched asunder the iron hands of the despotic Mexico! And wreathed the brow of the 'Queen State' with the glorious chaplet of 'civil and religious liberty'" (my emphasis). In *Inez,* the Texas Revolution is recast as a morally justified insurrection against a tyrannical power. While the language evokes the rhetoric of proslavery southerners in the sectional debates that dominated U.S. politics at the time—that the federal government and abolitionism were infringing on their "liberty"—it replaces those domestic "enemies" with Mexico.

By framing an obvious imperial incursion as a righteous rebellion, *Inez* is part of a southern imperialist ideology shaped by novels published between the U.S.-Mexican War (1846–48) and the beginning of the Civil War. During this time, writing by proslavery southerners generated a form of nascent southern nationalism through their depictions of military conflicts with Mexico and Cuba. These novels of adventure allowed authors to imagine, through fiction, a southern empire that could sustain free market and free labor values along with the continuation of racialized slavery. Beginning with the Texas Revolution—at the height of the southwestern land boom, just before the Panic of 1837—proslavery southerners were the driving force behind a series of imperialist endeavors into Mexico and the Caribbean. A decade after the Revolution, the annexation of Texas and large swaths of western land at the end of the U.S.-Mexican War set off a chain reaction of expansionist efforts throughout the 1850s. With the Compromise of 1850 posing a limitation to slave states in the West, southerners sought other avenues for enlarging slaveholding territories farther south. Cuba in particular became a regular target, and the 1850s featured a series of attempts to annex the island as slave territory. By the end of the decade, the southern imperial impulse culminated in an explicit form of Confederate nationalist rhetoric.[1]

Works such as Joseph Holt Ingraham's dime novel *The Texan Ranger; or, The Maid of Matamoras. A Tale of the Mexican War* (1846); Evans's *Inez;* and Lucy Holcombe Pickens's novel, *The Free Flag of Cuba; or, The Martyrdom of López, a Tale of the Liberating Expedition of 1851* (1854) gave voice to and shaped the ideology behind an emergent southern nationalism founded on a "benevolent" imperialism. Southern authors borrowed from popular British adventure tales by authors such as Daniel Defoe and, of course, Sir Walter Scott to create a regionally based national discourse through heroic archetypes. In the form of the adventure tale, the novels reinscribed the region's efforts at imperialism as being driven by liberal capitalist impulses, in which honor and economic freedom become the defining modes of discourse. What makes Mexico despotic in *Inez* is the hindering of southerners' and the southern economy's expansion into new territories on their terms—namely, to expand slavery and the plantation economy. In these depictions, slavery is the benevolent institution that differentiates southern imperialism from (as proslavery southern authors would have it) more exploitative forms of imperial expansion. According to the rhetoric of the novels, slavery enabled a form of free labor in the new southern empire in which all white men could achieve greater socioeconomic mobility. The genre also contributed to the creation of a unified southern nation where none existed—all under the banner of a new and "free" slave empire. Not only did this fiction presage the Confederate nationalism that drove the outbreak of the Civil War, but these imperial narratives were necessary to its ultimate creation.

The Southern Nation and the Adventure Novel

Joseph Holt Ingraham's 1845 novel, *Montezuma, the Serf; or, The Revolt of the Mexitili,* is a historical romance set in a fictionalized version of the Aztec Empire.[2] The hero of the novel, as the title indicates, is a serf who leads an uprising against the emperor and nobles. Although Ingraham is careful to assign the label of "serf" to Montezuma, his role in the fictionalized society bears similarity to the type of slavery that would have been familiar to nineteenth-century American readers. The novel often interchanges the terms *slave* and *serf,* and the feudal system emulates an extensive plantation, in which the serfs or slaves inhabit houses surrounding the castle occupied by the emperor and aristocrats.

That Ingraham would choose to write a novel set during a (highly) fictionalized segment of Mexican history on the eve of the U.S.-Mexican War is not unusual. Mexico and western lands had been the object of attention since the Texas Revolution, and the debates over annexation were at the forefront of American politics in 1845. What is unusual, however, is Ingraham's choice of topic: a slave rebellion, in which the novel's hero is the enslaved leader. For an author like Ingraham, a proslavery southern sympathizer who was born in Maine but had been living in Mississippi for most of his life, penning a novel supportive of a slave uprising was at odds with his political leanings.

The novel's use of economic language in its portrayal of that uprising is even stranger for an adopted southerner. In a speech inciting his fellow slaves to revolt, Montezuma evokes a free labor ideology, wherein individuals earn their wealth and should be able to claim the results of their hard work: "What right, brethren, has the emperor to seize upon the fruits of your toil? By what claim does the knight and noble hold the wages earned by the sweat of your brows? If you earn twelve silver *xu* a day, by what authority does the emperor take eleven—aye, a twelfth, if he choose—and cut off your heads and cast your bodies into the kennel if ye dare to murmur?"

(1:33). The slaves are entitled to freedom not because they are beings deserving of basic human rights but because they secured those rights with labor. This version of Mexican serfdom bears more resemblance to the industrial system in the North—a vague repurposing of the critiques advanced by labor advocates. In this construction, Mexican serfs are more like free white laborers in the North than enslaved black men and women in the South. A slave uprising in this context would be a method of reform, to ensure that their basic freedoms are protected. The uprising would also function as a way of protecting the slaves' wealth and allow them to reap the benefits of hard work—essentially, establishing a better labor system more in line with free market ideologies.

The novel's characterization of the slave uprising fits with the imperial demands that governed the South and the entire United States at the time of its publication. At a moment when the nation was on the precipice of war with Mexico, novels such as Ingraham's lay the ideological foundation for expansion into Mexico and the growth of slavery in those new lands. The Mexican "serfs" in *Montezuma* are, indeed, slaves. Yet the depiction of that serfdom and the revolt invests those slaves with characteristics that adhere to liberal capitalist principles. Through such language, Ingraham's novel retains a modified system of slavery that would correspond with the aims of proslavery southerners while also making the inhabitants of new territories sympathetic figures who model an ideal of economic progress and modernization.

Montezuma is one of a series of imperial adventure novels published by proslavery southerners throughout the 1840s and 1850s. Just as much of the cultural work of southern writing from the antebellum period has been discounted by critics, the role of the adventure novels in circulating an early form of regionally based nationalism has been largely ignored.[3] Novels such as *Montezuma* and Evans's *Inez* contributed to the idea of a southern nation and paved the way for the expansion of the South as it was defined by slaveholders in the context of the progressively acrimonious debates over slavery. The novels frame the invasions of Mexico and later Cuba in a favorable light, specifically as a method by which slavery—and the regional culture created around its existence—could be sustained and augmented in the context of a liberal capitalist economy.

Between 1846 and 1860—the years surrounding the U.S.-Mexican War and leading up to the Civil War—the American literary marketplace was flooded with adventure novels. Starting with the debates over Texas annexation in 1845 and culminating at the end of the war in 1848, cheap dime novelettes featuring Mexico and the war by authors such as Ingraham, George Lippard, and Ned Buntline were incredibly popular.[4] The trend continued into the 1850s with the publication of adventure tales set in areas of the far West, Southwest, Caribbean, and South America. *Inez* was just one example in a series of novels highlighting stories of exploration and military adventure: works such as William Clark Falkner's *The Spanish Heroine* (1851), William Gilmore Simms's *Vasconcelos: A Romance of the New World* (1853), John Rollin Ridge's *The Life and Adventures of Joaquin Murieta* (1854), and E.D.E.N. Southworth's *The Hidden Hand* (1859), to name just a few, continued the fascination with exploits and conflict in the West and greater South.[5]

Forming what critic Michael Denning calls "the genre of 1848," the novels were popular artistic responses to the U.S.-Mexican War and the resulting territorial expansion in the decade thereafter.[6] In her examination of the genre, *American Sensations* (2002), Shelley Streeby argues that these adventure novels played a key role in shaping the mid-nineteenth-century imperial imaginary in the United States.[7] For those like *Montezuma* that were published in the midst of debates over the war and during the actual years of the conflict, the novels were usually written and released so quickly that they took on an ephemeral or even documentary quality, serving as barometers of popular opinion regarding the war and U.S. politics.[8] For the novels that appeared in the decade after, like *Inez,* they were a response not only to the imperial growth of the United States but also to the urbanization and industrialization fueled by that growth.[9] Although the novels were not uniform in their responses to the war and later conflicts, the common thread was their attempts to negotiate the dynamics of an emerging nation in the midst of global expansion.[10] Taken in sum, the adventure novels that constitute the genre of 1848 present an examination of the war's imperial motivations and its aftermath, wherein "the debates about the war, expansion, and Manifest Destiny resound throughout the pages" (Streeby 21). As Jaime Javier Rodriguez describes it, in the literature, "the war forces the U.S. into a self-consciousness about its own national construction; it becomes aware—momentarily, perhaps—of itself as a common nation among nations" (50).

Yet as the examples of *Montezuma* and *Inez* demonstrate, novels by proslavery authors evolved radically different conceptions of imperial expansion and "nation," with slavery being the divisive flashpoint. Although it is often overshadowed by the Civil War in terms of its historical significance, 1848 was, in many ways, a watershed moment in global empire building, and particularly in the evolution of sectional politics and questions of nationalism in the United States.[11] A long line of historians cite 1848 as the true starting point for the conflicts that led to the Civil War, and the U.S.-Mexican War was an early training ground for future Confederate soldiers.[12] Sectional animosity over the issue of slavery culminated in the decade after, and the crux of these debates was the existence of slavery in the same newly acquired territories that formed the settings of the popular adventure novels. "Thus," historian David Potter observes, "the slavery question became the sectional question, the sectional question became the slavery question, and both became the *territorial question*" (49, my emphasis).

Over time, a generalized idea of U.S. nationalism defined by manifest destiny yielded to a southern nationalism defined by the imperative to extend slavery and the regional economy across the continent.[13] Beginning as early as the 1830s "flush times" and the Texas Revolution in 1836, settlers moved into and claimed land in southwestern territories and Mexico to establish plantations and farmsteads operated primarily by slave labor. In *A Glance at the Currency and Resources Generally of the Republic of Texas,* native Virginian James Cocke remarked in 1838 that Texas was a clear boon to the expansion of the southern slave-based plantation economy: "There can be nothing in the history of cotton planting, in Louisiana, Mississippi, Alabama, or any other cotton-growing section of the United States, *equal* to what may be *now seen* in the cotton fields of this country!" (12).[14] Similarly, although many proslavery southerners had mixed feelings about entering into the U.S.-Mexican War, none denied the benefits to the economy in doing so, particularly the importance of promoting slavery and the South's agricultural trade.[15] Writing in his commercial journal in 1846, James De Bow outlined the prospects of commercial growth for the southern states that would come with territorial acquisition: "We [New

Orleans] have as much to do with the Rio Grande valley, as with the Ohio or Mississippi. . . . On any settlement of the war with Mexico, . . . trade must become enormous" ("Progress of American Commerce" 422).

Under the perceived threats to southern sovereignty—that is, to slavery—southern leaders began to rally around a goal: to create a southern nation in order to expand slavery and the economy into the new territories but also to make sure that southern nation fit into an idea of progressive, liberal capitalism that drove the nineteenth-century world. During the congressional debates over the Wilmot Proviso in 1847—which proposed eliminating slavery in all of the territories acquired after the U.S.-Mexican War—South Carolinian and ardent proslavery advocate John C. Calhoun argued that ownership of slaves was a right to property protected by the Constitution. Therefore, the proviso was in direct violation of federal laws and "in derogation of that *perfect equality* which belongs to them as members of this Union" (455, my emphasis). In his defense of slavery, Calhoun uses the language of equality and liberty to rationalize the continued existence of a system founded on inherent inequality and bondage, thus burying the impulses of slavery-based, capitalist expansion under the rhetoric of communal liberty and a struggle for individual equality: "*Resolved.* That it is a fundamental principle in our political creed, that a people, in forming a constitution, have the unconditional right to form and adopt the government which they may think best calculated to secure their *liberty,* prosperity, and happiness" (455, my emphasis).[16]

With these rhetorical maneuverings, Calhoun balances two impulses: a desire for individual profit based on the principles of liberal capitalism; and the desire to maintain the southern, slavery-based plantation system. It was language that would be reworked again and again for the next decade, with proslavery southerners unifying around the idea of a retromodern slave state in the name of "freedom." For instance, the increased militancy of the slavery debates in 1850 would lead Mississippi senator Albert Gallatin Brown to declare that "at the first moment after you [northern, abolitionist politicians] consummate your first act of aggression upon slave property, I would declare the Union dissolved" (McCluskey 477). A few years later, and just two years before the Civil War, Virginia journalist and Confederate sympathizer Edward Pollard would write in his proslavery imperial manifesto, *Black Diamonds* (1859), "Shall the institution which has built up the commerce and industry of such large portions of the *civilized* world, that has so identified itself with the *progress* of the age, that is so beneficent to *national* strength and character . . . that inspires *independence,* refines the soul, and nourishes a graceful pride . . . be condemned to extinction [?]" (107, my emphases). With each new territorial incursion, "southern nationalists sought to reconcile the imperatives of equality—within the [southern] union, among themselves—with the brute realities of inequality and labor exploitation on which their slave societies were founded" (Onuf 39). On these terms, the illogical and impossible was achieved: the expansion of slavery became the expansion of freedom, liberty, and modern, progressive economic structures—especially the strengthening of free labor practices for white men.

The adventure novels by southern sympathizers legitimize this discourse by presenting the imagined slave empire under the guise of a benevolent form of liberal capitalism and southern nationalism. Popular fiction is necessary for this project because it disseminates and standardizes the idea of a unified nation and community in ways not as easily accomplished through other literary forms. In *Imagined Communities,* Benedict Anderson details that the idea of "nation-ness" came about in the eighteenth century through the development of print capitalism and the creation of national languages in widely circulated novels and print newspapers. These literary forms "made it possible for rapidly growing numbers of people to think about themselves, and to relate themselves to others, in profoundly new ways" (Anderson 36). In this sense, fiction—and specifically narrative fiction—is a mode of telling a community and nation into being, for it constructs continuity within a group that would not exist otherwise.[17] In other words, according to critic Gregory Jusdanis, literature and fictional narrative "promote the collective internalization of public norms, conventions, and symbols" (122). Popular and sensational literature such as the adventure novels therefore played a fundamental role in the construction and propagation of southern nationalism precisely because it is narrative driven, entertaining, and was written for mass consumption.

Imperial adventure novels had been performing this cultural work since the eighteenth century, only in service of the expanding British Empire. Adventure tales by authors such as Defoe, Scott, and Edward Bulwer-Lytton were some of the best-selling texts in Britain and the United States.

In the same way that the popularity of mid-nineteenth-century U.S. adventure novels corresponded with the general timeline of western wars and territorial growth, the earlier British novels emerged in tandem with the European age of exploration. And also like the genre of 1848 in the United States, the novels written by popular British authors were crucial to shaping the idea of a British world power to its subjects by positively reimagining and mythologizing the possibilities of colonial expansion under the banner of nationalism.[18] As early progenitors of the genre, the narrative patterns and character tropes of the British adventure tales set the stage for the later fictional representations in the United States.

As a form, the adventure novels of the eighteenth and nineteenth centuries fashion a collective idea of empire and nation by normalizing the actions of colonizers—primarily white, male, and upper-class. This objective was especially important for conveying the imperatives of empire to proslavery southerners in the context of the U.S. territorial debates. Despite popular assumptions, southern intellectuals were not united in their attitude toward all major events and issues of the era, and the U.S.-Mexican War and territorial expansion were divisive topics. Incorporating portions of Mexico also entailed potential socioeconomic mobility for lower-class whites and bringing citizens of color (Mexicans) into the South. Calhoun, for example, did not endorse the U.S.-Mexican War, despite being a proponent of Texas annexation, because it threatened the southern elite and presented the potential for too much racial intermixing.[19] Many other proslavery southerners, however, saw it as a way for everyday white southerners to get ahead, just as the 1830s flush times had offered prospects for the previous generation. Figures such as De Bow advocated for opportunities both to strengthen slavery and to diversify the economy. For those who wished to maintain the southern slave system, supported Texas annexation, and desired a war with Mexico to acquire new territory, the task was to present imperial expansion as a way of building on and extending the existent southern social and economic system, rather than upending it.

To diminish the objections to imperial expansion and aid in the creation of a potential community, the novels create heroic archetypes that connect to the experiences of the (presumably white, presumably middle-class) readers.[20] Although the heroes of the adventure tales invariably possess the privilege inherent in class, gender, and race, the novels depict them as everymen in unusual situations. For example, Daniel Defoe's titular character in *Robinson Crusoe* (1719) is a wealthy British aristocrat, yet he demonstrates basic survival skills and ingenuity while trapped on a Caribbean island. This blend of upper-class identity with a pragmatic work ethic connects the story of his survival on a tropical island with the daily lives of those reading the novel in England (or later, the United States).

Likewise, with its publication date directly before the beginning of the U.S.-Mexican War, Ingraham's novel *Montezuma* sets the stage for an emergent southern empire as defined by proslavery whites. The distinguishing feature of the slave system in Ingraham's fictionalized Mexico is the hierarchy of slaves and nobles. Rather than inherently degraded—as most proslavery writers of the time would have portrayed an African American slave—the slave leader and hero of the novel, Montezuma, is inherently dignified: "His stature was lofty, and his port noble; while the highest manly grace and beauty were stamped upon his face and person. His dignity was that of virtue; his beauty that of a gentle temper and cheerful heart. He was doated [*sic*] on by his father, idolized by his sister, honored and beloved by all of his degree in the city; but despised so closely had nature allied him to them, by all the nobles of the court." Because of these natural gifts, Montezuma is incredibly industrious. He earns respect and admiration through hard work, loyalty to family and community, and his ability to rise above his humble origins. As the novel takes care to note, Montezuma's father is "a poor net-maker . . . whose sole merit was his honesty, and whose only income was the daily pittance earned by the toil of his hands" (1:7). Depicting the hero in this way is almost a direct answer to politicians like Calhoun, who saw anyone of color as being innately inferior.

The adventure tales create a rationale by which the heroes—and allegorically, the upper-class, white male leaders of the respective empire—can enter, conquer, and move about new spaces with impunity on behalf of an entire nation. Like Defoe's Crusoe, despite being a serf, or "slave," Montezuma is an empathetic figure in the context of a foreign space. As such, the novel narratively imagines southern economic growth driven by a form of liberal capitalist enterprise benefiting the common (white) man of talent. The result is a story of imperial expansion that brings "individuals together into a common social experience, thereby enabling them to discover their shared identity" (Jusdanis 122). Through the adventure novels and their heroes, readers could vicariously participate in that movement, and the narratives translated the dynamics of national identity formation and imperialism, ultimately with the same general end: to unite the nation around the idea of territorial expansion already occurring, the ultimate expression of manifest destiny.

Montezuma also lays the groundwork for the version of free market engagement that relies on the existence of slavery in newly acquired territories. In this way, the southern adventure novels were once again following a pattern established in earlier British fiction. As many economists and economic historians are quick to point out, capitalism requires the constant expansion of markets for the circulation of commodities. And in the eighteenth and nineteenth centuries, market expansion equated to geographic imperial expansion.[21] Yet that constant expansion also threatened the stability of the existing nation-state. This paradoxical quality, critic Ayşe Çelikkol argues, is what promoted the rise of the adventure romance in British literature: the adventure tales became a way of reconciling "limitless exchange and global cooperation" with the persistent need for an established "British" identity (4).[22] Novels such as *Guy Mannering* (1815) by Sir Walter Scott depict heroes that draw from both the basic principles of liberal capitalist philosophy and "traditional" British cultural identity: for example, the figure of the individual, self-reliant British hero in the form of the maritime smuggler. Or in *Robinson Crusoe,* the representative Englishman who can also control the "savages" on a Caribbean island and create a one-man British colony through his own hard work and maintenance of "civilized" manners. In these characters, the adventure novels validate economic expansion by reframing it as part of British cultural heritage.

Montezuma performs a similar role in its representation of the slave uprising and the proposed social system that would emerge thereafter. The empathetic portrayal of Montezuma does not translate to all slaves, just certain individuals who demonstrate the characteristics worthy of esteem and, more important in a novel born out of free market ideologies, potential social and economic mobility. As a result, the new system Montezuma proposes will maintain the aristocratic hierarchies of serf-nobleman-emperor, but those divisions are determined by an individual's demonstration of merit. One character openly questions Montezuma regarding the system:

> "Wouldst thou slay the emperor and nobles, and let each man be his own governor?"
>
> "No . . . this were exchanging tyranny for anarchy. I would not destroy the throne, but *purify* it. The emperor would be the ruler of his people—not their master."
>
> "You would destroy, then, the barriers that stand between you and the nobility, leave their rank open to the deserving among yourselves, and from vassals and appendages to the power of the nobles, become free and independent citizens, with none but political subjection to the emperor."
>
> "It is what we aim at . . . alone." (1:36, my emphasis)

This conversation outlines a rule of governance according to a meritocracy, and the emphasis on "purifying" the system, rather than dismantling it, indicates the theoretically humane intent behind such reforms. There would still be masters—or noblemen and emperors—but those at the bottom would be cared for by more just and rational leaders.

This modified version of slavery or serfdom is predicated on the continued existence of enslaved populations and repeats the "New Man" philosophy of Whigs such as Kennedy, Hooper, and Baldwin or the "ordered progress" advocated by Simms. And in this new system, there will always be certain individuals on the bottom rungs of the social and racial ladder. Throughout *Montezuma,* several characters are designated as naturally "slavelike" and thus deserving of their role in Mexican society. Of course, these are also the preternaturally "evil" characters in the novel or the physically disabled (one is a hunchback), whose "corruption" implies that society as a whole would be more productive if they are kept enslaved.[23] As one character remarks to an enslaved man, a central villain in the novel: "Thy race are not like others. You alone feel delight in human woe and evil" (1:97). The language parallels the biological determinism and racism evinced by proslavery southerners such as Calhoun or "scientists" such as Samuel Cartwright in "Diseases and Particularities of the Negro Race" (1851), which attributed physical and psychological "defects" to inherent racial inferiority.[24] And like African Americans in proslavery rhetoric, this class in Ingraham's fictionalized Mexican society would gain from a supposedly benevolent slave system, in which they could be controlled for the benefit of more "deserving" classes.

Ingraham's novel dances the line between advocating a version of liberal capitalism in its emphasis on hard work and individual merit while still promoting the continuance of a strict, racialized slave system. What allows for an imperfect resolution of these two ideas in the novel is, again, its depiction of the hero, the noble slave. As in any standard Simms or Sir Walter Scott romance, the end of the novel reveals that Montezuma is, in fact, the descendant of nobility, thus raising him above his life as a serf. In this way, he is an example of ideal free market values in his talent and ambition but also receives a "pass" in terms of his natural origins or race. Therefore, the hero of *Montezuma* possesses the same traits as the heroic southerners of the historical romances: self-made, hardworking, yet blessed with a version of natural aristocratic leanings characterized by virtue and honor. Ingraham's novel creates a version of southern plantation society under the guise of Aztec history, in which a free labor ideology is promoted by the existence of a merit-based slave or caste system. With "natural" hierarchies (i.e., racialized slavery) in place, all white men with talent can better access the opportunities available in this fictional free market system.

The novel's construction of a certain type of slavery and a particular caste system within Mexican culture becomes a way to justify expansion to those, like Calhoun, who would doubt Mexican citizens' worth in comparison to white, Anglo-Saxon southerners and who, in turn, doubted the value of a southern empire.[25] In the case of *Montezuma,* the noble hero functions in a space foreign to readers, and certain Mexicans are sympathetic, and technically, already American—or better yet, southern by the standards of proslavery advocates. This depiction counters the racist objections of many proslavery southerners, who wanted to expand but worried about the "inherent inferiority" of the Mexican government and people.[26] The world of Ingraham's novel mirrors sentiments by southerners such as De Bow, who argued in a February 1846 issue of *De Bow's Review* that "Mexicans are possessed of great natural capacities, which only require proper cultivation and a favorable field for their development" ("Mexico" 131). A southern, slave-based system could provide this "proper cultivation," according to most pro-annexation, pro-expansion southerners.

Montezuma lays the imaginative foundation for a southern empire in Mexico. By fictionalizing a Mexican society that mirrors an ideal southern, slaveholding society, Ingraham's novel anticipates an empire that extends southern slavery but upholds the ideals of liberal capitalism. As with Simms's historical romances set during the Revolution, Ingraham's novel presents an ideal lineage for the southern nation in Mexico. In this vision of empire, expansion occurs through a legitimized and peaceful merging, rather than conquest.

Thus, the novels by southern sympathizers in the genre of 1848 mirror the language of southern politicians of the era to create idealized visions of a southern proto-nation, in which the lands seized during the Texas Revolution, U.S.-Mexican War, and later the filibusters in Cuba were "earned," not taken, by virtue of hard work and the egalitarian aims of the southerners migrating, fighting, and settling to the south and west. The adventure tales offer an alternative to engaging with the market that promoted the existence of slavery, benefited all white southerners financially, and (at least in the minds of these southern authors) invented a version of imperial expansion that incorporated those being conquered without disregarding existing social structures. In doing so, the novels effectively reverse the standard logic of free labor at the time. Following a pattern of rationalization that was ubiquitous in proslavery discourse, the qualities of "self-made" men in the novels are only apparent in an expanded slave system.

The three novels discussed at length in this chapter—Ingraham's *The Texan Ranger,* Evans's *Inez,* and Pickens's *The Free Flag of Cuba*—together represent the genesis of a unified southern nationalism based on the principles of liberal capitalism, in which extending slavery translated into extending a more egalitarian, benevolent economic and social system. These fictional representations envision a unified defense of southern traditions and republicanism in the face of northern or free-soil aggression, all while upholding the need for imperialism fueled by the desire for economic growth. As such, the southern novels of the genre of 1848 imagine a nation that fit within a developing global world while still relying on the defining element of regional southern culture—slavery.

Sowing the Seeds for Expansion: *The Texan Ranger*

Critical literary studies typically include Joseph Holt Ingraham in a long list of forgettable nineteenth-century authors and texts. At the time his

U.S.-Mexican War novels were published, Ingraham had been living in Mississippi for almost two decades and primarily earning his living through the sale of cheap, sensational novels.[27] Most of Ingraham's published texts were "novels of mild adventure," as a later family member would describe them, which probably accounts for the lack of critical attention.[28]

Despite the dismissal of his work, Ingraham's literary career paralleled trends in popular American fiction and the expansion of the South before the Civil War. As Henry Wadsworth Longfellow would reflect: "I think he may say he has written the worst novels ever written by anybody. But they sell" (Hilen 2:108). In 1835, he published an account of his travels through the region, *The South-West, by a Yankee.*[29] While Ingraham never makes an ardent defense of slavery, he does rationalize and justify its existence. For example, in a scene describing his encounter with a group of slaves who had just been sold to a sugar plantation in Louisiana, he remarks: "They all appeared contented and happy, and highly elated at their sweet [*sic*] anticipations. Say not that the slavery of the Louisiana negroes is a *bitter* draught" (1:190–1). Later, in his observations of a slave auction, he more boldly writes, "Do not mistake me: I am no advocate for slavery; but neither am I a believer in that wild Garrisonian theory, which, like a magician's wand, is at once to dissolve every link that binds the slave to his, and demolish at one blow a system that has existed, still gaining in extent and stability, for centuries" (2:32). Ingraham's self-avowedly "pragmatic" approach to slavery echoes the view of many Americans during this era, southern and northern alike, a sentiment shown by favorable reviews in many national magazines, such as the one by Edgar Allan Poe that appeared in the *Southern Literary Messenger* in 1836.[30] It also reveals the extent to which Ingraham saw the strength of the slavery-based southern economy, the system "still gaining in extent and stability." This impartial and even approving attitude toward slavery must have carried over to his views of the region, for Ingraham remained in Mississippi for the rest of his life.[31]

Building on this early positive appraisal of slavery, the language of Ingraham's adventure novels parallels the rhetoric assumed by proslavery southern intellectuals and politicians of the time. In the mid-1840s, the issue of Texas annexation created a sense of unity among southern politicians in an otherwise fractious political climate, wherein the focus was cementing and strengthening the role of slavery in what was seen as an already "southern" state.[32] Then President John Tyler (1841–5) appointed first Abel Upshur, then John C. Calhoun, as secretary of state. Both ardent proslavery advocates, Upshur and Calhoun made the annexation of Texas and protecting the interests of southern slaveholders their primary goals. In a letter to British diplomat Richard Pakenham in 1844, Calhoun cites the fates of black men and women in free states as primary examples of the need to maintain slavery in the United States and Texas: "The census and other authentic documents show that, in all instances in which the States have changed the former relation between the two races, the condition of the African, instead of being improved, has become worse. They have been invariably sunk into vice and pauperism, accompanied by the bodily and mental inflictions incident thereto . . . while, in all other States which have retained the ancient relation between them, they have improved greatly in every respect—in number, comfort, intelligence, and morals" (*Works of John C. Calhoun* 5:337). He concludes, "In this view of the subject it may be asserted, that what is called slavery is in reality a *political institution,* essential to the peace, safety, and prosperity of those States of the Union in which it exists" (5:339, my emphasis). Redefining slavery as a "political institution," one that promotes the well-being of all involved, recasts southern expansion into western territories as a benevolent act on the part of slaveholding southerners that would also profit the region's whites.

Ingraham was embedded in these debates from the beginning, an attitude reflected in his writing. As his observations over a decade earlier in *The South-West* reveal, he oscillated between presenting a fairly unbiased view of slavery to explicitly defending the institution. By the time his novels featuring Mexico and the war were published, he had been living in Mississippi and benefiting from the region's social and economic structures for more than a decade. In addition to his attitudes toward southern slavery and the region's economy, Ingraham was connected to many of the central figures who took part in the U.S.-Mexican War. *The South-West* is dedicated, for example, to John A. Quitman, a proslavery Mississippian and U.S.-Mexican War hero who also served two terms as governor of the state and later supported the invasions into Cuba in the 1850s.

By the time his next Mexican-based novelette, *The Texan Ranger; or, The Maid of Matamoras. A Tale of the Mexican War* (1846), was published,

Ingraham had taken his earlier fictionalization of Mexican history and culture in *Montezuma* and projected it onto the military conflicts then taking place in Texas and Mexico. Published the year the war officially began, the novel extends the representation of Mexico and Mexicans in *Montezuma* to the specific context of the war, using the lineage created in his earlier novel to depict the conflict and new Mexican territories as ideal conduits for a southern empire. The novel justifies Texas annexation and war with Mexico by presenting Texans as humane, industrious adventurers and *some* Mexicans as already American—even southern—in their sentiments and lifestyles.[33]

The novel begins with a portrait of the hero, who is a soldier for the Mexican army—not a Texan Ranger, despite the title. Like Montezuma, "Bonne Lance," as he is called, exhibits the predictable traits of a romantic hero: he is handsome, brave, intelligent, and kind, and his men respect him. In short, he possesses the natural "nobility" so important in any romance or adventure novel. Yet also like Montezuma, he earns that respect and those natural gifts by demonstrating skill in battle and strong leadership. Bonne Lance, in short, is a Mexican character who has all of the qualities of a New Man, an ideal laborer and just leader in a free market.

This position includes his role as a Mexican officer battling the U.S. Army. Bonne Lance approaches combat from a businesslike perspective, viewing the Americans as equal adversaries, rather than villains. He casually observes the opposing army's prowess—particularly the Texan Rangers—to a fellow soldier, noting that they are formidable enemies: "These Saxon [American] officers were educated to war, in one of the best military schools in the world. It is to the severe and searching course of military studies, and the martial exercises they are subjected to there to which the bravery and gallantry of the American army is to be referred. There are no better officers in the world than those of the American army. They know no cowardice. They can never fly" (14–15). It is an odd evaluation from a commanding officer of the opposing army but not so unusual in a novel that frames the conflict in a positive light, especially in favor of the Texan forces described here. It also reinforces Bonne Lance's role as an opportunist in the truest sense of the free market. As with any good businessman, the war is not personal for him. And when another fellow officer accuses Bonne Lance of traitorous thoughts for his positive evaluation of the Texans, he replies, "I do not despise the enemy as you do" (19). The "noble" Mexican chieftain then becomes a hyper-rational mouthpiece for the American cause.

Bonne Lance, in turn, treats the soldiers he commands as contract military. He frequently asserts that they will only fight if they are paid—there's no sense of national or cultural loyalty. At one point, when his soldiers have not been paid for their services in some time, Bonne Lance actually withholds them from battle: "Doubtless Prince Cima [the fictional Mexican ruler] had some experience of the credit of the generals of the republic and thought one fair maiden in hand better than gold in promises! . . . . The next morning the pay came and I rejoined the general. Then it was his fault not mine! I and my Rancheros are as free as air; and go at no man's bidding unless we have justice done us!" (15). The passage begins with the language of finance and economy—wages, payment for services rendered, credit—and ends with the abstract, idealistic terms of freedom and justice. Bonne Lance equates the two, and rather than acting through national loyalty, he and the troops are governed by loyalty to individualism and economic mobility. As he remarks to another character later in the novel: "I have no country but my saddle, no loyalty but my sword, Castellan! Like the birds of the air I and my brave rancheros light where we will, and the region wherein we descend we call our country as long as we remain upon it" (32).

By narrating the military engagements from the perspective of this honorable, free market soldier, Ingraham recasts the war as an economic venture, not a violent conflict, and the United States' enemies as business counterparts, who would be more sympathetic to American readers. The Mexican heroes, divested of any sense of national allegiance or cultural attributes, make the Mexico of the novel amenable to the extension of southern nationalism: they have the tools in place; they are just lacking the larger ideological structure. By this logic, Mexican citizens are more easily assimilated because southern nationalism would benefit them—and so would slavery. In this way, *The Texan Ranger* enacts a form of ideological imperialism through its representation of the enemy soldiers.

Likewise, from the perspective of the Mexican characters, the U.S. troops and the Texans (or southerners) are honorable military men performing their duties with skill. Their actions in the novel reinforce Bonne Lance's earlier evaluation. In battle, "the brave [Texan] rangers temper their war-like courage with the sweet virtues of humanity" (44). They are efficient and vicious, but humane, and there is a particularly ridiculous anecdote about a ranger giving a wounded Mexican soldier water during battle. As with his Mexican heroes, Ingraham creates Texans that are naturally noble yet still common men who have earned their places in the world. For example, the novel devotes a large section to a description of General Zachary Taylor, a Virginian, career soldier on the western frontier, U.S.-Mexican War hero, and of course, a future president. The description of Taylor greatly contrasts with that of the Mexican officers (with the exception of Bonne Lance): his dress is plain, his manner simple, and his appearance rough. But he is devoted to his southernized nation and commands the respect of his soldiers: "With great military experience, a profound tactician, skillful in the operations of war, and as brave as he was judicious, he had also won the esteem and confidence of his country" (24). Taylor and the other U.S. soldiers—again, particularly the Texan troops—embody the balance between free market individualism and natural nobility, a pattern established earlier in *Montezuma*.

This characterization extends to the Americans' motivations for the war (or Saxons, as they are known in the novel).[34] Continuing *The Texan Ranger*'s favorable assessment of the enemy, another Mexican character observes at one point that "the Americans have no other object in view in this war they are commencing than establishing peace and a permanent treaty with Mexico" (37). This very convenient rewrite of the war's aim falls in line with the businesslike characterization of the conflict on both sides and attributes the same balance of competency and natural nobility to U.S. imperialism that Ingraham assigns to all of his heroes.

Yet unlike the Mexican troops, the Texans *are* acting through loyalty to a national cause—the southern cause. This is made especially evident in the battle scenes between the Texan forces and Mexican soldiers. In one scene, the rangers take up common cries to arms during the U.S.-Mexican War, "The Alamo!" and "San Jacinto!"—both major defeats during the Texas Revolution. They win the battle decidedly, even though they are vastly outnumbered (41–2). By evoking the conflicts specific to Texans and the Texas Revolution, the novel emphasizes an allegiance to a particular form of nationalism, one of Texas and the slaveholding South, rather than the United States more generally. In this representation, Texans (and southerners) are merely claiming land that is already theirs, land they "earned" more than a decade earlier. They and the Mexican heroes are thereby linked and equated through common qualities and common territory.

The novel's explicit depiction of slavery cements the linkage between the Texans and their future imperial conquest in Mexican territory. Although U.S. slavery is only mentioned briefly in *The Texan Ranger,* an African American character plays a central role in one climactic scene. One of the Mexican heroines, Marguerita, is engaged to a Texan soldier.[35] Before the events of the novel begin, Marguerita has assisted two U.S. soldiers, one a Texan, in escaping from captivity in Mexico. When the novel commences, she is still imprisoned by her uncle, after being betrayed by a black servant in her father's house. The man is a former slave who fled Texas two years earlier. Although technically he is a servant and despite the fact that Mexico did not recognize slavery at the time, the novel always refers to him as a "slave."

The narrative also carefully designates the man as inherently corrupt, just as certain slaves in *Montezuma* are corrupt by nature. When Marguerita confides in him and asks for his aid in freeing the soldiers, "he proved treacherous; and for money gave her name to the authorities as the person who had aided the flight of the two prisoners" (69). The scenario implies an identical argument to the one made by Calhoun just two years earlier, during the Texas annexation debates: that black men and women who leave slavery lose their morals and become driven only by monetary gain. They cannot thrive in the free market because they lack the natural nobility to maintain a moral compass. In his representation of an African American former slave, Ingraham continues a racist paradigm established in his earlier Mexican novel, wherein slavery enables control over populations that would otherwise bring harm to themselves and others.

The novel compounds this idea in a truly odd scene between Marguerita and the black servant, which casts him as a pure villain: "She gave him all her jewels and the money she had. He took them and demanded all that he had asked for. She cast herself upon his mercy. He had none. She implored him to be silent. He was deaf." Then Ingraham introduces a sympathetic element in the servant's story, but in this scene, it is twisted to heighten his treachery:

> "The gold—enough to buy my wife and two boys in Bexar [Texas], or I betray you," he thundered out.
>
> "I have no more, slave," she cried, in the energy of despair. "Do your worst! At least *they* are free!"
>
> The demon-souled African left the beautiful, trembling girl, who had done what she did for the two prisoners out of generous, impulsive love to the nation, to which *one* she fondly loved belonged. (70)

The scene employs a trope that would normally create empathy between the readers and the character, at least in an abolitionist text: a formerly enslaved man working to free his family from slavery in Texas. However, in the context of this novel—wherein slavery promotes freedom—free labor without slavery threatens social and moral stability. The black servant, once enslaved in Texas but now free in Mexico, is the villain ("thundering," "demon-souled"), and the would-be imperial sovereign (the "trembling girl" loyal to the United States) is the victim. And in the perverse logic of the narrative, the enslaved wife and children in Texas are freer than the Mexican woman. By employing the tropes of an adventure novel in this imperial context, Ingraham flips the standard narrative of free labor. If southern slavery were to be expanded into this territory, greater freedoms would be achieved for the hardworking yet naturally noble characters who deserve such freedoms, while the innately "inferior" would be protected by the expansion of the benevolent institution.

By the end of the novel, imperial expansion is rewritten as a unification of two similar systems, with the southern slavery upholding a superior ideology of regionally defined nationalism founded on liberal capitalist ideals. The novel establishes the similarities between the Mexican and Texan heroes and highlights the Mexican characters' lack of national loyalty (except to the United States or Texas) to pave the way for an easy imperial transition.[36] Therefore, the novel ends rather abruptly and easily: Marguerita reunites with her lover in New Orleans, while Bonne Lance marries another Mexican noblewoman who is also sympathetic to the U.S. cause. In the novel, however, slavery is a stronger bond than even love and marriage. The final paragraph very quickly wraps up the war, establishing the smoothest possible imperial conquest for the slaveholding southern nation: "The events of the subsequent days in the brilliant victories of Palo

Alto and of the Rio Grande, the taking Matamoras, and other events of the campaign are too familiar to be here repeated. We have ended our romance with the consummation of the happiness of our heroes and heroines" (90). Ultimately, the form of the imperial adventure novel in *The Texan Ranger* builds on a lineage created with the historical romance in *Montezuma*. In doing so, fiction such as Ingraham's dime novels set the stage in the midst of the U.S.-Mexican War for future projections of southern imperial power that would arise during the subsequent sectional conflicts.

The Southern Slave Power and Territorial Expansion: *Inez*

When Augusta Jane Evans dedicated *Inez: A Tale of the Alamo* to the Texan patriots who so bravely fought for "liberty" and "freedom," the U.S.-Mexican War was already seven years past. According to the apocryphal story associated with the novel, Evans wrote *Inez* in 1850 while still a teenager and after living in San Antonio during the U.S.-Mexican War.[37] Like any of the imperial adventure tales, Evans's novel is set during wartime with a plot that uses actual military conflicts as the background for a fictionalized tale.[38] Yet the novel's commentary on southern imperial thought is complicated by its publication date, 1855.

Inez was published just one year after the Kansas-Nebraska Act (1854), which revived the sectional conflicts over slavery that had been simmering for years. Beginning with the Compromise of 1850—which allowed slavery in Texas, instituted the Fugitive Slave Act, and designated California a free state—the inclusion of each new territory sparked a fresh debate over the continuance of slavery. In 1854, the admittance of Kansas and Nebraska to the union resulted in extreme violence on the frontier, with proslavery and free-soil activists clashing in the territories and southern and northern politicians clashing in Congress.[39] The reaction of proslavery factions—which were quickly becoming synonymous with "southern" factions—was to more ardently defend the continuation of slavery and southern states' rights.[40]

The rhetoric of those debates permeates the novel's representation of the Texas Revolution. Ingraham's earlier pro-southern, imperial novels emphasize empathy and commonality across cultures to the end of establishing a precedent for future imperial endeavors. Evans's novel, however, takes it for granted that the cultures are vastly different. Instead, the imperative in *Inez* is to take an already strong and unified society—the southern slave system—and create a much stronger, more unified nation through the extension of slavery and a better form of social life represented by the plantation. By looking back to the origins of southern incursions into Mexico, *Inez* more firmly establishes the imperative for a southern imperial power at the moment when (as proslavery factions perceived it) the southern way of life was most in peril.

If nothing else, Augusta Jane Evans (later Wilson) is now known for being one of the most ardent supporters of slavery and ultimately the Confederacy. Her 1864 novel, *Macaria; or, The Altars of Sacrifice,* was one of the few Confederate novels written and published during the war.[41] Otherwise, during the nineteenth century, Evans was recognized for her immensely popular domestic novels featuring women.[42] She was also one of the few proslavery authors from the antebellum period who achieved fame and popularity after the war. Her 1866 novel, *St. Elmo,* rivaled *Uncle Tom's Cabin* as the third best-selling novel in the nineteenth century.[43]

Evans's first novel clearly engages with the themes of nationalism and southern community that would be the hallmark of Confederate ideology less than a decade later. As an imperial adventure tale, *Inez*'s plot is fairly straightforward: it tells the story of the Hamiltons, a family from Mississippi who relocate to Texas in the 1830s due to financial difficulties. The family consists of the father; his daughter, Florence; and her cousin Mary Irving. While residing in San Antonio, tensions between the Texan settlers and the Mexican government culminate in the Texas Revolution. The majority of the novel details the war through the experiences of the Hamiltons, their friends and love interests, and the titular character, Inez, a Mexican woman and member of the local elite.

The fact that the novel was written by a southern sectionalist and proslavery advocate is apparent from the first pages. On the title page, Evans is not named as the author, and the title takes prominence, with the words *Inez* and *The Alamo* in much larger print. The focus, then, is on a symbol of Texas identity and the Spanish name of the primary Mexican character: in other words, the imperial power and the land it will encompass. The dedication page to the "Texan patriots" reinforces the primacy of Texas and the South, and taken as a whole, the opening pages make it clear that the particular national unity and patriotism advocated in *Inez* exists within the U.S. South, or Texas.

Compounding the initial emphasis on regional allegiances, the novel begins in the southeastern United States. The Hamiltons move to the Texas territory in 1835 after Mr. Hamilton loses his Mississippi plantation through a series of poor business decisions. In this sense, the story parallels Evans's own biography: like Mr. Hamilton, her father suffered businesses losses, and the family was forced to give up their plantation in Columbus, Georgia. The Evanses moved to Texas in 1845, where Mr. Evans ran a small store in San Antonio until the end of the war, when they decided to move back to the Southeast (Fidler 24–35).

By beginning the novel in the geographically defined southern United States and framing the wartime adventure story with discussions of finance and economic loss, Evans continues the pragmatic, businesslike attitude toward war adopted by Ingraham in the earlier novels. Settlement in Texas is motivated by economic considerations first, not U.S. patriotism or ideology. Evans then recasts the Texas Revolution and territorial expansion as part of the economic trajectory of the South's development as a region, later a nation. The novel's setting during the 1836 revolution—and not during the U.S.-Mexican War—is telling, for it implies that the most recent territories and states are simply part of the natural progression of southern economic growth and imperial acquisition.

As always with the southern adventure novels, that growth is contingent on the presence of slavery to expand the southern economy and promote the best version of liberal capitalist policies. The fictional Hamiltons' migration into Texas echoes a common tale for many southerners at the time, who saw the West as an open space of opportunity. This is never clearer than in the initial descriptions of the Hamiltons' home in San Antonio: "Half hid by a majestic live-oak which shaded the front . . . stood a small white house. It was built of adobes and contained only three rooms. Instead of reaching these by a broad flight, one step from the threshold placed you on the ground. . . . Before the open window was placed the table, arranged for the morning meal. How pure the cloth looked, how clear the glass; and the bouquet of fragrant roses which adorned the centre, how homelike, fresh and beautiful it seemed!" (41–2). In this description, Evans is careful to differentiate the Hamiltons' new home from the lush images of plantation manors that dotted the southeastern states. While the live oak and white house evoke the plantation home they left at the beginning of the novel, the three rooms and lack of a grand staircase highlight the modest accommodations. This is a middle-class family slowly building up its fortunes in the new territory, not members of the landed gentry.

Evans then pauses the narrative to take sides in the 1850s sectional debates: "An air of comfort—American, *southern* comfort—pervaded the whole. The breakfast was brought in by a middle-aged negress, whose tidy appearance and honest, happy, smiling face presented the best refutation of the gross slanders of our Northern brethren. I would that her daguerreotype, as she stood arranging the dishes, could be contrasted with those of the miserable, half-starved seamstresses of Boston and New York, who toil from dawn till dark, with aching head and throbbing heart, over some weary article, for which they received the mighty recompense of a shilling" (42, my emphasis). In this description, Evans rehashes the proslavery arguments made by Calhoun during the 1840s annexation debates or those circulating in the 1850s regarding western territories: slavery protects those enslaved and then allows white men the freedom to pursue economic mobility through free labor. By incorporating proslavery arguments into a scene of middle-class domesticity, Evans again presents the paradoxical idea that establishing slavery in the new territories would also secure opportunities offered by the free market and the future expansion of the southern economy. In this imagining, southerners achieve social mobility in the open space of the West in order to secure the "southern comfort" promoted by slavery. The Hamiltons' home in Texas is a small replica of the southern plantation but one better equipped to promote the liberal capitalist ideals of free labor for all white settlers who would seek out financial opportunities in newly claimed lands.

Even with the novel's fixation on economic growth and the extension of southern society into new territories, one of the most striking features of *Inez* is its rabid anti-Catholic sentiment. In her close reading of the novel, Elizabeth Moss argues that the Catholic-Protestant conflict is an allegory for sectional conflicts, in which the "tyrannical" and "evil" Catholic Church (represented by the villainous character, Father Mazzolin) evokes the supposed tyranny of the North, while "rational" and "egalitarian" Protestantism (represented by Mary Irving) is a stand-in for the virtuous, slaveholding South. At one point, Mary even uses the term *balance of power* during an extended argument with her cousin Florence regarding the evils of Catholicism, a fairly obvious reference to the debates taking place in Congress over the "balance of power" between slave and free states (*Inez* 168).[44]

Still, however much the anti-Catholic rhetoric may dominate (and detract from) the narrative, it is just one portion of the novel's portrayal of the southern empire. As an adventure novel, *Inez* engages equally with the topics raised in Ingraham's earlier works: detailed battle scenes, intrigue and cross-dressing on the part of Inez (who dresses as a man to aid the Texan soldiers), and the trials of the Texans against the Mexican military. Throughout all of these interweaving narratives, Evans offers a story of southern imperial history within a global context that ensures the expansion of slavery and also maintains the principles of liberal capitalism. Europe, the Catholic Church, and the supposed aristocracy they represent are antithetical to that narrative. In a long tirade against Catholicism, the Protestant heroine Mary Irving claims that "the Pope of *imperial* Rome, surrounded as he is with luxury, magnificence, and hosts of scarlet-liveried cardinals," maintains class hierarchies in order to "keep the masses in ignorance" and better control them (151–2, my emphasis). That same level of control is enacted on a micro level in *Inez.* One southern transplant notes that Mexican Catholics "are allowed no choice: bred from infancy in the Romish faith, they are totally unacquainted with the tenets of other creeds. Implicit obedience to the Padre is their primary law, the grand ruling principle of life, instilled from birth" (47). The evil influence, as the novel presents it, has the potential to spread, even to white Protestants: midway through the novel, Mr. Hamilton becomes ill, and under pressure from Father Mazzolin, he converts to Catholicism. Before he dies, he urges Florence to convert as well and to follow all of the directives of the priest, "to be guided . . . in all things" (81). The arrangement quickly becomes toxic, with Father Mazzolin dictating all of the family's movements to his own evil ends, whatever those might be, and Florence submitting entirely to his control until Mary finally intervenes on her behalf.

The Catholic Church is just one of the many scapegoats in the novel for "non-benevolent" forms of imperialism and an easy marker for readers to identify non-southerners (i.e., nonwhites) or elites who would not participate in the evolving southern nation. The form of control enacted by Father Mazzolin over the Hamilton family and his parishioners is a small representation of the global control exerted by, as the novel depicts it, the despotic imperial might of Spain via the Mexican government. Throughout the novel, Father Mazzolin counsels and directs the Mexican military to, as one Mexican soldier declares, "fight [the Texans] till all submitted, or the last American child was driven to the far bank of the Sabine" (98). To further the depiction of Mexico as part of a global dictatorial force, the interactions between the historical figure Stephen Austin and Mexican politicians are always framed with the same language of righteousness and desire for liberty that characterizes the novel's opening pages.[45] When Austin is imprisoned by Mexican officials at the beginning of the novel, Father Mazzolin celebrates: "A breach is made which can only be closed by the bodies of hundreds of these cursed heretics; and Santa Anna is bloodthirsty enough to drain the last drop. Alphonso Mazzolin, canst thou not carve thy fortune in the coming storm?" (34). Thus, Mexico and its ties to the Catholic Church are portrayed as both inhumane and selfishly, economically driven—not like the purer motives of the southern settlers. When reflecting on the coming military clashes, one Texan declares that in the face of the "oppressive policy toward us" pursued by the Mexican government, Austin protested and was unduly punished. The result is increasing pressure from Santa Anna, who "is opposed by a few brave hearts, who scorn the servitude in store for them." (52–3).[46]

Inez, then, represents the potential for an egalitarian, southern space in new territories as an alternative to these tyrannical strawmen. On the eve of the Texians' (as they called themselves) declaration of independence in the novel, Evans describes the citizens of this new nation: "Mechanic, statesman, plowboy, poet pressed forward to the ranks, emulous of priority alone. A small but intrepid band, they defied the tyrant who had subverted the liberties of his country; defied Santa Anna and his fierce legions, and spurned the iron yoke which the priests of Mexico vainly strove to plant upon their necks. Liberty, civil and religious, was the watch-word, and desperately they must struggle in the coming strife" (94). In this configuration, the Mexican politicians, Santa Anna, and the priests representing the global Catholic empire are wealthy tyrants, while the Americans are white men of all classes simply trying to build lives for themselves, according to the tenets of the free market.

And once again, those free market principles, at least according to the nationalist rhetoric of the novel, are predicated on the continued existence of slavery. Just as the novel begins in the southern states and with southern economic development, it ends firmly rooted in the slaveholding South. The action of the novel concludes with the tragedies that marked the end of the Texas Revolution: the siege of the Alamo and the massacre at Goliad.[47] But the very end of the novel leaves the reader with a sense that the consequences of the revolution—one could easily say the U.S.-Mexican War—would be much more far-reaching and long-lasting. The characters who survive the battles eventually return to the South—just as Evans and her family did. In a convenient plot device, Florence Hamilton recovers her father's lost plantation and slaves in Mississippi when her new husband inherits them from a distant relative. A heartfelt reunion with a slave from her childhood, Isaac, brings the novel full circle, with the implication that these white southern characters could not attain their economic and social status without their experiences in Texas to lead them there—and slavery is the one constant through it all. The end of the novel reverts to the standard nineteenth-century romance plot, with a celebration of Florence's marriage and mourning for the deaths of others (including Mary Irving, in an appropriately melodramatic scene). Yet the final focus on sentimental and domestic tropes cements *Inez's* portrayal of southern imperialism: through the security of the domestic sphere represented by the plantation and their union, Florence and her husband reclaim the rightful place of white southern families and find financial and emotional prosperity that will continue to expand into the future.

By bookending a novel about the West and Texas with scenes from the Southeast, Evans declares that U.S. expansion begins and ends in the slaveholding South. That South counteracted the aristocratic imperialism of older global powers (Spain, the Catholic Church) and the "tyranny" of the North, with the new, supposedly egalitarian stability of the southern slave system functioning in a global free market. *Inez,* then, is a response to the territorial and slavery debates of the late 1840s and 1850s, one that uses imaginative representation to make a case for the proslavery southern nation. Through a typical tale of adventure—the tyrannical villain versus the indomitable heroes—Evans wrangles the ideal of a southern empire to match the values of a progressive capitalist society and mythologizes an expanding southern nation in the Southwest as it was happening. The same version of an imperial South would emerge in contemporaneous fictional representations of southern empire, only this time in the Caribbean.

The Southern Imperial Dream: *The Free Flag of Cuba*

In 1851, Narciso López, a Venezuelan-born Spanish army officer, led an ill-fated expedition into Cuba to "liberate" the island from the Spanish government. He and his followers, referred to as "filibusters" (as were, confusingly, their expeditions), were captured and executed by the Spanish government the same year. The disastrous 1851 filibuster was the last of a series of failed expeditions to Cuba led by López beginning in 1848, the year the U.S.-Mexican War ended.

Despite the actual failure of the filibuster, the imaginary that emerged around Cuba and López's expedition remained important in the potential formation of a southern empire founded on slavery, or what historian Robert May calls the "Caribbean dream." It would lead proslavery southerners such as Mississippi senator Albert Gallatin Brown to proclaim bluntly in 1858, "I want Cuba, and I know that sooner or later we must have it" (McCluskey 326). Indeed, López's filibuster was just one of the more famous attempts to acquire territory in the 1850s, a decade that was peppered with forays into the Caribbean and South America, largely led by U.S. southerners or with the support of proslavery southerners.[48]

Such expeditions were the product of a growing fascination with the Caribbean, and especially Cuba, after the end of the U.S.-Mexican War. Throughout the nineteenth century, writes Louis A. Pérez Jr., "it became all but impossible for the Americans to contemplate their future well-being without the presumption of possession of Cuba" (25). This was especially true of proslavery southerners, who were interested in claiming the area as an extension of a potential slaveholding empire.[49] This southern fixation amounts to what John Lowe calls the "Cuban imaginary," in which Cuba functions as a space or idea used "to frame and animate their investigation/presentation of contemporary historical events and to push their ideological/political projects" (61).[50]

The attempted forays into Cuba throughout the 1850s built upon and expanded the imperialist sentiment on the part of southern nationalists from the end of the U.S.-Mexican War, in which much of the fixation on Cuba was predicated on the ever-present desire to expand the southern slave-based economy into other parts of the world. In an 1854 article for *De Bow's Review* entitled "Cuba and the South," Samuel R. Walker declares: "With Cuba . . . what a splendid prospect of commercial eminence opens to the South! What wealth will float upon our waters! What a bright gem will she, 'the Queen of the Antilles,' be in the coronet of the South, and how proudly she will wear it!" (524). And just a few years later, Edward Pollard would write in *Black Diamonds* (1859):

> Looking into the possibilities of the future . . . we may see an empire as powerful and gorgeous as ever was pictured in our dreams of history. What is that empire? It is an empire founded on military ideas; representing the *noble peculiarities of Southern civilization;* including within its limits the isthmus of America and the regenerated West Indies; having control of the two dominant staples of the world's commerce—cotton and sugar; *possessing the highways of the world's commerce;* surpassing all empires of the age in the strength of its geographical position; and, in short, combining elements of strength, prosperity, and glory, such as never before in the modern ages have been placed within the reach of a single government. (108, my emphases)

Of course, the "noble particularities" refer to the slave labor system. The preoccupation with Cuba and its annexation allowed southern nationalists to envision the slaveholding South as an independent "circumCaribbean" empire that could sustain not only a unique culture but also an autonomous economy within an evolving global market.[51]

Lucy Holcombe Pickens's 1854 novel, *The Free Flag of Cuba; or, The Martyrdom of López, a Tale of the Liberating Expedition of 1851,* is one of the clearest—and perhaps most influential—examples of an artistic representation that built up and expanded the southern imperial imaginary in the Caribbean. Although it is a fictionalized account of the López filibuster,

Free Flag was published at a time when Cuba would have been at the forefront of U.S. politics: in the same year, two separate events took place that complicated U.S.-Spanish-Cuban relations. First was the *Black Warrior* affair, when a U.S. cotton-carrying ship was seized by Cuba, prompting calls to invade the island, primarily on the part of the southerners exporting the cotton. Second was the Ostend Manifesto, or a bungled attempt on the part of the United States to purchase Cuba from Spain.[52] In the context of renewed economic and political tension with the island, Pickens's novel offers another alternative model of southern imperialism. In this ideal, benevolence on the part of white, upper-class slave owners becomes a way to make slavery compatible with free labor ideologies and capitalist growth, one preferable to the botched efforts on the part of the federal government. If Ingraham looks to the past to lay the groundwork for southern incursions and Evans writes into being a southern imperial ideology as it took place, then Pickens's novel maps out a trajectory for a future global empire separate from the United States.

As an author, Pickens was not incredibly prolific. *Free Flag* was her only novel, which she published under the pen name H. M. Hardimann. But in terms of influence in the South and the southern imperial imaginary, she was a central figure. Pickens was the daughter of a prominent Tennessee family, by way of Texas, and would eventually marry Colonel Francis Pickens, a South Carolina politician and later Confederate. Pickens's portrait was even featured on Confederate currency, and she was dubbed the "Queen of the Confederacy."[53]

Free Flag details the events of the López expedition through two sets of romantic pairings: Ralph Dudley and his fiancée, Genevieve Clifton, both southerners; and Eugene de France, a southerner, and Mabel Royal, one of the few northerners in the novel. The rest of the characters are mostly historical figures, including López and Pickens's once fiancé, Colonel William Crittenden, as well as a cast of stereotypical black characters, who are largely relegated to minor or background roles.[54] The main plot features the men fighting in Cuba, while the women remain behind. By the end—and fitting with the actual events of the expedition—only a handful of the men survive, including Dudley.

In contrast to the reality of the expedition—in which a group of soldiers attempted a coup without the support of the U.S. government—the novel introduces López's filibuster as a fight between tyranny and freedom. The opening pages gesture toward Pickens's goal in curating the historical narrative for future posterity: "Then, dear reader, as I sit in memory's silent chamber, as one by one I take from the imaged wall those pictures which I strive to paint on the mental canvas of your mind, throw thou the warm light of sympathy around them; let their colors glow in the generous interest the fair and brace ever feel for the nobly unfortunate" (55). As Simms claims to "hold a lantern to history" in his historical romances, Pickens presents herself as shaping and revising the history of the expedition and, in doing so, convincing her readers of the rightness of the cause.[55] In the novel, that cause is motivated by a collective, ground-up impulse for the common man or masses. To reinforce this idea, the novel always refers to López and the other filibusters as "Liberators" or "patriots"—even though their patriotic loyalty is focused on "liberating" Cuba from Spain in order to merge it with the slaveholding South. These assertions of autonomy and freedom for the everyman point to an understanding of free market capitalism as an avenue to self-driven economic, social, and political equality. The ideology of liberal capitalism gives legitimacy—or a benevolent cast—to an empire founded on slavery and white supremacy. In framing the campaign as a demonstration of commonly held honor and an avenue to liberation, *Free Flag* is an example of how proslavery southern nationalists and their supporters (namely Pickens) could maintain a benevolent artifice while achieving territorial gain and ensuring a slaveholding economic power in the South.

Building on Pickens's initial avowal to reshape the popular conception of López's expedition, the opening pages pit the filibuster—and the southerners who participate—in direct opposition to the United States as a whole.[56] The novel begins with a conversation between López himself and General John A. Quitman, a politician and soldier from Mississippi who supported the filibusters (and to whom, incidentally, Ingraham dedicated his first book, *The South-West*). The men discuss a recent proclamation by President Millard Fillmore that explicitly disavowed any attempts at filibustering on the island. The fictionalized Quitman angrily denounces the move: "*He has no right to will away the lives of freemen.* . . . It is his duty, and should be his pride, to shield and protect American interest. It is not his province to wantonly assign away to a foreign power the lives and liberties of men by whose sufferance he holds his position of limited—*not absolute*—power. He is not their master, nor are they his slaves, to be thus delivered up at pleasure to the mercy of a despotic oppressor" (60). The language draws on the common master-slave discourse of the day and evokes the very system the filibusters were wishing to extend. But the slippage here is also interesting: while *oppressor* ostensibly refers to Spain, it's unclear whether Pickens (via Quitman) is also applying it to Fillmore. In this depiction, Fillmore's actions are already alienating "patriotic Americans"—mostly southerners—and the rhetoric echoes the sectional language used by Evans in her representation of the Texas Revolution in *Inez.*

But the element in the novel that truly aids in creating this benevolent form of southern imperialism is the primary female character, Genevieve. In many ways, Genevieve functions as a stand-in for southern nationhood. The daughter of a wealthy plantation family, she is engaged to Ralph Dudley and possesses all of the Old South stereotypes of southern womanhood: delicacy, passivity, aristocracy, beauty. As a representative Old South figure, Genevieve plays an allegorical role in the novel. With the treatment of her character, Pickens demonstrates a recuperation of the Old South that moves it into the future through imperial ventures. The benevolence here, very oddly, is not toward the Cubans but toward proslavery southerners themselves—they must be drawn into the fold in order to ensure future southern prosperity.

Genevieve's allegorical role as an Old South figure in the new imperialist discourse is shown in her constant objections to her fiancé's, Ralph's, participation in the filibuster. At one point she asks him to abandon the expedition, "to forsake a wild visionary scheme for an unattainable result; to give *me* that love you lavish on a people wholly unworthy of it. The Cubans are not worthy of freedom" (66). Genevieve's response reflects the racism and fear of many proslavery southerners of the time, including John C. Calhoun during the earlier U.S.-Mexican War. In contrast, Mabel Royal, the northern lady, is an ardent supporter of the filibuster. In his introduction to the new edition, Orville Burton cites this reluctance as evidence of the novel's nonsectional bent, and most critics who have studied the novel usually read Mabel or Dudley as the central characters, given Pickens's clear allegiances.

Yet it is Genevieve who is set up as the most interesting and complex character from the beginning, and the novel devotes more space to developing her personality than any other: "There certainly is a spell in unconscious loveliness that immediately reaches the heart, a mystic fascination in the perfect harmony of beauty, which rouses every deep sympathy, and draws you towards its possessor with an influence nothing else can exercise" (63). So it was with Genevieve. For most of the novel, the happiness and future of this striking character are always at stake: regularly, the novel breaks from the action scenes in Cuba to return to her life in the United States, as if to monitor her development as the filibuster itself develops. In this sense, Genevieve becomes the stand-in for reluctant southern nationalists. In the novel, persuading her means persuading the rest of the South and converting them to the benevolent mission of southern imperialism.

Ultimately, because it features a filibuster that failed, *Free Flag* achieves the aims of southern expansionists whose dreams were never realized through fiction and the character of Genevieve. The novel constantly frames the failure of the filibusters as the catalyst for a southern imperialism that would exist for future generations, in which Cuban independence and subsequent annexation are not just distinct possibilities but a definite future path. That ideal of a future southern empire is especially true in the most traumatic moment of the novel: when the filibusters are executed in Cuba. After López's death scene, Pickens-as-narrator declares: "Thy wondrous martyrdom kindles a sacred enthusiasm in the chivalrous and brave; the holy sympathy, the generous daring of La Fayette—of Kosciusko, thrill America's noble sons. Thy name, thy bright and honored name, oh, thou lover of freedom, shall be their watch-word to victory. The day of Cuba's redemption comes surely on" (185–6). Although the rest of the filibusters die, Dudley is spared to carry on the momentum of López's cause and transmit it to Genevieve and southerners in the United States. With moments like these, Pickens takes a general impulse present in the antebellum period, adapts it, and invents a lineage of southern imperial identity through benevolence. In doing so, novels such as *Free Flag* were actively creating a new, independent imperialist identity that was necessary for future Confederate nationalism.

Yet the undercurrent in the novel's promotion of "liberty," "republicanism," and "honor" is—as with all of these novels—ultimately economic in nature. The final three chapters all concern the financial state of the

South and specifically how Cuba fits into its future imperial expansion. And again, the novel uses Genevieve to negotiate the South's imperial future. When Dudley returns home from Cuba, he discovers that he is completely bankrupt, and he receives sage financial advice from, of all people, his slave, Marmion. After chastising Dudley for squandering his family's wealth, Marmion offers a possible solution: to keep the plantation together and the slaves from being sold, the estate could be mortgaged off and left in the hands of a trusted family friend who would handle the creditors. In the interim, advises Marmion (in horrifically rendered dialect), "you ken go to Callyforny, an' nothin' thought of it; when you cum back, den all'll be straight an' hushed up, an' no hard feelins 'gainst nobody. Lis'en to yo' ole white-headed sarvunt, Marse Ralph, 'cause poor Marmion's bin faithful to you, an', please God, he want to die whar he wus born, in sight of his ole house whar he used to wait on his blessed marster, an' de great Ginel whut's swarin' in glory" (202). In an odd turn for a proslavery novel, Dudley follows Marmion's advice, mortgages the estate, and leaves for the West. In other words, to repair his situation, he follows the trends established by southerners before him—Ingraham decades earlier, Evans's family, and the Hamiltons in *Inez*—and travels into newly acquired western territories to earn his fortune. And he is only able to do so with the support of a benevolent slave system and his slaves. When he returns three years later, Dudley and Genevieve marry and settle on his plantation.

As Dudley's, and thereby Genevieve's, future is at stake, so is the future of the slaveholding South. The novel implies that in following the patterns established by previous southern imperialists in the far West, Ralph Dudley will complete the future "liberation" of Cuba and eventually the South will establish a benevolent, slave-based empire. The final lines ensure this future, declaring that Cuba's "freedom," with the catalyst of López's failure and the guidance of southerners such as Dudley and Genevieve, is surely at hand: "Poor Cuba! Long has she wept; but a radiant smile is breaking over her sadly-beautiful face, for a start has arisen—a bright joy-promising star—whose destiny is to pour the rays of hope into her sad despairing heart" (212). The language echoes the description of Genevieve at the opening of the novel, and the implication is that she, Cuba, and the South all follow parallel paths. Once Genevieve and Ralph's future is secured, so is the future southern nation. Thus, the Old South, through the figure of Genevieve, is brought into the fold of a new southern, Caribbean empire, which will only continue to expand and flourish in the future.

Capitalism demands the expansion of markets and territories, and as the global cotton trade grew in the nineteenth century, the U.S. economy invariably demanded more land and labor. The response of proslavery southern authors was to lay the groundwork for a new form of imperialism through artistic representations that rationalized and justified the growth of U.S. slavery. But that distinction relied on there being a separate southern nation—which could not exist and still maintain a unified United States.

Novels such as *The Texan Ranger, Inez,* and *The Free Flag of Cuba* were vital to establishing a particular idea of the South as a separate nation and highlight the interchange between imaginative writing and imperial expansion during the antebellum period. The imperial adventure novels offer a vision of a global southern empire fueled by liberal capitalist impulses. Yet as always, the underlying goal was to sustain the fiction of a benevolent system of southern culture and slavery.

4

NARRATIVES OF REFORM

The Proslavery Social Problem Novel

Despite typical assumptions about the antebellum South, the region was not a monolithic entity when it came to an understanding of slavery. Southern intellectual thought evolved over decades, making it possible to defend the system while also seeing it as a moral wrong and contradictory to the aims of a liberal democracy. George Tucker's *The Valley of Shenandoah; or, Memoirs of the Graysons* (1824) details a slave-owning family's decline while presenting a positive impression of the slaveholding South. In the novel, Edward Grayson, the son of a prominent, plantation-owning family, wrestles with his views on slavery, telling his northern friend, "We, of the present generation, find domestic slavery established among us, and the evil, for I freely admit it to be an evil, both moral and political, admits of no remedy that is not worse than the disease" (1:61). Maria J. McIntosh's *The Lofty and the Lowly; or, The Good in All and None All-Good* (1852) is another proslavery novel that advocates for the continuance of slavery and paints a favorable portrait of the white southern way of life.[1] Yet at various points the narrative pauses to articulate a sustained critique of the South—particularly the southern economy and slavery—such as when the southern-born Mrs. Montrose declares to her northern relative, George Browne: "As to the want of ease [in the North] of which you complain, is it not the necessary result of that enterprise and industry which changes only by elevating? And is not this a sign of a healthier and happier system than that in which all is stagnant? The perfect repose sometimes seen in a landscape of a summer noon is beautiful in painting or poetry, yet some of us have felt that the beauty may be too dearly bought" (1:95).

Both passages represent a southerner's evaluation of the slave-based plantation economy during the antebellum period that is nonetheless couched in a clear defense of slavery. The first is an outright critique of the institution, declaring it a moral and political "evil." Yet it deflects the issue by pronouncing the "remedies" to the problem as equally wrong. The second is more circumspect in its criticism but just as trenchant. Rather than limiting her focus to slavery, the speaker, Mrs. Montrose, encompasses the entire system of which the institution was part: the South's plantation-based economy, the "stagnant" and backward structure that demanded and perpetuated slave labor. The "beauty too dearly bought" is antebellum southern society founded on a lagging plantation economy and an immoral system of human bondage. Whatever accusations are leveled at slavery in either novel, however, both ultimately come down on the side of perpetuating the existent social, economic, and cultural institutions that structured the region.

But how can novels uphold the institution of slavery and yet simultaneously condemn that institution as immoral and "evil"? Both Tucker's and McIntosh's texts reconcile these contradictions and criticize slavery through the language of economic progress and reform. Reframing slavery as an economic problem in their fiction deflects the question of morality and instead interprets human bondage as part of a larger economic system—in this case, free market capitalism. Positioning slavery as part of or even a by-product of global capitalism, proslavery southern authors could absolve both themselves and the region of any immediate culpability. In the skewed logic of these proslavery texts, the process and progress of capitalism is answerable for both the creation of the slave system as well as its eventual destruction—not the individuals who created and sustained the system in the first place.

The variances between the two novels reflect how shifts in the southern economy and the global market during the antebellum period altered proslavery southerners' proposed reforms over time. Tucker's novel was written in the early decades of the nineteenth century, before the Panic of 1837 and at a time when the southern plantation economy was much more stable. McIntosh's novel is a post-1837 text, when the South's agricultural economy was declining and abolitionist sentiment had increased. If Tucker's southerner speaks from a position of relative security, in which his view of the evils of slavery are much more direct and overt, McIntosh's southerner—in her somewhat obviated criticisms—must navigate the more complicated economic and political climate of the years leading up to the Civil War.

These southern "social problem" novels represent the evolution of proslavery thought and its approach to reform. In that evolution, southern authors participated in the same transatlantic exchange that characterized the entire antebellum period. In articulating their proposals for reform, southern authors drew from the popular British fiction by authors such as Elizabeth Gaskell and Samuel Richardson to articulate a critique of southern slavery without advocating for outright abolition. Both Tucker and McIntosh use economic language and the patterns of literary genre to project a version of reform in their fiction that would effect the balance between the continuation of slavery and the acknowledgment of its inherent moral and ethical wrongs. In doing so, they continue the project of writing the slaveholding South into a narrative of global economic progress.

"Present Inconvenience" versus Long-Term Prosperity: George Tucker and the Economic Seduction Novel

Midway through *The Valley of Shenandoah; or, Memoirs of the Graysons,* two of the primary characters engage in an extended conversation over the existence of slavery. James Gildon, the son of a New York merchant, is visiting his college friend in Virginia, Edward Grayson, the son of a prominent, plantation-owning family. As the pair rides through the family estate, Gildon remarks, "Don't you feel, Edward, when riding over these vast domains of yours, something like a feudal Baron?" (1:60).

Edward's response is to vehemently denounce the system of human bondage that was the foundation of his family's wealth. Calling it "an evil, both moral and political," he rejects the idyllic vision of the plantation South imagined by Gildon. His reaction indicates that underneath the feudal ideal cherished by many white Americans (both North and South) lay slavery and also the problems with the plantation system that structured the region's economy.

The rest of the novel sustains this critique. Rather than a celebration of the early, post-Revolutionary plantation South, *The Valley of Shenandoah* is the narrative of a family's decline. The Graysons are not the "feudal Barons" of Gildon's fantasy but a family in economic and social crisis, like many upper-class families throughout the South in the late eighteenth and early nineteenth centuries. Their downfall is precipitated at the beginning of the novel by the numerous debts left after the head of the family, Colonel Grayson, passes away. The problems are then compounded, one after another, by personal disasters and poor economic choices spurred on by the demands of plantation culture. Against the backdrop of the family's financial losses, the Graysons' daughter, Louisa, begins an affair with Gildon. The episode ends disastrously: the novel implies that Louisa might be pregnant, and she eventually dies, while Edward dies in a duel with Gildon in an attempt to defend her honor. By the end of the novel, a once prominent and respectable Virginia family is virtually extinct and penniless, with only Mrs. Grayson surviving.

In spite of the problems that would eventually lead to his family's ruin and his own admission of the evils that structure their way of life, Edward hedges in his rebuttal to Gildon's praise of the plantation South. He cannot commit to abandoning a system that he so clearly identifies as evil. Rather than calling for emancipation—the clear solution—he dismisses all remedies, dubbing them "worse than the disease" (1:61). He goes on to rationalize and explain away both slavery and the plantation system, treating both as if they are semipermanent fixtures of southern life that must be accepted: "The theme is an ungrateful one—like any other *natural defect or misfortune which is incurable*" (1:62–3, my emphasis). Yet he contradicts himself in the very next sentence. They *are* "curable," but white, upper-class southerners simply do not want to take the steps toward implementing that cure: "We are fully aware of its [slavery's] disadvantages—that it checks the growth of our wealth—is repugnant to its [the South's] justice—inconsistent with its principles—injurious to its morals—and dangerous to its peace. Yet after giving the subject the most serious and attentive consideration, and finding it admitted of no other safe remedy but what time may bring some centuries hence, they are fain to acquiesce in their inevitable destiny" (1:63). In these reflections, Edward extends the evils of slavery to include the poor economic practices promoted by one-crop plantation agriculture and a reliance on slave labor, of which all white slaveholders, including himself, are guilty. However, his pronoun usage indicates an attempt to extricate himself from his own culpability in the system. What begins with Edward identifying as a fellow southerner (*we*), ends with an implicit distancing from the region (*its, they*). He finally settles on a convenient stopgap to the problem: eventual emancipation or recolonization "some centuries hence."

Edward's reflections on slavery in this passage are indicative of a trend among southern intellectuals in the late eighteenth and early nineteenth centuries. The constant tension between defending, rationalizing, and explicitly critiquing the southern slave system points to the ways in which southern intellectuals of the era attempted to acknowledge the problems with slavery and the South's economy but avoided dealing with those very problems. Like the fictional Edward, George Tucker and his contemporaries wrestled with their positions as slave-owning southerners of the aristocratic order. They drew their ideals from the more progressive Enlightenment principles that structured the formation of the United States, yet their daily lives clearly contradicted those very ideals. As a result, upper-class southern intellectuals who found fault with the slave system but perpetuated its existence were never free from the moral contradictions their lives presented.

The Valley of Shenandoah is a necessary fictional response to these ideological conflicts. Although upper-class southerners evaded any direct admission that slavery should be dismantled in their nonfiction and public lives, the imagined space of fiction provides a venue for critiques without real-life consequences. To balance the tension between overt criticism of slavery and a reluctance to dismantle the system entirely, Tucker's novel adopts the form of the eighteenth-century sentimental novel of seduction and applies it to economic commentary. In many of its basic plot structures and character types, *The Valley* is a tale of seduction so common to eighteenth-century sentimental novels such as Samuel Richardson's *Clarissa* (1748) and Susanna Rowson's *Charlotte Temple* (1791; U.S. publication followed in 1794). These novels ostensibly present a "true story" of a young woman's seduction and subsequent disgrace in order to illustrate the potential dangers for innocent young women who read too many novels of romance. Only in *The Valley,* the more "sentimental" aspects (Louisa's seduction, Edward's duel) are generic conventions employed to illustrate the economic theories advanced by Tucker and his contemporaries. Instead, the novel presents an entire community that is undermined by its own follies and financial ineptitude.[2] The Graysons serve as a cautionary example for other southerners, just as the young women led astray in the previous novels are examples for young female readers. As an "economic seduction novel," *The Valley* melds the trends of popular literature of the time—the seduction romance—with a depiction of the South that highlights the region's economic problems and criticisms of the slave system.[3] The form allows Tucker to address the debates over slavery and the economy in ways not available in nonfiction representations.[4] In the context of fictional narrative, Tucker could advocate for and imagine possible reforms to the southern economy and slavery without fully committing to abolition or actually changing the plantation system in the "present generation."

Like the fictional Edward Grayson in *The Valley of Shenandoah,* southern intellectual elites in the early nineteenth century foresaw the problems inherent in the South's plantation economy and the continued existence of slavery. In the wake of a revolution driven primarily by Enlightenment philosophies and liberal thought, many Virginia intellectuals viewed slavery as antithetical to the doctrine of universal human rights preached during the Revolutionary period. For example, Thomas Jefferson points out the moral evils represented by slavery in *Notes on the State of Virginia* (1787), and after inserting a very large caveat on the inherent "inferiority" of the black race, he outlines a plan for the gradual emancipation of slaves through a recolonization project in the western territories of the United States.[5] Some upper-class intellectuals also predicted that the dominance of a plantation-based economy would hinder the region's development economically. In 1796, St. George Tucker, a prominent Virginia planter and politician (and not coincidentally, George Tucker's cousin) published *A Dissertation on Slavery, With a Proposal for the Gradual Abolition of It in the State of Virginia,* which echoes many of the same arguments in Jefferson's *Notes.*[6] *A Dissertation* also accounts for slavery's role in Virginia's finances and contends that the institution continues to exist in the United States because of the profit it brings: "What else . . . could have influenced the merchants of the freest nation . . . to embark in so nefarious a traffic, as that of the human race . . . ? What, but similar considerations, could prevail on the government of the same country, even in these days, to patronize a commerce so diametrically opposite to the generally received maxims of that government [?]" (15–16).[7] On the surface, these vaguely progressive ideas on human rights and modern economics seem at odds coming from members of the planter elite profiting from human bondage.

However, for a landowning, Virginia aristocrat of the early antebellum period, taking a critical stance against slavery and the plantation system presented an inherent problem. Jefferson did little to counteract the evils he describes in *Notes,* nor did any of the other Virginia intellectuals act on their supposed beliefs.[8] Emancipating one's slaves meant giving up property and an accustomed way of life. While southerners such as Jefferson and St. George Tucker recoiled at the human degradation slavery represented, they were ultimately conservatives and balked at changing a system that was so clearly profitable, at least for a select few. For example, in *A Dissertation,* St. George Tucker proposes a plan similar to Jefferson's in *Notes,* which involved the gradual relocation of former slaves to western territories. To qualify his plan, St. George remarks that "it will be attended with a gradual change of condition in the blacks, and cannot possibly affect the interest either of the creditors, or any other description of persons of the present generation" (2). As a solution for their moral predicament, the default answer for Virginia politicians and the more philosophical plantation owners was that immediate emancipation would be disastrous but that gradual emancipation may, possibly, be a solution—but only in the distant future.[9]

George Tucker fit neatly into the tentatively progressive, largely conservative intellectual climate that dominated turn-of-the-century Virginia, yet he more readily acknowledged the long-term effects of slavery on Virginia society and its economy. Tucker wrote *The Valley of Shenandoah* directly before he accepted a professorship in political economy at the University of Virginia, and the novel was a last-ditch attempt to save his depleted finances.[10] Always improvident with money (a sad coincidence considering his chosen line of study), Tucker had lost his second wife and encountered financial difficulties with his plantation in the Virginia countryside. As a result, most of Tucker's nonfiction works are concerned with slavery and the plantation system's effects on the regional economy.[11] In one of his earliest publications, a small 1801 pamphlet written in response to the slave rebellion organized by Gabriel Prosser in 1800, Tucker shares his cousin's view that slavery was economically motivated, calling the issue of emancipation a "present inconvenience" to slaveholders that would have long-lasting benefits to the entire region (*Letter* 4).[12] He then extends the argument further and asserts that slaves, as human beings, cannot be kept in isolation and ignorance forever; as the slave population grows, Tucker argues, so, too, will the opportunities for education and interaction between slave communities.[13] In contrast to his contemporaries, Tucker actually acted upon his theoretical writings and freed his slaves upon retirement from the University of Virginia—but only at the end of his life.

In the context of the imagined yet historically grounded South of *The Valley of Shenandoah,* Tucker could balance these vying progressive and conservative impulses by putting his theories into practice in ways that neither he, his cousin, nor any of the other southern intellectuals of the era would do in their real lives. During the conversation with James Gildon, most of Edward Grayson's arguments parallel the nonfiction of Tucker and his contemporaries. First is the repetition of the phrase *present generation,* which is taken almost verbatim from St. George Tucker's *Dissertation* and his critiques of slavery. The second is the idea of potential reform through gradual emancipation, which is conveyed through the temporal placement of the characters and, by extension, the readers. The phrase *present generation* presumably refers to the fictional Grayson's era, or the post-Revolutionary generation; however, the stress on *present* in the novel implies that the situation has the potential to change, which also creates an imperative for the early-nineteenth-century reader. Like Jefferson and St. George Tucker, the fictional Edward proposes that a system of recolonization would be the best possible solution if only slaveholders would commit to the plan (although he seems to exclude himself from these reflections). Therefore, if slavery is only presently established in the context of the novel, it could be phased out of existence by the time of the antebellum era or beyond, even "centuries hence," as Edward puts it.

In other sections, the novel makes a case for future emancipation through its stark portrayal of slavery and slave life. Many of the Graysons' slaves are described as content, even happy, and "the bonds of [the Graysons' estate] sat lightly upon them" (1:65). Yet Tucker does not hesitate to depict the physical and psychological violence integral to the system, including abusive overseers, the separation of families, and implicit references to sexual assault of female slaves.[14] Late in the novel, the Graysons are finally forced to sell their estate, including the slaves, and the novel gives a detailed account of a slave auction, one unusual for a novel so clearly sympathetic to the southern planter elite. The narrative is forthright in recognizing the obvious inhumanity of the proceedings: "One not accustomed to this spectacle, is extremely shocked to see beings, of the same species with himself, set up for sale to the highest bidder, like horses or cattle; and even to those who have been accustomed to it, it is disagreeable, from their sympathy with the humbled and anxious slave." Still, even in this explicit condemnation of the practice, the narrative walks back its portrayal of the brutalities of slavery with a qualification that not all forms of slavery are necessarily "bad": "The weight of his fetters, the negro, who has been born and bred on a well regulated estate, hardly feels. . . . He his, in fact, a member of a sort of patriarchal family" (2:206). The very next sentence, however, is another strong condemnation of the auction: "But when hoisted up to public sale, where every man has a right to purchase him, and he may be the property of one whom he never saw before, or of the worst man in the community, then the delusion vanishes, and he feels the bitterness of his lot, and his utter insignificance as a member of civilized society" (2:207). This ambivalent back-and-forth is characteristic of each scene that directly represents slavery. Like Edward in his halfhearted rebuke to Gildon, the novel's articulation of critiques to slavery remain only half-fulfilled.

The ambivalence toward slavery in *The Valley of Shenandoah* indicates a general pattern in Tucker's writing and that of his contemporaries. Although the novel clearly depicts the violence and moral wrongs of the slave system, as fiction, it mediates the representation and intensity of those critiques, portraying slavery as one small component of a much larger, more problematic plantation system. For example, the passage in which Gildon and Edward discuss the evils of slavery only takes up 10 pages of an almost 650-page novel, and the slave auction itself, while graphic, occupies only a short chapter. That misdirection, though small, has larger implications for the way in which upper-class southerners represented the region and its social structures. Placing emphasis on the plantation system as a whole separates upper-class southerners—and the readers of the novel—from being direct agents in perpetuating slavery. Instead, the language implies that the plantation system and backward economic practices are the true culprits in promulgating an immoral system, then sidesteps the question of direct abolition. These rhetorical acrobatics in their texts allow southern authors such as Tucker to criticize the practice of slavery and admit the moral faults but also suspend the immediate guilt incurred by slave owners themselves—much in the same way that Jefferson and the Tuckers put off emancipation as a present inconvenience. Therefore, the problem is not slavery alone, or even bad slave owners, but the South's conservative attitudes toward older social mores and plantation-based agriculture as the basis for its economy.

The emphasis on long-term economic development as a method of negotiating any criticism of slavery emerges in most of Tucker's nonfiction. In a later economic text, *The Laws of Wages, Profits, and Rent, Investigated* (1837), Tucker outlines slavery's negative influence on the Virginia economy and predicts that gradual emancipation would also promote more industry on the part of white southerners: "A course of bad crops, a recurrence of epidemic diseases, and lastly, extreme indolence, ignorance, or improvidence in the people would all conduce to the same end" (62). The argument picks up on a common accusation leveled at the slaveholding South: that racialized slavery cultivated an aversion to manual labor and hard work on the part of southern whites and discouraged the development of a white laboring class. According to this logic, the absence of a steady source of labor and a strong laboring class would have the same deleterious effects as natural disasters—that is, unless slavery and the one-crop agricultural system are gradually phased out.

Following these theories, Tucker frequently predicted that the practice of slavery would naturally end as the South moved away from the plantation system that perpetuated it. In his trajectory of long-term population growth, slavery is a stage in the economic progress of the southern region and the nation as a whole, while urban areas and manufacturing are more important for a sustainable economy: "[Slavery] cannot exist in the most advanced stages of society, where the utmost degree of industry and economy are required in the great mass of the community to provide the means of subsistence . . . it is found that the labour of the slave does not repay the cost of rearing him; and consequently, as slavery at that period would be a tax on the master, it cannot exist" (Tucker, *Laws* 48). If finances are constantly funneled into the upkeep of slaves and agriculture, then a large portion of capital does not go to other investments, and a large sector of the labor force remains inert. Therefore, according to Tucker's economic analysis, slavery cannot be the dominant mode of labor organization indefinitely, nor can the South progress as a plantation economy only.[15] To compete with the rest of the country, or the world, white slave owners and southern elites must not hinder the natural progression of economic forces: "No country can attain a great height in manufactures, in commerce, or in agriculture, where one half of the community labours unwillingly, and the other half does not labour at all" (Tucker, *Letter* 21).[16] Without explicitly arguing for abolition or emancipation, Tucker contends that the South would have to abandon its long-held conservativism and adapt to the modernizing global economy by allowing for the gradual disappearance of slavery and the plantation system—with, again, the emphasis on "gradual" and no assumption that slave owners of the present generation would act on these theories.[17]

The Valley of Shenandoah adopts the form of the seduction novel as a method of connecting with readers and warning them against the perils of regressive economic practices, farming techniques, and the financial mismanagement of the plantation elite—with slavery only occasionally coming to the forefront as a topic of conversation. The novel itself begins with a financial crisis: after his father's death, Edward and his mother learn that Colonel Grayson had financed several failed land speculations and cosigned on a number of loans for his neighbors. By the novel's opening, these problems, in addition to a steadily decreasing return on the plantations' harvests, have left the Graysons virtually bankrupt. However, as the novel makes clear, their situation is by no means unusual. In yet another conversation, Edward explains the family's financial state to Gildon, who only sees the apparent wealth of upper-class Virginians: "You forget . . . that you are in an agricultural and a slave-holding country, the inhabitants of which have always been remarkable for spending their incomes before they made them, and for rating them very extravagantly. As the profits of a landed estate come in but one or twice a year, the means of the proprietor are then ample, and if he is not in debt he is likely to become so, by underrating the unforeseen contingencies [weather, insect infestations, fluctuations in the market], and by getting into habits, formed when his purse was full, which cannot be changed when it is empty. Consequently, in order to continue them, he is compelled to run in debt" (1:110–11). Similarly, Colonel Grayson lived beyond his wealth on the basis of his family's good name and the assumption that the harvests on his two plantations would more than make up for the loans issued—never taking the trouble to modify his spending and lending or to monitor the management of his farms.

The Graysons follow the patterns of the seduction novel heroines to become representative figures of the fading, conservative South reliant on a declining plantation economy, which in turn relied on slave labor, the perpetuation of credit and debt, and a single method of earning a profit through one-crop agriculture for its existence. The title and preface are the first indications of the novel's debt to the eighteenth-century sentimental genre. An important trait of most seduction novels, particularly given their cautionary intent for young readers, was to establish the veracity of the story being told and frame the text as a documentary act. For example, the full title of Hannah W. Foster's 1797 sentimental novel is *The Coquette; or, The History of Eliza Wharton.* The story was, in fact, based on the tale of a young woman who died in childbirth after being abandoned by her lover.[18] Rowson's *Charlotte Temple* is also subtitled "A Tale of Truth." In both cases, the novel ends with a description or re-creation of the young woman's tombstone, with the authors taking pains to present "evidence" for the heroine's sad story. Likewise, the full title of Tucker's novel is *The Valley of Shenandoah; or, Memoirs of the Graysons;* as with *history* or *truth,* the term *memoirs* points to the documentary structure of the narrative. Thus, the "tale of truth" presented by the novel is the story of the family and the area as a whole, and their example presents an exhortation to the readers to consider the consequences of poor economic practices and financial imprudence. While Tucker's nonfiction delineates the problems with the South's economy and slavery through bare statistics, the seduction novel shows it in a more empathetic form through the fates of the characters.

The use of the "found manuscript" trope common to many eighteenth- and nineteenth-century novels further cements the novel's documentary and cautionary function. According to the preface, the narrative has been pieced together from the papers of a dying man whom the narrator (presumably Tucker) encountered while traveling in New York.[19] With the editorial framing that precedes *The Valley,* Tucker once again presents evidence for the story. The preface claims that the novel is both "a history of real life" and "one of those fictitious representations by which inventive genius has occasionally . . . sought to supply to youth the wisdom and experience of age" (v).[20] As Rowson exhorted her "fair readers" to learn from the "reality" conveyed by *Charlotte Temple,* Tucker's preface urges his readers (fair or not) to learn from the "true" example of the Graysons. The novel, then, relies on a form of realism but taps into a more dynamic representation that Tucker's works of political economy cannot and one that could connect to readers' experiences in a more visceral way than dry statistical data.

Beyond the cautionary tale of financial mismanagement, *The Valley of Shenandoah* also presents the dire consequences of the social conservativism that contributes to the region's lagging development. In *Progress of the United States in Population and Wealth in Fifty Years* (1843), a census-based statistical analysis of the nation's economic growth, Tucker points out that the South suffers from a lack of economic diversification outside of one-crop agriculture, which is the result of upper-class southerners' reluctance to deviate from the social and economic organization of the plantation (129–31, 141).[21] Although southwestern states such as Mississippi and Louisiana were still prospering from the cotton and sugar trade up through the 1850s, Tucker's analysis consistently reveals the economic systems driving such growth were unsustainable in the long term.[22]

Rather than being led astray by the example of novels and promises of love, the Graysons' ruin is precipitated by their collective refusal to abandon the traditional social mores that characterize the plantation aristocracy, which is quickly fading in the face of economic progress. Tucker puts these ideas into practice by representing the actual decline of the region's upper class in *The Valley of Shenandoah* through the seduction plot. One element is the aforementioned tendency of all members of the plantation elite toward "indolence" and a disregard for practical business matters. This is especially true for the young women, and Louisa Grayson's ignorance of the family's financial affairs partially leads to her seduction. While her mother and Edward attempt to recoup the family's estate, Louisa is left to entertain herself with "ladylike" activities. Her idleness gives Gildon the opportunity to woo her (1:93). Those favorable circumstances are compounded by Louisa's role as the daughter of a landed Virginia family. On the plantation, "the little country flower," as she is often called in the novel, is a mere innocent child: "The circumstances of her education, temper, and situation at the time, peculiarly exposed her to [Gildon's] seductive influence. Treated, from her infancy, with extraordinary delicacy and tenderness, experiencing nothing but kindness and indulgence from both parents, she was all softness gentleness, timidity, and affection" (1:91). As the novel presents it, the traditional roles for upper-class young women have a reverberating effect within plantation culture and breed generational ignorance, which only worsens the poor economic practices that hinder the region. The seduction plot drives home this point when, at the end of the novel, Gildon leaves Louisa for a socially and financially savvy northern merchant's daughter, and Louisa wastes away in the Virginia countryside, unmarried and ruined.[23]

Yet Louisa is not the only Grayson affected by the family's adherence to aristocratic values and an outdated economic system; the novel is, after all, about the fall of the entire family. Edward, despite whatever prudence he evinces in critiquing slavery and the southern economy, is also guilty of his own social prejudices and ignorance, holdovers from the practices of an earlier generation. To ascertain their finances, he takes stock of the family's fortune, including a distant plantation being run by an overseer. Employing an overseer was common practice for the absentee owners of large or multiple estates, yet it represents another version of the indolence that infected most of the South's gentry. As in any business, the longer the owner was away, the more poorly the plantation was run. In this case, none of the Graysons had been to the estate in months, even years, and the overseer runs it as his own farm: he mistreats the slaves, spends more time cultivating his own crop to the neglect of the Graysons' harvest, and has let the maintenance of the great house fall apart. Although the overseer is clearly cheating the family of money, Edward is reluctant to believe ill of him, even when he witnesses the problems firsthand—or perhaps he is simply unwilling to take on the burden of running the farm himself. In either case, despite his doubts, he trusts his father's judgment of the manager, "a smooth, plausible, voluble man, who had got the blind side of Col.

Grayson in his lifetime, and had maintained himself in the good opinion of the family ever since" (2:33). If Louisa represents an impossible ideal of genteel female innocence, Edward represents a southern aristocrat of the old order, one quickly passing into obscurity.[24] In a modern economic world characterized by capitalist models of free trade, the aristocratic codes that once dictated Virginia society hold little value.

Edward reverts to those outdated codes in order to seek satisfaction for the honor of his sister, which proves to be the family's death knell. When he learns of Gildon's treachery, Edward travels to New York to challenge him to a duel. At one point, a friend from the South attempts to dissuade Edward from his mission, claiming that Gildon "deserved no serious notice from Edward" (2:276). But Edward will not be deterred and "declared that his course was fixed and unchangeable, and that he would punish such unprincipled baseness, or perish in the attempt" (2:277). The tunnel vision in regard to family honor is represented as yet another element of the conservativism verging on outright backwardness that pervades the plantation South as a whole. One northern character in the novel remarks, "These chaps have been so accustomed to lord it over their slaves, that they think they are to do as they please every where" (2:280).

Edward's tenacious search for "satisfaction" through the duel is yet another way in which the novel critiques the plantation system while obviating direct censure of slavery itself. In his discussion of southern honor codes, Bertram Wyatt-Brown points out that honor as a general concept allowed upper-class white southerners to overlook the more basic problems with the antebellum South: "Holding men in bondage could not have worried too many Southerners so long as they were committed to the age-old morality. Honor, not conscience, shame, not guilt, were the psychological and social underpinnings of Southern culture" (22). As the novel presents it, however, those bastions of southern antebellum culture eventually lead to its destruction. Edward challenges Gildon to a duel, and the episode costs the family financially and Edward his life.[25] With the depletion of his family's wealth and landholdings and his inability to move beyond the cultural traditions of the plantation system that created his former wealth, Edward Grayson is an increasingly powerless figure in turn-of-the-century America. Honor means nothing when a man is dead and his family is left destitute.

This episode is the denouement for the entire Grayson clan, the culmination of the seduction plot set in motion by the cycles of an unsustainable plantation-based economy. True to the form of the cautionary tale, the Graysons are victims of the economic and social practices that originally led them astray, in which their "seduction" at the hands of aristocratic values and poor economic practices parallels Louisa's more literal seduction. Edward is, of course, dead; Louisa eventually dies of heartbreak; and Mrs. Grayson lives alone in a small cottage, for the family has sold the plantation. A family friend in the novel observes, "Here is a family possessing every virtue and grace, fitted to enjoy happiness and comfort beyond any other I ever knew, that are overwhelmed with every species of affliction" (2:293). Yet the novel makes clear that these "species of affliction" did not merely happen. The Grayson family as a whole meets the same fate as Charlotte Temple, Clarissa, and Eliza Wharton in the earlier seduction novels: death, shame, and virtual extinction due to poor choices and an inability to evolve in a modernizing world.

In line with the pattern established by the seduction genre, the Graysons' fates are cautionary. If Charlotte Temple is a "striking example of vice" for her female readers (*Charlotte Temple* 132), the Graysons and the plantation elite are warnings for antebellum readers who uphold the plantation system and its reliance on slavery as the ideal of southern society. The novel ends with a final injunction: "And thus, gentle reader, you may see, in this true, but melancholy history, something of the life and manners which prevailed about twenty-five or thirty years ago, in Virginia, and especially in that part of it which is called the Valley of Shenandoah" (2:320). As the following decades would demonstrate, that ideal would slowly become the marker of southern identity but also the problem with which potential southern reformers would wrestle in their calls for economic modernization.

The Impending Crisis

With his ambivalent position on slavery and his emphasis on the inevitability of the plantation system's decline, George Tucker was a product of the public position espoused by most southern intellectuals at the beginning of the nineteenth century. As the decades passed, however, regional divisions over the issue required that most Americans, especially self-identified southerners, take a more definitive side. For this reason, between the 1830s and up to the Civil War, novels by southerners that featured slavery shifted away from narratives that presented a tenuous balance between critique and acceptance and were replaced with rigorous defenses of the system—the proslavery and "anti–Uncle Tom" novels of the 1850s that were published in response to Stowe's *Uncle Tom's Cabin.*

Maria J. McIntosh has long been grouped into the "anti-Tom" genre, for good reason. McIntosh was an ardent defender of slavery and what she saw as its crucial role in the national and global economy. In 1853, she published a small pamphlet titled *Letter on the Address of the Women of England to Their Sisters of America in Relation to Slavery,* in response to an antislavery petition that had been circulated in England.[26] Her proslavery novel, *The Lofty and the Lowly,* was published directly after *Uncle Tom's Cabin,* and reviews of the novel frequently contrasted the two.[27] Yet like Tucker, McIntosh identified the problems with the southern economy and slavery and perceived that both "may be a beauty too dearly bought."

The moment in which McIntosh wrote her proslavery novel is best characterized by the familiar refrains "Commerce is king" and "Cotton is king." Taken together, the two popular quotations from the nineteenth century draw attention to the disparate yet intrinsically linked impulses that defined the era. The first, attributed to the nineteenth-century British economist and social theorist Thomas Carlyle, was cited frequently by nineteenth-century American economists and served as the perennial motto for *De Bow's Review* (see again fig. 2, p. 8).[28] The quote points to a large-scale change occurring in the global economy throughout the mid-nineteenth century, in which free trade and laissez-faire capitalism had become the dominant way of life. After the Panic of 1837, the United States was ever more invested—both literally and metaphorically—in free market, transatlantic capitalism. While this allowed for the growth of industry in the North and England and increased the demand for raw materials from the South, the trend also highlighted the larger problems with the southern agricultural economy. The system of trade that made the southern United States one of the wealthiest areas in the world was gradually rendering its plantation-based economy and social structures obsolete. Cotton prices plummeted in the late 1830s, and the subsequent panic left many planters (as well as northern and foreign investors) in debt. Although commerce and manufacturing flourished in the northern states, most southern states still focused on agriculture and mining. For an economy in which manufactures were important commodities, agriculture alone would not be sufficient to support southern finances.

The now-famous declaration "Cotton is king," from the South Carolina politician James Henry Hammond in 1858, indicates the political climate that developed concurrently with these global economic shifts.[29] Debates over slavery and its expansion into new territories forced southern authors and intellectuals to confront the issue in a much more direct fashion. The United States' expansion into southwestern territories in the 1830s and 1840s intensified public debates over the existence of slavery, and in the 1850s, these problems worsened, with one conflict after another: the Compromise of 1850; the attached Fugitive Slave Act; the publication of *Uncle Tom's Cabin* (1852); the Kansas-Nebraska Act (1854); and the *Dred Scott* decision (1857).[30] Hammond's most famous speech to the U.S. Senate defied abolitionist and free-soil advocates by declaring that the South and slavery—by this point the two were synonymous—were too important to the global economy to be undermined by outside interference. "The greatest strength of the South arises from the harmony of her political and social institutions," he contends, and that harmony came from the region's unification around the existence of slavery ("On the Admission of Kansas" 317).

In addition to intensified ideological clashes, the very same economic changes that made the South increasingly obsolete also drove proslavery southerners to cling more intently to the plantation system and slavery. The 1830s southwestern land boom as well as the profitability of cotton manufactures in the North and England forestalled the imminent economic decline George Tucker had predicted in 1824. Rather than diverting the South from an agriculture-based economy, the growing transatlantic commercial trade encouraged southerners and those migrating to the southwestern states to focus more intently on one-crop cultivation. As Hammond would proclaim in 1858, "No, you dare not make war on cotton. No power on earth dares make war upon it" ("On the Admission of Kansas" 317). His declaration of economic power was an attempt to assert the region's economic autonomy in the face of abolitionism and the federal government's efforts to curb the spread of slavery. Unifying around slavery also meant unifying around an economic system that continued to benefit white southerners, at least in the short term. By the end of the decade, not only was the United States divided according to its economic practices; the country had split into two distinct regional factions over the continued existence of human bondage.

Therefore, in the decade before the Civil War, southern reformers such as McIntosh were in a precarious position. If southerners defended the systems that made the region prosper for so long (including and most especially slavery), they were also forced to recognize the problems that gradually rendered the region's economy regressive in a rapidly modernizing transatlantic market. The difficulty became how to remain unified around a homogeneous regional identity defined by slavery yet still articulate critiques that would help situate the South in the modern global economy.

Most upper-class white southerners staunchly defended slavery and the plantation system by positioning both in opposition to capitalism, which they characterized as more exploitative.[31] Historian David Donald observes that these anticapitalist slavery supporters "were defending not the social order which they knew, with flaws so glaring they had to be admitted, but an idealized paternalistic society which, as they believed, had formerly flourished in the South before it was undermined by the commercialization of urban life" ("Proslavery Argument" 16). As the debates over slavery became more heated and divided, southern proslavery advocates aligned the system with quasi-feudal, precapitalist economic models that counteracted the evils of the free market. Directly after the Panic of 1837, for example, the South Carolina judge William Harper argued that slavery provided an antidote to the imbalance in wealth promoted by capitalism: "In periods of commercial revulsion and distress, like the present, the distress, in countries of free labor, falls principally on the laborers. In those of Slave labor, it falls almost exclusively on the employer. . . . a consequence will be, that there will be less inequality and less suffering" (95). While slavery may not be as profitable, at least it protects those enslaved. In this bizarre paradigm—and one that would be rehashed over and over by proslavery advocates—slavery provides the beneficent contrast to free labor.

The most prominent example of proslavery sentiment disguised as anticapitalism was George Fitzhugh, whose tirades against the evils of the free market in *Sociology for the South* (1854) and *Cannibals All!* (1857) went hand in hand with his promotion of slavery. According to Fitzhugh, "free trade" created all of the major problems in the nineteenth century, particularly the poverty resulting from widened class disparities: "It has been justly observed that under this system the rich are continually growing richer and the poor poorer" (*Sociology* 51). The solution, he claimed, is slavery employed in all areas of society, including manufacturing: "The association of labor carried out under a common head or ruler, would render labor more efficient, relieve the laborer of many of the cares of household affairs, and protect and support him in sickness and old age, besides preventing the too great reduction of wages by redundancy of labor and free competition. Slavery attains all these results. What else will?" (59). In this vision of the nineteenth-century economy, slavery is a remedy to capitalism, a system that exacerbates inequality and promotes individual suffering, while the principles of the free market signal the decline of morality and community.

Continuing the alignment of slavery and the southern plantation economy against modern capitalism, abolitionist writers used virtually the same premises in their arguments. According to these claims—which have uncanny parallels to those of southern intellectuals earlier in the century—slavery and the plantation system prevented the South from advancing economically. In 1846, abolitionist Daniel Goodloe argued "that slavery absorbs the great bulk of Southern capital [and] must always present an obstacle to extensive [manufacturing] operations. . . . Slavery sits like the Old Man of the Sea upon the necks of the people, paralyzing every effort at improvement" (13).[32] And in his 1857 text, *The Impending Crisis,* Hinton Rowan Helper used census statistics to prove the very same point, emphasizing that the presence of slavery also resulted in a higher rate of poverty for lower-class whites.[33] Slavery, in this context, became the catalyst for a growing class disparity that traversed racial lines.

However, there were those who saw slavery as already integral to the global free market and, further, saw its potential to remain a key factor in the modern economy. Maria J. McIntosh was certainly an example of this trend; she and other like-minded southerners advocated for slavery to continue but also pointed out potential reforms to the southern economy that would align it with modern economic theory and make the system more humane. As McIntosh would observe in her 1853 proslavery pamphlet, "We claim not that we or our fathers have done for them [enslaved men and women] all that we ought—we acknowledge that more, far more might and should have been done" (*Letter* 16). In navigating midcentury regional politics and global economic theories in their writing, southern authors such as McIntosh attempted to resolve the vision of a modern southern economy with the traditions that defined southern identity—slavery and the social organization of the plantation.

Across the Atlantic, British authors and economic theorists had been dealing with the changing global economy for decades, and many of the southern proslavery advocates looked to British thinkers for inspiration on how to merge traditional social structures with new economic practices. The forerunner among them was Thomas Carlyle, who, in addition to supplying the motto for *De Bow's Review,* was also frequently featured in southern periodicals and proslavery texts.[34] Proslavery U.S. authors drew parallels between the debates over industrialization in England and the conflicts over slavery in the United States, and for many proslavery authors, England's social problems found their echoes in the growing economic and social disparities in the United States. In mid-nineteenth-century Britain, increased urbanization and the thriving factory system raised questions regarding the treatment of workers, the poor working and living conditions in cities and factory towns, as well as the growing poverty rates. Carlyle, like many of his fans in the South, saw industrialization and the growing dominance of capitalist economic practices as hints of an impending social and economic disaster. In his book *Past and Present* (1843), Carlyle points out that as Britain grew wealthier from the boom in cotton manufactures and factories, the laboring classes were gradually distanced from its benefits: "In the midst of plethoric plenty, the people perish; with gold walls, and full barns, no man feels himself safe or satisfied" (9). In a proposal that paralleled the ideal of the "New Man" advocated by southern Whigs, Carlyle argued that the solution is to adopt communal strategies, in which naturally "talented" men would influence those of lower intellect and "character." With these "Captains of Industry" as the proper models, "to be a noble Master, among noble Workers, will again be the first ambition with some few,—to be a rich Master only second" (266). Although it denotes the common language for employers and workers in the British factories, Carlyle's use of the term *master* conjures up the image of the "benevolent master" that dominated proslavery rhetoric of the time. The difference is that rather than railing against free trade (like Fitzhugh or Harper), Carlyle saw the potential to integrate old systems into the new.

The similarities between Carlyle's theories and those of proslavery southerners indicate a discourse that responded to the economic and political changes occurring on both sides of the Atlantic, in which mid-century authors attempted to merge traditional conceptions of plantation slavery with new economic paradigms. For instance, although he always argued in his paper's editorials that slavery was one of the cornerstones of southern society and its economy, James De Bow did not position it in opposition to the tenets of the free market. In an editorial hopefully titled "The Southern Industrial Revolution" (1850), he writes: "But what shall we say of the South—the old South, which fought the battles of the Revolution—which gave the statesmen, the generals, and the wealth of those early times—which concentrated then the agriculture, the commerce, and, even to some extent, the manufactures of the continent, but which has lost, or is losing everything else, save that agriculture; and even this last resource growing less and less remunerative, threatens in the event to complete her beggary? How much has the South promised, and how little has she fulfilled?" According to De Bow, the region's decline was due to its reluctance to expand industries outside of agriculture: "We [southerners] have been content to be solely agriculturalists, and to exhaust the fertility of an abundant soil, believing that all other pursuits being derivative only, were of less importance, and even dignity." He argues that the South must "diversify, or find new employment for labor" (78). He then suggests a list of new investments, from railroads and manufacturing to increasing foreign commerce—all under the premise that both slave and free labor can be employed in each new industry (79).[35] McIntosh, too, pointed out the regressive southern economy, even as she defended it in her writing. In her only major work of nonfiction, *Woman in America: Her Work and Her Reward* (1850), she identifies what she calls "feudalism" as the primary source of economic decline: "There [in a feudally based system] the distinctions are not of the various grades of talent, but of the common clay and fine porcelain, the folly of the last being more excellent than the wisdom of the first" (46). The description outlines, without directly identifying it as such, the typical southern plantation and its pseudoaristocratic social organization. The plantation system, and its inability to adapt in the context of free market capitalism, creates a self-defeating lineage for the region, in which prosperity is dictated by birth and not talent.

De Bow's and McIntosh's nonfiction works reveal that some proslavery authors sought ways to resolve the new economic order with the continued existence of slavery. But in a political climate in which slavery was set up in opposition to the principles of free market capitalism, finding a rhetorical balance was difficult. For proslavery political economists such as De Bow, there had to be a theoretical middle ground in the discourse of intensified sectionalism, wherein the South could at once embrace the advantages of industrialization and the free market and also retain the plantation structure and slave labor that defined its culture and identity as a unified society.

This is the dynamic from which McIntosh's proslavery novel, *The Lofty and the Lowly,* emerged: an increasingly industrialized, free market economy that demanded change and modernization on the part of the South but a political discourse in which southerners more urgently advocated for the continued existence of slavery and the plantation ideal. This particular set of historical circumstances makes McIntosh an odd, inscrutable figure for a modern historian or literary critic. She was a defender of the southern way of life who also saw the economic decline of the region; she was a defender of slavery who did not see slavery existing indefinitely into the future. Like Tucker before her, she took up the task of envisioning a future South in her fiction—and also like Tucker, she used a popular literary genre promoted by British novelists to imagine that future.

The Proslavery Social Problem Novel

In her 1854 novel, *North and South,* British author Elizabeth Gaskell depicts a series of debates between her two main characters and love interests, John Thornton, a northern mill owner, and Margaret Hale, a recent transplant from the South. In response to Hale's critiques of the cold, businesslike North, Thornton responds: "I would rather be a man toiling, suffering—nay, failing and successless—here, than lead a dull prosperous life in the old worn grooves of what you call more aristocratic society down in the South. . . . One may be clogged with honey and unable to rise and fly." Irate, Margaret retorts: "You are mistaken. . . . You do not know anything about the South. . . . Now, in the South we have our poor, but there is not that terrible expression in their countenances of a sullen sense of injustice which I see here. You do not know the South." To which Thornton responds, "And may I say you do not know the North?" (81).

In a very different context, Maria McIntosh represents a similar regional exchange in *The Lofty and the Lowly; or, Good in All and None All-Good.* After visiting friends in the U.S. North and observing their factory town, southerner Alice Montrose reflects on plantation slavery and slaveholders' roles in the system: "Mr. and Miss Grahame's interest in their work-people . . . made me ashamed of my useless life. I tried at first to excuse myself, under the plea of different circumstances, and to persuade myself that I had none whom I could teach and influence as she did these people; but then I remembered the negroes, and how much I could teach them" (1:205). Like the exchange between Margaret Hale and John Thornton in a fictionalized England, Alice's experience as a southerner moving between regions highlights the varying economic systems and cultures that made up the mid-nineteenth century United States, and further, forces a recognition of the inherent moral problems in the South's slavery-based economy.

If read without the accompanying publication information, authors, or titles, these passages could easily come from the same novel. The first repeats the regional stereotypes of the nineteenth-century United States: the South as aristocratic and agrarian; the North as capitalist and industrialist. It also assumes a sectional tone that suggests the growing antagonism over slavery and the economy. The second passage evokes the language of labor reform and working conditions, and with the exception of the racialized terminology, it could take place in an English or northern industrial town. Its tone denotes the attitude of progressivism and a desire to promote communication and openness, rather than reactionary defensiveness.

These passages reveal how dominant ideologies shaped by economic networks led to the creation of distinct literary forms across spaces and societies that grew from transatlantic trade reliant on slave labor. The commonalities are even more incongruent given that the first passage is taken from a British industrial reform novel, while the other is from a proslavery novel. The two could not be more different in authorship and composition, yet the formal overlaps indicate how an emergent capitalism system in the nineteenth century forced authors and intellectuals from widely different areas and backgrounds to confront the resulting social changes and ethical issues occurring on a global scale.[36]

The economic paradigm of the mid-nineteenth century gave rise to a new genre of reform fiction: the social problem novel. In England, authors such as Gaskell pointed out problems with factory labor but still visualized the future of British manufacturing in their novels with those more humane changes in place.[37] However, the social problem genre was not limited to critiques of industrialization, and while there were plenty of examples of American texts that also critiqued factory labor practices, southern proslavery authors adopted the same form as a way to negotiate the economic and political pressures that shaped the region's development before the Civil War.[38]

The Lofty and the Lowly is a "proslavery social problem novel," one that critically assesses the problems with southern economic practices and slavery while still upholding the southern identity performed by proslavery southerners in the 1850s. McIntosh participated in the global circulation of popular fiction that emerged from the debates over the free market and the factory system, and *The Lofty and the Lowly* is a response to contemporary theories of economic modernization through its discussion of reforms to slavery and the southern economy. Yet as a self-identified proslavery southerner, McIntosh also used her fiction to advocate for the plantation system and the continued existence of slavery. In adapting the form of the social problem novel to the context of the U.S. South, McIntosh created a fictional world that maintained both: slavery and the social organization of the plantation in a modernizing global economy.

To enact their ideas of reform, authors of the social problem novels on both sides of the Atlantic employed "reconciliation narratives."[39] Like Tucker's economic seduction novel, these fictional narratives create imagined spaces in which authors could introduce cooperation and understanding between divergent groups, then make it possible to present reforms without posing a direct threat to existing systems. The sense of greater understanding as a means of alleviating social ills is ultimately what connects McIntosh's fiction, and specifically her proslavery novel, with the British social problem novels. In these texts, reconciliation is effected through the interactions of characters, which illustrate both sides of a particular issue. For example, in one of the earlier British social problem novels, Frances Trollope's *The Life and Adventures of Michael Armstrong, the Factory Boy* (1839–40), the wealthy heroine, Mary Brotherton, is first made aware of the working conditions in the factories when she encounters Michael on his way home from work. Her interest in Michael sets her on a course of social improvement: she adopts factory children and educates the rest of her wealthy neighbors on the abuses of the current system.[40] Likewise, Elizabeth Gaskell's novel *North and South* promotes cross-cultural understanding through the direct contact between characters and their discussions of social problems. The varying sides of the debates over industrialization are represented through the conversations of fictional characters.[41]

McIntosh's earlier novel, *Two Lives; or, To Seem and to Be* (1846), also adopts a reconciliationist plot in reference to modern economic systems, and it sets the precedent for her later proslavery novel. *Two Lives* features two girls born in the South who must move north after their father and caretaker dies. While one girl, Isabel, is self-sufficient, prudent, and unpretentious, her cousin Claire is indecisive, dependent, and only concerned with pleasing others. Through their examples, the novel emphasizes that independence and common sense are needed to survive in nineteenth-century society, and those qualities can only be exercised through a proper understanding of the financial system. Claire has no sense of finances or money matters, while Isabel takes pains to learn about them. When their uncle, an investor in the stock market, loses the family's fortune, Isabel forces him to explain the situation, despite his protests. She remarks: "Perhaps [women] would understand more about it, if men would talk more frequently to them of it.... Perhaps [my aunt] has not a taste for business, but I have decidedly" (216). She then assumes responsibility for their finances by paying her uncle's debts with her own investments and supporting the family by going to work herself. In this sense, the reconciliation promoted by the novel is between the increasingly complicated financial system of the mid-nineteenth century and average Americans, particularly women.[42]

With these reconciliation plots, most social problem novels aim to reform the systems in place, not dismantle them. Despite the criticisms leveled at the factory system in *Michael Armstrong* and *North and South* or the problems presented by the unstable stock market in *Two Lives,* the novels ultimately espouse the basic tenets of modern capitalism as being for the general good. After enumerating the evils of the current factory system in *Michael Armstrong,* a character nonetheless insists, "If used aright there cannot be a doubt that this magnificent power [industrial technology] might, in all its agencies, be made the friend of man." (205). Or in the passage from *North and South,* Thornton's comment on the "clogged" life in an aristocracy indicates the benefits of self-reliance, opportunities for social and financial mobility, and individual creativity in a free market. *Two Lives* also upholds these ideals through the example of Isabel. Although she experiences hardship, Isabel's tale is resolved happily due to her knowledge of finance and ability to adapt to market conditions.[43] With her example, McIntosh's *Two Lives* enjoins the readers that once individuals understand the workings of the modern economy, they have the opportunity to prosper, and future financial problems can be alleviated and even avoided.

In many ways, McIntosh's personal biography made her particularly attuned to writing in the reconciliationist style of the social problem novel.[44] Born on a large plantation along the Georgia coast, McIntosh came from a prosperous, aristocratic southern family similar to the Tuckers of Virginia. She was also an only child who grew up watching her mother run the plantation after her father's death in 1806, when McIntosh was three. Her mother died when McIntosh was twenty, leaving the plantation to her care. She ran the estate for twelve years, until 1835, when, motivated by the decline in profits for plantations on the Atlantic coast, she sold the estate and moved to New York. After suffering financial loss during the Panic of 1837, in which her entire life's fortune disappeared, McIntosh turned to writing to earn her living.[45] She lived out the rest of her life in the North on the profits of her books. However, like most upper-class southerners of the time, her position and wealth originally rested on the profitability of slavery and the plantation system. With her firsthand experience running a large plantation, owning numerous slaves, and investing in the markets, McIntosh's perspective on the South was that of a businesswoman who understood the practicalities of a southern plantation and the larger commercial markets of which it was a part.[46]

In her proslavery novel, *The Lofty and the Lowly,* McIntosh draws from her personal experience and the context of antebellum economic development to approach the question of slavery from a reconciliationist standpoint. In a climate of intensifying sectional divisions and southern economic decline—and in which public discourse aligned free market capitalism with northern and foreign interests—the novel overlaps with the British industrial fiction of the era. As a proslavery social problem novel, *The Lofty and the Lowly* depicts a version of economic reform that promotes cooperation between regions, classes, and even races while also maintaining slavery and the plantation as the South's defining points of identity. Because *The Lofty and the Lowly* is typically lumped into the anti–Uncle Tom genre, often these reconciliation patterns are ignored in the few critical studies of the novel.[47] However, the underlying economic concerns that permeate McIntosh's proslavery novel bear more similarity to the British industrial novels and parallel her direct experience with plantation slavery and global markets.[48] Recategorizing *The Lofty and the Lowly* as a proslavery social problem novel reveals the interconnected nature of southern writing to the rest of the globe and demonstrates how southern authors—even or especially the ardent proslavery advocates—conceptualized their positions in a larger global economic and social context.[49]

Yet there is no denying the fundamental quality of *The Lofty and the Lowly:* it is proslavery and adamantly so. Yet in keeping with the social problem genre, the novel's fictional version of southern life portrays necessary reforms and future developments of nineteenth-century society as a whole, not just the continuance of the southern slave system. In the preface, McIntosh claims she began writing *The Lofty and the Lowly* in 1850—before the publication of *Uncle Tom's Cabin.* If her chronology is true, the novel can be read as a general reflection on the role of the South and slavery in a modern global economy and transatlantic society, rather than just a reactionary defense of the institution. Through the reconciliation plot, *The Lofty and the Lowly* identifies what many proslavery advocates viewed as the potential benefits of slavery and the plantation system while still adapting both to liberal capitalist principles. By the end, the novel posits gradual reforms to slavery and changes to the plantation economy—without the complete disappearance of either institution—through the interchange between its characters and an espousal of individual and regional economic self-reliance.

The Lofty and the Lowly's narrative consideration of broader economic questions emerges first in the novel's most noticeable characteristic: movement. No one character ever remains in the same place for any substantial length of time. And for a novel that upholds slavery and the southern way of life in the plantation system, only a small portion of the plot takes place in the South or on a plantation. Much like the opening of *The Valley of Shenandoah,* the events in *The Lofty and the Lowly* are preceded by the death of a family patriarch: Mr. Montrose, the son of a wealthy Georgia family, moves to the North and marries a northern lady but then dies, leaving his wife and two children in Boston as well as a number of debts and a failing business. Even the opening lines of the novel evoke movement: the first paragraphs are a letter written by Mrs. Montrose's brother, Mr. Browne, to her brother-in-law in the South informing him of the death and the family's financial circumstances. A conversation between Mr. and Mrs. Browne over the future of the Montrose family follows the reprint of the letter, with Mr. Browne lamenting his brother-in-law's lack of business sense and his sister's helplessness.

The conversation between the Brownes establishes the physical and social geography of the novel from the outset and points to *The Lofty and the Lowly*'s role as a social problem novel. For one, the connections between the characters emulate the trading patterns and economic networks in the United States: from the southern plantations represented by the Montrose family to the northern commercial towns inhabited by the Brownes and, finally, the interregional travel and trade within the United States mirrored by the movement of the Montrose family. The conversation also reiterates the common social stereotypes of each region and establishes the representative groups. Browne is "the model of a successful [northern] merchant. Shrewd and cautious in business. . . . Close in his calculations, and a rigid economist; his expenses have always been kept far within the limit of his income" (1:8). He is also cold and businesslike to a fault, while his wife and children are the typical wealthy northerners, superficial and materialistic. In contrast, Mr. Montrose, the southerner, was careless with money and generally lacking common sense when it came to business, but he was a warm and generous family man.

What follows is a six hundred–page novel composed of constant shifts and travels, in which the characters' movements emulate the changes occurring in the nation as a whole. The novel is set during the 1820s and 1830s, the time of the Industrial Revolution, the vast expansion of the western United States, and the initial cotton boom in the South. As these widespread changes occur, Mrs. Montrose moves to the South with her children—Alice and Charles—to live with her brother-in-law, Colonel Montrose, and his family. The rest of the novel's plot is fairly simple: the southern Montrose family travels extensively through the North during vacations, while the two Montrose sons eventually join the army and the navy, then travel internationally. All of this travel introduces a new set of northern characters, who extend the geographical reach of the novel and furnish the romantic drama for the southern characters, while connecting the characters to major events that shaped the mid-nineteenth-century global economy.

Movement within the novel also permits the cultural and regional interchange necessary for the ultimate aim of *The Lofty and the Lowly:* the reconciliation plot. As with most reconciliation narratives, romance encourages a sense of understanding between representative characters. The former factory owner Mary Brotherton and a former factory boy marry at the end of *Michael Armstrong;* in *North and South,* the southerner Margaret Hale and the mill owner, John Thornton, marry after spending most of the novel arguing over regional differences. The novels suggest that together, these couples can encourage moderate reform without total revolution.

In *The Lofty and the Lowly,* the primary love interest is between Robert Grahame, a northern factory owner, and Alice Montrose. Following the pattern of the reconciliation plot, Grahame is a successful businessman and inventor and the model of a capitalist individual, while Alice is the stereotype of southern womanhood according to aristocratic plantation values—"lovely," docile, and innocent. Their romance is the core of the novel, and their interactions take on allegorical significance as each stands in for their respective regions.

However, the characters' extensive movement goes beyond simply uniting North and South through representative character types; it broadens the parameters of the novel beyond regional, or even national, dimensions. The travels break down the isolationism brought about by sectional divide to highlight the integrated nature of American social and economic life as a whole. Within this vast narrative geography, slavery and industrialization are not "southern" and "northern" institutions, respectively; they are part of a global nineteenth-century society. The characters' travels and interactions with other social groups reveal how the inherent problems in the South as well as the North can be modified to fit into the modernizing global economy.

The Lofty and the Lowly first identifies the stereotypes associated with each region: the economic stagnation and laziness of the South encouraged by the plantation system; and the mercenary quality of the North bred by free market capitalism. Donald Montrose, the son of the Georgia planter Colonel Montrose, becomes the primary conduit for the critique of southern backwardness and falls prey to his northern cousin, George Browne, who is a degenerate gambler. After a series of losses to Browne, Donald signs over the deed to the family's plantation in Georgia. Though Browne is partially to blame for leading Donald astray, the loss is mainly due to Donald's refusal to familiarize himself with money matters. When Donald signs over the deed, the narrator reflects: "To a prudent mind, it may seem strange that the mention of large interest did not serve as a counterpoise. . . . But Donald was not prudent; like all the self-indulgent, he was ever prone to sacrifice the future to the present. Besides, . . . he had been taught in his Southern home, that the first characteristic of a gentleman was to prove himself untainted with a narrow, money-loving, or as they termed it, *Yankee* spirit; and that this was to be done, not by a wise and systematic benevolence, but by thoughtless profusion and disregard of money. To have kept a regular account of his losses and gains, would have savored of the petty shopkeeper in his opinion" (1:130). Donald's financial recklessness and dissolute behavior mirrors the pattern of the average plantation owner described by Tucker in *The Valley of Shenandoah,* in which southern aristocrats squander money with the promise of future returns on crops.[50]

Donald's problems with money also reveal the materialism of the North and the moral problems that stem from a fixation on profit in a capitalist system. Browne eventually signs Donald's debt over to his father, who then demands regular payment of usurious interest.[51] The Brownes' fraudulent abuse of Donald's debt cements the early characterization of the heartless, shrewd northern merchants at the beginning of the novel, and Mr. Browne's intense focus on accumulating wealth infects his family: "These views, too, had had their legitimate effect on all, in indurating their hearts, degrading their aspirations, and presenting to them life in its most superficial aspects" (1:245). The idea of character being shaped by experience and education once again highlights an underlying belief present in all of McIntosh's works as well as that of the British industrial novelists: a broader understanding of the world and opposing viewpoints will effect positive social change. The novel implies that had either the Brownes or Donald experienced anything beyond their immediate worldviews and social spheres, perhaps the fraud and debt would not have occurred.

Using these basic reforms to regional stereotypes as the foundation, the reconciliation plot of *The Lofty and the Lowly* maps out a trajectory for the South that maintains slavery and the "traditional" southern social organization of the plantation but still fits the region within the development of the global economy. The narrative implies that once each region can "fix" its respective cultural flaws, then both can work together to reform existing systems, with slavery being the main focus. Again, this is accomplished through travel and interactions between characters. While traveling in the North, Alice Montrose visits Robert Grahame's factory town. While there, she is impressed by the general prosperity of the factory workers, including the Grahames' efforts to maintain better working conditions and provide education for the factory children. When she returns to the South, she rethinks the condition of the slaves: "I tried at first to excuse myself, under the plea of different circumstances, and to persuade myself that I had none whom I could teach and influence as she did these people; but then I remembered the negroes, and how much I could teach them" (1:205). Consciousness now awakened, Alice begins a school in which she teaches the slaves on her family's plantation to read and write.

Because it follows these patterns of small-scale reconciliation, McIntosh's defense of slavery paradoxically connects her novel to the British industrial texts. The social problem novels rarely present complete revolution; the plots of reconciliation are always enacted without undoing the entire system in question.[52] Alice's actions after her experience in the North assume that slavery will still exist—she does not become a radical abolitionist. The interchange between regions, nations, and characters in *The Lofty and the Lowly* models change based on the ideal principles of democratic, liberal capitalism, only here it occurs within the existent southern economy based on slave labor.[53]

In order to correct the evils of plantation society, including slavery, the novel indicates that the southern characters must draw from the lessons of the free market displayed in the North. In the second volume, Alice and her mother move north to live on their own after the death of Colonel Montrose. While there, in a parallel to McIntosh's own life, the Panic of 1837 depletes the small fund of money available to them. The financial disaster forces Alice to support the family by taking in sewing and needlework. Although it is difficult, especially compared to the sheltered life she led in the South, another character observes, "she is every day acquiring that practical wisdom necessary to the successful prosecution of business" (2:154). Rather than being a blight on her character, as with Mr. Browne, Alice's gradual understanding of simple finances and self-supporting labor align with Christian values to ennoble her. She defends her work to her brother Charles and declares, "I have felt since I began to try to make something, how very good our Heavenly Father was to give man work to do when he lost his happy Eden" (2:182). Alice's move to the North and away from the Montrose plantation forces her into the sort of self-reliance and economic self-sufficiency so often lacking in the South.

The Lofty and the Lowly further promotes economic self-sufficiency and liberal capitalist ideals by placing individual characters within the larger context of the international economy. The scope of the novel is deliberately non-regional, so when Robert Grahame, the northern factory owner, travels to England to sell and promote his new invention for cotton manufacturing,[54] he is not only a representative of the prosperous American economy but an emblem of future progress for civilization across the globe: "Robert Grahame was . . . an American. His whole nature had been cast by the circumstances of his life in an American mould, and had grown rigid there. He instituted no comparisons between his own and other countries; he saw, and was willing to admit their superiority in many things, but *they were,* and America *was to be.* America was the land of hope, of promise. The matured man excels in many things the youth; but have all his attainments equalled the youth's imaginings? America is to her children what they see she may become" (2:142). Couched in this nationalist rhetoric is the basic principle of success and progress in a free market economy. Additionally, McIntosh takes care to frame this ideal of progress as less about one nation, class, or group triumphing over another but, rather, of groups understanding and interpreting one another while always looking to the future. Robert, as the ideal American, plays a role in the novel's reconciliation plot on an international scale by understanding other nations and being willing to adapt for the long-term good.

The plot of *The Lofty and the Lowly* projects these visions of long-term, global economic and social progress onto small-scale, regional reforms, indicating that changes within a region will then have reverberating consequences nationally and internationally. The effect is to situate slavery more firmly at the foundation of the global economy but also to trace out the path of future modernization for the South through reforms to the slave labor system. The primary African American character in the novel is "Daddy Cato," a longtime slave on the Montrose plantation who the family frees after the death of Colonel Montrose, and his character exemplifies this theory of "reformed" slavery. When Alice and her mother move to the North, Cato follows them, and his labor contributes to the household income. However, rather than taking his money, Alice creates a bank account for him, and he gradually builds a small savings from his work as a free laborer in the North. McIntosh represents Cato with the paternalistic benevolence espoused by most proslavery authors: his genuine love for Alice motivates his loyalty to her, and he is far too simple and inexperienced to live on his own. Cato himself claims that freedom and working for oneself are overrated, for a slave: "Ent he got he house, and he meat, and he hom'ny, and he taturs, and he fowl, and he egg, and he clothes ebery winter and ebery summer, wha' he want wid money?" (2:101). Cato's fate in the North, though it also follows the pattern of self-sufficient labor in a free market, presents a version of reform rather than outright revolution to the slave system.

The novel also asserts through its reconciliation plot that these changes must be incremental. In her 1853 proslavery pamphlet, *Letter to the Women of England,* McIntosh claims that interference from abolitionist groups exacerbates the problems of slavery and regional schisms and that gradual reform from within is the best course of action (22). As if to illustrate these theories in fiction, McIntosh represents an interaction between northern abolitionists and *The Lofty and the Lowly*'s southern heroes. While Alice and Cato are in the North, local abolitionist leaders see Cato traveling to and from the cottage and assume he is a slave who has been brought north by his master. Charged by a recent meeting, the group gathers at Alice's home to confront the slaveholder, only to find a timid Alice and a confused and frightened Cato. The scene ends with (conveniently enough) the interference of Robert Grahame and Cato's personal assurance of his freedom and contentment to the abolitionist group. He remarks afterward: "You see, maussa, dem an't so bery bad arter all, only I tink dem crazy 'bout free. Free bery good ting, but free ent all; when you sick, free won't make you well, free won't gib you clo'es, nor hom'ny, let 'lone meat. Free bery good, but free ent ebery ting" (2:175). The fictional confrontation between the abolitionists and the Montroses works on several levels: not only does it present a fictional imagining of the problems that arose from the Compromise of 1850 and the Fugitive Slave Act, but it also "proves," in a sense, McIntosh's idea that interference from abolitionist groups is ineffective when compared with more gradual methods of reform and understanding between the groups. Cato's contact with the group and understanding their position, and vice versa, accomplish more in the novel than the mob gathered about the Montrose home.

The novel's reconciliation narrative models a version of gradual emancipation within the existing southern economy. Toward the end of the novel, Donald Montrose, the heir to the Montrose plantation, also visits the Grahames' factory town. He, like Alice before him, is impressed by the industry and living conditions of the workers. And it also forces him to reflect on the condition of his slaves: "The contemplation of all this, and the reasons which Robert Grahame alleged for it, awakened an interesting train of thought in the mind of Donald. 'I too,' he said to himself, 'am a Christian man. God has made me, too, a ruler over others. What have I done to advance their higher interests? Will not God require their souls of me? Has he not in some sense committed them to me? . . . This is wrong and my conscience condemns it'" (2:297). Upon Donald's return to the South, he establishes what he calls a "colony" for slaves separate from the plantation, in which slave families run their own farms under his supervision, and he provides a school and church for them to attend. The system is essentially a form of sharecropping, but in the context of McIntosh's novel, it represents an attempt at reforming slavery without its entire abolishment.

By the time the novel reaches its end, both regions have undergone a rigorous reevaluation of their basic social and economic principles, especially in regard to slavery and sectional divisions. The conclusion, then, follows the checklist of most reconciliation narratives in the social problem genre, in which the representative character types marry: Alice and Robert marry, as do Donald and Mary Grahame, Robert's sister. The marriages are the symbolic flashpoints for the South's evolution in a larger international context. They indicate the reforms in progress, those yet to come, and those that can be enacted in the future to merge the slaveholding South into the modern global economy. As the novel concludes, "And thus by the affinities of spirits devoted to the same noble ends—to the advancement of man's happiness and of God's glory—the North and the South, the Lofty and the Lowly, have been drawn together, and the experience of life has taught to each and all of them, that there is good in all and that none is all-good" (2:323). Ultimately, mutual understanding and modifications to existing systems become the greater goals within the broader framework of a free market, international economy based on liberal capitalist ideals. And underlying those goals, as always, is slavery.

While many southern authors such as Kennedy and Simms looked to the past in their revision of southern society in historical romances—or attempted to create a version of the southern nation in the present, as with the imperial adventure novels—Tucker and McIntosh used economic language to project a version of the future South in the context of a global capitalist economy. Reading these novels in light of their attempts to reform—and rationalize—the existence of slavery demonstrates how proslavery southerners envisioned the region as it would evolve while still retaining the structures that benefited and defined the South for so long. While these attempts were ultimately misguided and futile, they illustrate how southern sympathizers and proslavery advocates wrestled with a desire to promote a modern (perhaps even progressive) South within the bounds of a conservative southern culture as it was defined by slavery and the plantation.

5

"FREE LABOR" AND THE FREE MARKET

Slave Narratives

The image of the slave in the swamp is a common trope in representations of the antebellum South. Accounts of slave uprisings in the early nineteenth century make reference to the use of swamps to hide the revolutionaries, and antebellum slave narratives feature stories of fugitives who effect their escapes through the swamps. In her 1856 novel, *Dred; A Tale of the Great Dismal Swamp,* Harriet Beecher Stowe presents a fictionalized revolutionary community in the swamps of the Carolinas—modeled after the real-life rebellions of Denmark Vesey and Nat Turner—that operates outside of the slave system. And more recently, critics have held up the figure of the slave in the swamp as formative in shaping discussions of antebellum southern literature and culture.[1] In all of these imaginings, the swamp is a space in which slaves could attain a form of economic independence and self-governance, neither of which could be accessed in the plantation South. The image of the swamp, as a result, relegates the limited freedom attained by slaves to liminal, marginal spaces within antebellum southern society and, by extension, its economy.

Contrast the figure of the slave in the swamp with Frank McWorter—also known as Frank McWhorter or simply "Free Frank"—an enslaved man in Kentucky during the early part of the nineteenth century.[2] During the War of 1812, McWorter established a saltpeter manufactory and hired his time from his owner. Since saltpeter was a key ingredient in manufacturing gunpowder, McWorter's enterprise was incredibly successful, and he eventually purchased both his and his wife's freedom by 1819.[3]

The example of Free Frank connects to a larger pattern in antebellum writing by black Americans, wherein skilled black labor is represented as central to the functioning of the national and global economies of the nineteenth century. While Frank's example was indisputably rare, it demonstrates that manifestations of autonomy on the part of enslaved men and women were not limited to marginalized spaces such as the swamp. Rather than peripheral, Free Frank's enterprise in Kentucky provides an example of the economic positioning documented by many black authors of the antebellum period, specifically the autobiographical slave narratives popular in the decades leading up to the Civil War. These narratives represent the labor of enslaved men and women as integral to the economy and social life of the antebellum South and, by extension, the rest of the nation and the global networks of which it was a part.

Slave narratives published from the 1830s up through the 1850s were the most popular form of writing by black Americans at the time. Not only did these texts bolster the growing abolitionist movement, but their popularity coincided with the decades in which debates over free labor and labor organization were more important as a result of the growing factory system in Britain and the United States. In their narratives, authors such as Frederick Douglass, Henry Bibb, William Wells Brown, and Harriet Jacobs highlight the economic determinants that governed the lives and identities of slaves in the South. The narratives present black labor in the South as part of the growing pool of skilled laborers in the developing global economy, much in the manner of Free Frank earlier in the century.

Within the context of the nineteenth-century slavery debates and the dominance of free market capitalism, the popular slave narratives respond to questions of labor, the national economy, and international commerce during the decades leading up to the Civil War. As such, they are counterpoints to the imagined versions of the South created by proslavery southerners in their fiction. Yet the narratives are also shaped by the same economic forces that drove the historical romances, sketches, adventure novels, and social problem fiction. In the same way that bringing writing by white southerners into conversation with British texts reveals the centrality of regional writing and representations of slavery to the nineteenth-century literary marketplace, understanding slave narratives as part of the southern literary canon highlights their importance in shaping ideas of region as well as the function of race and regional identity in national and global contexts.

Black civil rights activists intertwined the language of abolitionism and universal equality with that of modern capitalism in order to promote a particular vision of black American life as the nation developed to the end of the century. In this vision, enslaved black Americans did not exist on the periphery of the modern economy, nor were they written into invisibility, as demonstrated by proslavery texts. As slave labor was essential to the growth of the global economy, so, too, was skilled black labor a cornerstone for future economic development in the United States. With this vision, authors of the antebellum slave narratives wrote themselves into the trajectory of economic prosperity and individual freedom within modern capitalist systems.

A Person with a Price: Abolitionism, Free Labor, and "Wage Slavery"

Historians of transatlantic slavery have long theorized the connection between the development of capitalism and industrialization with the concurrent rise of North American slavery, the growth of plantation economies in the Atlantic South, and the subsequent response of abolitionist movements in both Britain and the United States.[4] Yet seldom do these studies interpret the role of slaves themselves in the plantation economy beyond their position as chattel. Further, most slave narratives are read by critics as attempts on the former slaves' part to distance themselves as much as possible from any signifiers of bondage and the degradation of slave life in the South.[5]

However, if read with a particular emphasis on representations of individual labor, slave narratives written in the 1830s, 1840s, and 1850s reveal a much more dynamic characterization of the slave's role in the southern economy. In a reading of Sojourner Truth's 1850 autobiographical narrative, for example, Xiomara Santamarina describes the conflicted interpretations of Truth and her narratives as a "problem of class" (37). Rather than adhering to the standard depiction of slave labor as inherently degrading, Truth "insisted on the value produced by the hardworking slave" (39). As Truth's narrative indicates, slaves and former slaves represented their lives in the plantation economy in ways that were just as contradictory as the representations by white southerners, slaveholders, and proslavery advocates. Truth's narrative and the absence of such discussions in histories of slavery point to the importance of understanding slavery as an economically productive system *in addition to* a racialized form of human bondage.[6]

To discuss how former slaves conceptualized their labor in the southern economy and, perhaps more important, how they represented that labor to the rest of the world, this chapter examines a set of slave narratives written between 1830 and 1860. These decades are considered the peak moment of the slave narratives' composition and popularity, with dozens of narratives being written or transcribed, then published.[7] To narrow down the discussion, this reading highlights narratives written by former slaves themselves, not those with ghostwriters or what William Andrews calls "amanuensis-editors." Like Andrews's foundational study of the narratives, *To Tell a Free Story* (1986), the focus of this interpretation is on the rhetorical choices made by individual authors in representing their lives, rather than on the content of the narratives exclusively.

Indeed, the narratives are never without the influence of their rhetorical context. Ultimately, the goal of the slave narrative was to use an individual life to represent the whole of the slave system in all of its appalling manifestations. Whether influenced by their abolitionist editors and sponsors, the abolitionist papers in which they were published, or by their white reading public, as John Sekora puts it, "clearly the meaning of slave writing did not inhere exclusively in the text of a narrative alone. Meaning flowed into and out of a narrative in a series of acts of power" (500). That rhetorical situation makes the chosen content of the narratives and their representation of individual lives under the southern slave system that much more significant.

Typically, the narratives are read for their emphasis on the brutalities of slavery. These scenes are often sentimental appeals to the reader and a way to show that slavery's degradation went beyond bondage.[8] The brutal treatment of female slaves and the violent rupturing of families become particular symbols of the psychological and physical violence wrought by the system.[9] There is a reason *Uncle Tom's Cabin* begins with Tom's sale and the destruction of his family, for the dismantling of family structures—or sometimes the inherent lack of family structures—presents slavery as an institution that at its core operates on the dehumanization of those enslaved.[10]

Yet the narratives also reveal a very particular economic awareness on the part of the former slaves. As Walter Johnson details in *Soul by Soul* (1999), the market was central to the lives of antebellum southerners, slave or not. In this system, a slave was simply, as Johnson puts it, a "person with a price" (2). Likewise, the market is central in the slave narratives' representations of individual lives. In the conventional openings for most narratives, the authors describe their earliest memories, or lack thereof, but they are also careful to identify their owners and catalog their owners' properties (land and slaves). Describing one's family meant also describing one's master, his holdings, as well as the constant threat of violence, and the narrators make a point of noting that their masters were frequently their fathers.[11]

The level of detail in such descriptions indicates the narrators' awareness of the economic system in which their physical bodies held value. In his 1845 memoir, after relating his early separation from his mother, Frederick Douglass describes his master, his master's economic standing, and his property holdings: "He was not considered a rich slaveholder. He owned two or three farms and about thirty slaves" (5). Likewise, in his 1847 *Narrative,* William Wells Brown lists his master's financial portfolio in detail: "My master owned about forty slaves, twenty-five of whom were field hands. . . . in addition to his practice as a physician, he carried on milling, merchandizing and farming. He had a large farm, the principal productions of which were tobacco and hemp" (13–14). For many of the authors, describing their owners' property also meant describing the sales and transactions that defined their early lives. Moses Roper begins his 1838 narrative with a dramatic tale of his birth: because Roper is the "bastard" son of his master, his mistress "went into my mother's room with full intention to murder me with her knife and club" (9). To preserve the peace, he and his mother are sold. In the next paragraph, however, that drama devolves into a dry description of slave property division; Roper is sold again at age six or seven after the death of his second master. What follows is a list of different transactions in which Roper is sold to a series of owners. The almost relentless quality of these descriptions—from the dryness of the language to the lists of properties to the litany of sales—underscores the dehumanization at work in the slave system but also highlights the prevalence of economics in the lives of slaves and former slaves.

In turn, the former slaves present a consistent knowledge of their own worth on the market. Henry Bibb's 1849 *Narrative* chronicles his numerous attempts to escape. At the end of a successful venture, Bibb tallies up his total "cost": "In the first place they paid eight hundred and fifty dollars for me; and when I first run away, they paid one hundred for advertising and looking after me; and now they had to pay about forty dollars, expenses travelling to and from Cincinnati, in addition to the three hundred dollars reward; and they were not able to pay the reward without selling me. . . . And if it should be known that I had been a runaway to Canada, it would lessen the value of me at least one hundred dollars" (70–1). Bibb is describing himself, yet the passage takes on the quality of a ledger, in which the passage of time in his life is marked by the fluctuations of his market value. Much of that value is dictated by his physical attributes but also his abilities. Often slaves "hired out" their labor, like Frank McWorter, for which they would receive a portion of the profits, while their masters would "earn" the bulk. Many slaves used hiring out as an opportunity to learn new trades, and this system also enabled Douglass to earn enough money to escape from Baltimore and McWorter to buy his freedom. William Wells Brown's entire career as a slave in his narrative is governed by hiring out, and he is careful to document the monetary value of his earnings at each step. After learning that he will be sold, he confronts his master with these facts: "After you have hired me out, and received, as I once heard you say, nine hundred dollars for my services,—after receiving this large sum, will you sell me to be carried to New Orleans or some other place?" (64). This transactional tone in relation to their own lives parallels the authors' detailed descriptions of their masters' properties, and in the narratives, the lines between the individual identities of the authors and discussions of property value become blurred.

As Brown's, Douglass's, and Bibb's examples demonstrate, the former slaves' consciousness of their value in the southern market permeated their literary self-representations. The economic forces figure so deeply that they are often merged with emotional and familial ties. In 1843 Moses Grandy describes that when his wife was sold from him, he begged the trader to see her one more time. Barred from actually touching her, he relates that he gave her the money in his pocket and said good-bye from a distance (16). In the narrative, this memory of his wife becomes interchangeable with the money in his pocket, a moment in which she is defined both by her sale from him and his own monetary possessions.[12]

The narrators' awareness of the centrality of the market in their lives appears in the narratives alongside the descriptions of violence, divided families, and sexual brutality. That overwhelming presence then raises the question: if the goal of the narratives was only to serve the ends of abolitionism, as many scholars have argued, then why include moments of productive labor (as in the case of Truth's narrative) or the details of economic exchange? In short, the rhetorical impact of narratives by authors such as Bibb and Douglass reaches far beyond the immediate cause of abolition. The narrative awareness of economic forces expands the rhetorical situation of the texts to encompass the debates over free labor and industrialization that also dominated the 1830s, 1840s, and 1850s. Therefore, the slave narratives' representations of labor and economic systems are a response to the broader social and economic changes that were occurring within the region and throughout the international economy.

As a moment that marked the beginnings of dramatic economic change in the Atlantic world, the 1830s prompted a growing awareness of the need for social reform. The rise of industrial sectors in both the North and Britain—on top of the expansion of the United States into the Southwest territories—fostered a demand for staple crops. That demand promoted the growth of the southern plantation economy, which fed the development of the factory system in the North and Britain and placed greater emphasis on slave labor in the South. All of these factors brought the topic of abolition to the forefront of social and political debates in the United States and Britain. And as one of the abolitionist movement's most popular genres, the slave narrative rose to prominence in the midst of these developments.

However, just as this economic shift represented the two-sided development of plantation agriculture and industrialization, the growing prominence of abolitionism emerged in tandem with more heated discussions of working conditions and the rights of wage laborers, or "free laborers." Although the 1830s did not witness the sort of working-class organization that would emerge later in the century, this decade and the one following it represented what historian Kim Voss calls a "moment of class formation" in England and the United States (5). In the northern United States, skilled artisans and workers in textile factories began protesting for a ten-hour workday, rights to universal education, public relief for the poor, and fair labor contracts. These decades also saw the rise and fall of Britain's first radical labor movement, Chartism. In the United States, European-influenced reformers and Owenites such as Frances Wright and Stephen Simpson—the leader of the Working Men's Party in Philadelphia—advocated for reform. The Working Men's Party spurred the organization of the Locofocos, the radical labor-oriented faction of the Democratic Party that lasted up through the 1840s.[13] Throughout the decades leading up to the Civil War, numerous pro-labor newspapers such as the *Working Man's Advocate* (New York) and the *Mechanic's Free Press* (Philadelphia) also emerged, and labor advocates circulated pamphlets such as the *Ten Hour Day Circular* (1835) to outline the injustices endured by the American wage laborer and demand reforms. Although it was published in 1861, Rebecca Harding Davis's *Life in the Iron Mills* is set during the 1830s, and like Elizabeth Gaskell's fiction set in England in the same decade, presented an incisive critique of labor conditions in the factories and factory towns of the northern Untied States.[14]

The transatlantic debates over free labor and those over slavery were always connected, especially in terms of their rhetoric. Labor activists in both Britain and the United States frequently used the metaphor of slavery and the term *wage slave* to refer to working conditions in industrial sectors, and many activists evoked slavery as a parallel to the conditions of free laborers in their writing. Four years before she published *The Life and Adventures of Michael Armstrong, the Factory Boy,* Frances Trollope published her antislavery novel, *The Life and Adventures of Jonathan Jefferson Whitlaw; or, Scenes on the Mississippi* (1836). The book was based on her experiences traveling in the American Southwest, and the scenes on the novel's Mississippi plantation mirror those in the British factories in the later novel. In the Chartist newspaper the *Northern Star,* one article published in 1837, "Black Slavery!" describes the beating and subsequent death of a female slave. The passage is almost identical to the famous scene in Frederick Douglass's 1845 narrative that describes the beating of his Aunt Hester: blood oozing, lacerations on her back, screams. The piece concludes, "In struggling for universal liberty, we know no distinction between black and white; while we abominate the cant of the money mongering hypocrites who affect to bewail the miseries of Colonial Slavery and labour at the same time, to make the conditions of the British freeman to be full as bad; we hope never to forget that the black slaves are our brethren." For many labor activists, slavery—either as a metaphor or through realistic descriptions—was a means of tapping into the "struggle for universal liberty" at a moment when a rapidly changing economy raised issues of human rights on both sides of the Atlantic.[15]

The slave narratives themselves emerge from a context directly connected to labor movements in both England and the United States. William Lloyd Garrison attained much of his prominence as an abolitionist in America through his association with the antislavery movement in Britain, which successfully abolished slavery in British dominions in 1833. The British Anti-Slavery League, with which Garrison had connections, also had several Chartists as members and was supported by the labor movement. In 1840, Garrison attended the World's Anti-Slavery Convention in London organized by Joseph Sturge, an abolitionist and Chartist. That year the *Liberator* reprinted a letter from a Scottish Chartist, Charles M'Ewan, with Garrison's annotations. The letter recounts a speech given by Garrison at the convention and is followed by an intertextual dialogue between Garrison and M'Ewan on the subject of the British working class. While Garrison chastises M'Ewan for his use of the word *slave* to describe free laborers, he ultimately upholds the need for the British government to enact reforms ("Scottish Chartists").[16] In a later issue, in 1847, Garrison takes the same tone in reply to another letter laying out the need for labor reform, agreeing, without any real conviction or plan, that the current "system"—one presumes he means contracts or working conditions—should indeed be revised ("Free Labor"). Frederick Douglass, too, had direct connections to Chartism and British labor reform after his first trip to England in 1845. During the trip, he met with several Chartist leaders and actually came out in support of the movement in a speech. When Douglass returned to the United States, he began his own abolitionist paper, the *North Star*.

While it clearly references the use of the star to guide escaped slaves to the North, the title also echoes that of a prominent Chartist newspaper, the *Northern Star.* And throughout the 1840s and 1850s, the *North Star* printed articles by Douglass and others criticizing both the American and British labor systems.[17]

Yet Garrison's halfhearted and somewhat contentious endorsements of British labor movements in the *Liberator* reveal the fraught relationship between American abolitionism and labor reform. For many antislavery activists, especially those in the United States, the arguments against slavery also upheld the virtues of the free market. In reaction to proslavery, anticapitalist advocates such as George Fitzhugh, abolitionist movements on both sides of the Atlantic drew their philosophies of political economy from eighteenth-century writers such as Adam Smith.[18] For many abolitionists, including Gerrit Smith and Theodore Dwight Weld, slavery presented a direct contradiction to the basic premise of capitalism and the free market: "free" labor and the autonomy of the individual.[19] American abolitionists rallied around the ideology of liberal capitalism, which held the promise of productive individual labor touted by laissez-faire principles, a contrast to the constrictive and decidedly unfree labor represented by slavery. Such outright endorsement of free labor as an antidote to slavery may have been a rationalization on the part of abolitionists who did, indeed, witness the problems with the American and British labor systems.[20] However, the repeated comparisons between slavery and the "truly free" labor in abolitionist writing reveals the movement leaders' fundamental trust in the liberal capitalist ideals of the free market.

Examples of such argumentation also appeared in the *Liberator* and provided the context for many of the well-known slave narratives. In an August 1833 article, John Greenleaf Whittier presents a list of arguments against slavery, one of the more prominent being its effects on labor and the economy in the United States. Drawing from the free labor–slave labor dichotomy, he writes: "In the free States *labor is reputable.* The statesmen, whose eloquence has electrified a nation, does not disdain in the intervals of the public service to handle the axe and the hoe. And the woman whose beauty, talents and accomplishments have won the admiration of all, deems it no degradation to 'look well to her household.' . . . But the Slave stamps with indelible ignominy the character of occupation" ("Whittier's

Reply").[21] In this vision of a liberal capitalist utopia, free labor empowers those who have access to it, while slavery quenches the liberating impulse and remains an "ignominious stamp" on the kinds of labor performed by the slave. More than two decades later, Garrison used the *Liberator* to promote a speech he gave in Wilmington, Delaware, claiming that "we demonstrated, not only on the plainest principles of political economy, but by a strong array of undeniable facts, the destructive and demoralizing tendency of the slave system, and the wonderful productiveness of free labor and free institutions" ("Lecture"). And in the midst of the controversy over the Kansas-Nebraska Act, the paper's poetry section printed "Song of a Kansas Emigrant," by Almira Seymour. Between odes to the "Patriot-Pilgrims" of the West, the poem cries:

> *Rights of Freemen for all!* With the hands of *free*
> *labor*
> We till the free soil that a just God has given;
> No chains for our children, no stripes for our neigh-
> bor—
> Who enter our borders, their shackles are riven. (Second emphasis mine)

In each of these depictions, the abolitionist paper frames the conversation over slavery so that free labor is a virtuous good beneficial to all of society, while slavery and bondage are both a moral and economic wrong.[22]

In turn, the relationship between the antislavery movement and the labor movement in the United States was antagonistic, tense at best.[23] Activists who spoke out against "wage slavery" criticized abolitionists for overlooking the problems with free labor in the North, and as the earlier quotation from the *Northern Star* indicates, many went so far as to claim that labor conditions for the working class were "full as bad" as—or worse than—the conditions of slavery. In "The Laboring Classes" (1840), a famous essay that originally appeared in the *Boston Quarterly Review,* the preacher and labor activist Orestes Brownson declares:[24] "In regard to labor two systems obtain; one that of slave labor, the other that of free labor. Of the two, the first is, in our judgment, except so far as the feelings are concerned, the least oppressive. . . . As to actual freedom one has just about as much as the other. The laborer at wages had all the disadvantages of freedom and none of its blessings, while the slave, if denied the blessings, is freed from the disadvantages. We are no advocates of slavery, we are as heartily opposed to it as any modern abolitionist can be; but we say frankly that, if there must always be a laboring population distinct from proprietors and employers, we regard the slave system as decidedly preferable to the system at wages" (10).

Despite his rather halfhearted protests to the contrary, Brownson's denunciation of the current free labor system echoes that of the proslavery southerner George Fitzhugh fifteen years later.[25] In using the standard "slavery versus free labor" comparison, his logic is drawn into an inadvertent defense of slavery.[26] Similarly, British labor reformers utilized the comparison to the ends of depicting slavery as the preferred state. In her analysis of the Chartist poetry that appeared in labor newspapers, Kelly Mays notes, "Working to show that the black slave's situation is not only different from but also better than that of the British worker, such poems appropriate and modify abolitionist representational strategies in order to generate sympathy and support for the specifically white British worker" (141). And as with Brownson in the United States, that rewriting ultimately becomes a presentation of slavery as an ideal counterpart to "'white slavery' in 'the land of the free'" (Mays 150).

If the language of labor activists distantly emulated that of proslavery southerners such as Fitzhugh, then often labor organizations evinced a similar form of racist logic prevalent in defenses of the slave system. Labor historians have highlighted the ways in which the nineteenth-century white working class in the United States unified around a racist ideology.[27] This stance identified black Americans as a threat in terms of labor competition but also presented slaves and former slaves as antithetical to the image of an industrial and progressive working class. "Chattel slavery stood as the ultimate expression of the denial of liberty," historian David Roediger writes, "but republicanism also suggested that long acceptance of slavery betokened weakness, degradation and an unfitness for freedom. The Black population symbolized that degradation" (66). The pattern also follows for Chartist labor reformers. Although British workers rallied around the antislavery cause in Britain, many held labor reform as a much higher priority than abolition.[28] Again relying on the slavery versus free labor dichotomy drawn by both abolitionists and labor reformers, working-class whites unified around the correlating racial designations.

Yet the nineteenth-century labor reform movement was deeply divided by classifications outside of race: the split between skilled versus unskilled labor more clearly defined the movement. In contrast to Britain or France, labor movements in the United States were dominated by skilled artisans and craft workers.[29] This fact presents an interesting, and somewhat contradictory, trend: while craft workers were necessary to the formation of labor movements in America, they also frequently excluded the less-skilled or unskilled workers from such movements. Citing the example of anti-Irish sentiment that ran through the ranks of the American working class in the 1830s and 1840s, historian Jonathan Glickstein points out that the racial divides have more to do with a working-class abhorrence of unskilled labor: "The self-definition undergone by northern white male craftsmen during the antebellum decades of incipient industrialization—during the so-called crisis of skilled labor—was shaped not merely or even primarily by skin color per se; it was shaped at least as much by confrontation with an assortment of negative reference groups of varying ethnicity, gender, and age. These latter groups were broadly linked together by their ostensible lack of a respectable economic expertise or competence" (*American Exceptionalism* 95–6). Included in these "negative reference groups"—in addition to Irish immigrants, women, and children—were slaves.

In all, during the 1830s and up through the Civil War, there was a climate in the United States that devalued the labor of slaves as unskilled and thus antithetical to the tenets of the free market that most labor advocates and abolitionists upheld. While abolitionists presented slaves' access to the free market as predicated on their escape from slavery, labor activists viewed slaves and former slaves as inherently degraded, either because of racial attitudes or because of the slaves' supposed distance from the free market. Thus, during the height of their popularity in the 1830s, 1840s, and 1850s, the context of the slave narratives was shaped by the intersections of debates over slavery and discussions of skilled and unskilled wage labor. Rather than being relegated to a no-man's-land of unskilled labor, the narratives reveal the very centrality of slave labor and, more important, skilled slave labor to the U.S. economy. Thus, former slaves' emphasis on their labor and economic value in the narratives reveals an engagement with economic modernization and, further, how the possession of skilled labor allowed slaves and former slaves to rewrite their roles in the modern global economy.

"Learn Trades or Starve!"

In light of the discourse surrounding free labor in the mid-nineteenth century, many slave narratives—especially those that are now designated as the canon of the genre (those by Bibb, Brown, Douglass, and Jacobs)—are counterpoints to the prevailing view that slaves and former slaves were unable to access the free market economy due to their "unskilled" status. Indeed, scholars have already observed the narratives' efforts to emphasize the labor and industry of former slaves. Some situate the narratives in the tradition of American exceptionalism and the American dream, while others interpret the narratives as responding to the emerging capitalist order of the eighteenth century.[30] Yet most of these studies subsume the emphasis on labor under the impulse of the "Protestant work ethic," in which industry, dedication, and hard work are ultimately rewarded. Further, discussions of labor in the narratives are often limited to the sections that take place in free states.

However, many of the narratives also channel the ideology of liberal capitalism and the free market that sustained the very system that kept them in bondage. While there are narratives that adopt the rhetoric of Protestant virtue,[31] narratives such as those by Bibb, Brown, and Douglass are also responses to the abolitionist and labor reform debates that labeled slave labor as fundamentally degraded. These former slaves present their enslaved selves not as long-suffering and hardworking victims but as hardworking and self-propelled individuals according to the free market ideologies that drove both the southern plantation economy and the northern factory system.

This sort of positioning becomes clear in light of the contemporaneous discussions of labor but also in the discourses surrounding the labor of black Americans in the decades following the initial publication of the narratives. Articles that appeared in Frederick Douglass's newspapers during the late 1840s and up through the 1850s consistently advocated for black Americans to embrace skilled labor as an eventual avenue to social and political equality.[32] Beginning in 1853, Douglass advocated for an industrial and mechanics school for black men and published a series of articles in his second paper, simply titled *Frederick Douglass's Paper.* His frequently quoted editorial "Learn Trades or Starve!" proclaims that free black Americans must learn skilled trades because the less skilled are going to new immigrants.[33] Another article a few months later similarly prescribes: "Make Your Sons Mechanics and Farmers, Not Waiters, Porters, and Barbers." Performing the skilled-unskilled labor divide that characterized the labor reform movement during these decades, Douglass's articles reveal how former slaves acknowledged the ongoing discussions of free labor in a changing economic climate.[34]

However, rather than devaluing slave labor, the narratives frame it in such a way that highlights the connection to skilled labor in a capitalist economy. In this sense, the more popular narratives—such as those by Bibb, Brown, Douglass, and later Jacobs—can be read as products of the rhetorical situation faced by black abolitionists. Discussions of the work of slaves and black Americans in these narratives, and in the later articles by Douglass, are the result of efforts to make slave labor legitimate and connect the role of black workers to an emerging capitalist order. Rather than applying the slave versus free labor dichotomy to all forms of enslaved labor, these narratives recalibrate the spectrum of labor in the southern economy to represent their subjects as active members of a free market economy in the South and the North.

To again present Douglass as an example, a significant moment in his 1845 memoir reveals the dynamics between slave and free skilled and unskilled labor in the southern economy. In a frequently cited scene from the *Narrative,* Douglass is hired out by his master in Baltimore to work in a shipyard as an apprentice and general assistant. While there, the white ship workers and carpenters threaten to strike, claiming "they would not work with free colored workmen. Their reason for this, as alleged, was, that if free colored carpenters were encouraged, they would soon take the trade into their own hands, and poor white men would be thrown out of employment" (95). In the wake of this discontent, Douglass becomes a target for the white workers and is severely beaten. This scene is often read, rightly so, as an example of white working-class racism, of the type Douglass himself would experience again when escaping to the North.[35]

However, the tendency to merge this scene with Douglass's later experiences as a free laborer elides the narrative's presentation of his experiences *as a slave* who is laboring. At this point, Douglass is not a free laborer, nor is he a skilled laborer, and the *Narrative* takes care to highlight this difference. Instead, Douglass points out that the physical violence he endures is as an unskilled slave laborer. After describing the labor dispute, Douglass comments in the narrative: "Now, though this did not extend to me *in form,* it did reach me in fact. My fellow-apprentices very soon began to feel it *degrading* to them to work with me" (95, my emphasis). With the use of the term *degrading,* Douglass's language mirrors discussions of labor in both the abolitionist writings and those of labor reform. Slave labor, as opposed to free labor, is degrading. But more important, unskilled slave labor is degrading when placed alongside skilled free labor. Jonathan Glickstein observes that such violent conflicts and outbursts can be read alongside "the pains that masters and journeymen proudly took to differentiate their own skilled and manly competence from more subsistent, unskilled drudge labor" (*American Exceptionalism* 88). Douglass's *Narrative* participates in this sort of pattern by recognizing the divide. After this abuse, Douglass's master places him in another shipyard, where he learns the trade of calking, quickly becomes a skilled laborer, and then escapes from bondage.

The narratives' careful distinction between skilled and unskilled labor by enslaved individuals taps into contemporary debates over questions of labor and draws in the abolitionist cause as part and parcel of the issues surrounding the free market and mid-nineteenth-century industrialization. In his study connecting the abolitionist movement to the emergence of free market capitalism, historian Thomas Haskell argues that market culture forced abolitionists to alter their rhetorical approaches. As the market increasingly dominated the transatlantic culture of the nineteenth century, individuals saw the connections between societies, countries, and locales in new ways.[36] The same argument applies to the authors of the slave narratives and their representations of the violence of slavery, their labor as slaves, and the southern slave system itself. The southern plantation economy, in this sense, is not an isolated space in the narratives but is integral to the transatlantic economy. In turn, slavery in these narratives is not a unique issue but one that affects the entire world, connected by an increasingly expanding and industrializing global economy. Thus, the work of the formerly enslaved narrators in presenting their lives is often contradictory: the former slaves must at once denounce slavery but also view it as a means by which they found value in their own labor as members of the free market system.

The authors of the narratives use the skilled-unskilled labor divide in labor reform debates to distinguish themselves as autonomous individuals in the free market system through their accomplishments as skilled laborers. Many scholars have observed that literacy is of central importance in the narratives, with the narrators highlighting their first encounters with reading and the efforts they took to learn in a system designed to keep them in ignorance.[37] The narrators often recognize their self-motivated education as a turning point in their lives. Yet the "moment of learning" in the narratives also corresponds with the narrators' move from unskilled to skilled labor, with their literacy functioning as part of their education as workers. To use Douglass again as a reference point, the 1845 *Narrative* pointedly enacts this learning process. Douglass describes his youth as one passed largely in ignorance, split between time on the Maryland plantation where he was born and the Baltimore house where he spent most of his childhood. While in Baltimore, he learns to read and write, and the narrative spends several paragraphs detailing the effects of reading on his psyche. Yet it is not until he is sent back to work on the plantations that he achieves his full "education." The scene in which he physically battles with Mr. Covey, his master-by-hire, is a pivotal point in the narrative, which Douglass acknowledges as "the turning-point in my career as a slave. It rekindled the few expiring embers of freedom, and revived within me a sense of my own manhood. It recalled the departed self-confidence, and inspired me again with a determination to be free" (72).

While it is easy to read this moment as simply a testament to Douglass's "manhood" through physical and violent defiance, it also indicates the shift in Douglass's education from that of a menial, unskilled laborer to that of a skilled, educated worker. On Covey's plantation, Douglass performs only the physical labor necessary for running a farm: baling hay, processing cotton, caring for livestock. But after he is released from Covey and after the altercation, as Douglass puts it, his "tendency was upward." Not only is the rest of the narrative characterized by his attempts to escape to the North, but those attempts are more realizable as Douglass becomes a skilled worker according to the definitions of the nineteenth-century free market. William Andrews observes that thereafter in the narrative, "the right at issue is pragmatic and economic, not abstract or romantic" (128). After a failed escape attempt from a Maryland farm, Douglass is sent back to Baltimore. There he begins his work in the shipyards, learns the trade of calking, and thereby escapes to the North.

Similarly, in his *Narrative,* Henry Bibb aligns his education as a laborer with his education more generally. In fact, most of Bibb's narrative is dominated by his movement through the various modes of labor and slave employment in the Southwest. Born in Kentucky yet hired out and sold to areas all along the Mississippi River, Bibb's narrative traverses almost all levels of the southern slave system. At the beginning of the text, Bibb describes the trajectory of his "education": "I confess that it was no disadvantage to be passed through the hands of so many families, as the only source of information that I had to enlighten my mind, consisted in what I could see and hear from others. . . . Among other good *trades* I learned the art of running away to perfection. I made a regular *business* of it, and never gave it up, until I had broke the bands of slavery" (15, my emphasis). Bibb's use of the words *trade* and *business* to describe his attempts at running away, though ironic, indicates the merging of debates over skilled labor with the general development of Bibb as an enslaved individual. As he presents it in the narrative, he develops skill in escaping, which sets him apart from other enslaved men and women. That, coupled with Bibb's repeated emphasis on a fundamental wrong of slavery—its robbing the individual of his wages and possession of his labor—foregrounds the importance of free and skilled labor throughout the narrative.

William Wells Brown's *Narrative* also characterizes his education as tied to his increasing skill as a worker. Like Bibb, Brown marks the story of his life as a slave in terms of his various employments and masters. Also like Bibb, Brown spent most of his life as a slave along the Mississippi River and not employed on a plantation. In fact, he takes care to differentiate between the unskilled work done by field hands from that of his work in urban areas or on steamboats. As the letter from Edmund Quincy printed at the beginning of the narrative declares, Brown's tale "presents a different phase of the infernal slave-system from that portrayed in the admirable story of Mr. Douglass, and gives us a glimpse of its hideous cruelties in other portions of its domain" (v).[38] Although in many ways this alternative perspective adds to the work of portraying slave labor as not entirely degraded when compared with free, much of Brown's employment as a slave was with a slave trader. In this sense, the narrative depicts Brown's labor as a slave as educating him in terms of both learning trades and exposing him to the literal and institutional violence of slavery. Paralleling Douglass's and Bibb's narratives, Brown characterizes his time as a skilled worker as the moment of awakening. While still a young man, Brown was employed in a St. Louis newspaper office, and he reflects: "I am chiefly indebted to [the editor], and to my employment in the printing office, for what little learning I obtained while in slavery" (27). In this way, although he is less ironic than Bibb, Brown also connects his increased experience as a skilled laborer with a growing desire to escape bondage. As with Douglass's "tendency upward" after his struggle with Covey, after his work at the printing office Brown obtains a job on a steamboat, where he is exposed to more forms of labor and more of the violence of the slave system. Ultimately, these experiences culminate in his determination to escape.

Aside from the emphasis on skilled labor, the narratives also highlight the diversity of slave labor in a way that undercuts the slave versus free labor dichotomy. The lives of the narrators vary depending upon where they were in the South, and their labor, like the work of free laborers, adapts according to the locale. So, while Douglass's narrative displays a blend of rural farmwork and port trades of the East Coast, Bibb and Brown are located in the growing Southwest and the Mississippi Valley. As such, their labor fits more with the expanding large-scale plantations, land speculation, and river-based employment that form the backdrop of the Southwest humor stories. Indeed, scholars have made the connection between the narratives and trickster tales.[39] Others, like Raymond Hedin, have described them as "road narratives," in which Bibb and Brown's constant movement and the episodic nature of the narratives represents an adaptation of the "picaro."[40]

However, Bibb's and Brown's presentation of their labor and lives as slaves in the Southwest fits more with the figure of the confidence man who populates the humor sketches. And in many ways, their lives were shaped by the same economic forces that coincided with the rise of Southwest humor. The Bibb and Brown of the narratives have traits of the free agents who swindle and sue their way into owning plantations and profiting from land speculation. With the former slaves, their cunning presents them as skilled, autonomous individuals and eventually allows them to obtain their freedom. Throughout his narrative, Bibb adopts the same slightly mocking tone that characterizes his reflections on the "trade" of running away, and many of his exploits involve tricking and cajoling his way to freedom. During his final escape, Bibb boards a steamboat and takes up with a group of deck passengers. He buys them drinks, and after an hour or so, he remarks, "I was thought to be one of the most liberal and gentlemanly men on board . . . they were ready to do anything for me" (168). So, when the porter comes around, Bibb's new "friends" buy his ticket for him. A famous scene in Brown's narrative also involves a "trick" he plays on a free black man. When Brown's master sentences him to a whipping at the local jail, Brown is sent with a note to give to the jailer. Knowing the goal of the errand, Brown gives the note to a passing man, who then receives his whipping. In a similar manner to Simon Suggs, Brown exercises his education through various employments to avoid the violence of slavery. While much has been done in scholarship with the ways in which the men explain away their misdeeds in the narratives, these moments of "shiftiness" reveal the manner in which the authors take care to present themselves as intelligent, able men in the growing Southwest economy.

Perhaps one of the best examples of a slave narrative that constructs an image of skilled slave labor is James W. C. Pennington's *The Fugitive Blacksmith; or, Events in the History of James W. C. Pennington, Pastor of a Presbyterian Church, New York, Formerly a Slave in the State of Maryland, United States* (1849).[41] The title is the first significant departure in the text from the rhetoric of most slave narratives and discussions of labor. Many of the narratives take pains to indicate the author's status as a former slave. For instance, the subtitle to Douglass's 1845 narrative is "An American Slave. Written by Himself," while William Wells Brown's is by "A Fugitive Slave. Written by Himself." These subtitles place emphasis first on the author's role as a formerly enslaved individual, then on their escape from bondage, and finally on their literacy, all of which would have marked them as unique, especially to white northern audiences. Pennington's narrative, however, characterizes him first as a blacksmith and tradesman. Although he is a "fugitive," the word *slave* is not included until the very end of the title, which highlights Pennington's skilled labor as a blacksmith, rather than his position as a slave. The title then implicitly ranks the importance of Pennington's identities in the order they are mentioned: first as a skilled tradesman, then by his name, then in his chosen profession (pastor) in the city where he is a free man, and finally, according to his origins as a slave in Maryland.

Likewise, the preface shifts the emphasis of the narrative from a description of the particular violence Pennington experienced while enslaved to the violence of the system as a whole, specifically the economic violence wrought by slavery. He writes, "The being of slavery, its soul and body, lives and moves in the *chattel principle,* the *property principle,* the *bill of sale principle;* the cart-whip, starvation, and nakedness, are its inevitable consequences" (iv–v, my emphasis). This is not to say that Pennington downplays the violence he and other slaves experienced and continue to experience at the time of the narrative's publication. Instead, his concern, as he notes later, is to "shew [*sic*] the cruelties incident to the system" (9). As with the title's shift in emphasis, the opening pages of *The Fugitive Blacksmith* reframe Pennington's life story to make it less about his degradation as an individual and more about the degradation inherent in the system itself. As a skilled tradesman and professional, Pennington, in fact, is far from degraded as his narrative presents it.

Continuing its modification of the format established in other slave narratives, Pennington's tale describes his early childhood and family life with an even greater emphasis on economics and skilled labor. The text begins with an overview of the type of agriculture in the area of Maryland where he was owned but then quickly moves to a description of his family. The overview of his master and descriptions of slave life, which occupy the first few chapters of most narratives, is tacked on in a final chapter at the end of the book, almost as an afterthought. Instead, Pennington highlights his early family life and his education as a tradesman. Part of the reason for this difference is that Pennington knew his parents, who were both enslaved. He and his eleven brothers and sisters lived in close proximity most of their lives, which was uncommon and rarely depicted in the popular slave narratives. Throughout his text, Pennington's family—most of whom were also trained as skilled workers—forms a close-knit unit that is highly unusual for their circumstances and one that is sustained long after Pennington escapes bondage. Part of the appendix, for example, consists of a letter he wrote to his family after he escaped and while they were still enslaved.

The description of his early childhood is also marked by his education as a skilled laborer; beginning "at the age of eleven" (4), Pennington is hired out and apprenticed to various masons and blacksmiths. He also learns to read through his trade. Later in the narrative, he explains: "My duties as a blacksmith have made me acquainted with the figures on the common mechanics' square. There was a day-book kept in the shop, in which the overseer usually charged the smithwork we did for the neighbours. I have spent entire Sabbaths looking over the pages of that book; knowing the names of persons to whom certain pieces of work were charged, together with their prices, I strove anxiously to learn to write in this way. I got paper, and picked up feathers about the yard, and made ink of—berries. . . . In this way I have learnt to make a few of the letters, but I cannot write my own name, nor do I know the letters of the alphabet" (42). As Pennington takes care to document, literacy was only achievable once he was able to perform skilled labor. Those abilities then form the core of his individual sense of self, as the title of his text indicates. After his early education in the opening pages, Pennington, for the rest of the narrative, often refers to himself as "a blacksmith" or makes mention of his blacksmith training. Through this emphasis on his trade, the skilled labor of the entire family, and the cohesive sense of community that stems from these abilities, *The Fugitive Blacksmith* portrays Pennington and his family as akin to middle-class tradespeople in the North and Britain, skilled workers in a free market who would be more sympathetic to the mid-nineteenth-century reading public.

The narrative creates an identity for Pennington that deviates from the typical characterizations of unskilled slave labor that circulated at the time—he is a skilled tradesman who is part of a proud family of skilled tradesmen. As a result, the narrative turning point does not just come with the shift from unskilled to skilled labor but at a moment in which Pennington witnesses violence that causes him to question his own alienation from his skilled labor.[42] While tending to livestock, his father is severely beaten by their master. Pennington describes his family's anger at the "insult" and the "open rupture" it caused in their lives; as he explains it, "The spirit of the whole family was roused." He then reflects, "Whenever I thought of the great contrast between my father's *employment* on that memorable Monday morning . . . and the barbarous conduct of my master, I could not help despising the proud abuser of my sire." He declares, "I never was a *Slave* after it" (7, first emphasis mine).

As Pennington presents it in the narrative, the wrong done to his family is the discrepancy between the value of their talents and labor, or "employment," and the manner in which they are treated by their master. As Douglass's fight with Covey turns him from a slave to a man, the alienation from skilled work leads to Pennington's awakening and his desire to be free. Shortly thereafter, Pennington himself is beaten, and he further declares: "I had always aimed to be trustworthy; and feeling a high degree of mechanical pride, I had aimed to do my work with dispatch and skill, my *blacksmith's pride and taste* was one thing that had reconciled me so long to remain a slave. I sought to distinguish myself in the finer branches of the business by invention and finish . . . but after this, I found that my mechanic's pleasure and pride were gone. I thought of nothing but the family disgrace under which we were smarting, and how to get out of it" (8–9, my emphasis). Although his and his father's beatings are appalling, the descriptions do not contain the dripping blood and moans to incite reader sympathy. Instead, Pennington adopts the appeals of an independent, free laborer who takes pride in his work, but the system in which he labors is inherently unjust. Much like the labor reformers who evoked wage slavery in their calls for better working conditions, the moment demonstrates the devaluation of individual labor in the slave system and, specifically, the talent needed for skilled labor. For Pennington, like the labor advocates of the era, his labor is his defining point of identity. Yet however much he may define himself according to his skill as a blacksmith, in the southern slave system, that skill is never possessed by him but by his owner. As a slave and personal property, his personal identity, or "inner world," is not only separate from his labor but is meaningless. When it is made clear that his labor is treated as something separate from him as an individual and the "pleasure and pride" he associates with this identity are worthless, he can no longer remain a slave.

Therefore, if the narratives by Douglass, Bibb, and Brown perform the transition from unskilled to skilled labor, then Pennington's is predicated on the existence of skilled labor in the southern slave economy in order to relate the story of his eventual escape. After the beatings, Pennington flees on foot, and the next few chapters detail his escape much in the manner of the Bibb and Brown narratives: like the confidence men, he relies on his wits to evade capture. Again, however, those methods of survival are often derived from his training as a blacksmith. At one point, when he is confronted with a potential captor, he sizes up the man, remarking, "My habits as a blacksmith had given my eye and hand such mechanical skill, that I felt quite sure that if I could only get a stone in my hand, and have time to wield it, I should not miss his knee-pan" (20). Later, when Pennington is discovered on the road and held by a group of farmers outside of Baltimore, he uses his past observations of the clientele in the blacksmith and mason shops to get out of the situation. He claims to have been part of a gang of slaves being sold by a trader, who took ill and died of smallpox. When he is able to provide the name and an accurate description of the trader, the men fear he is contagious and relax their guard; Pennington is then able to escape again (24–5).

Pennington's skills also mark him, for better or worse, within a system governed by the "chattel principle." After his escape, his pursuers often refer to him as the "blacksmith." While in hiding near a farm, Pennington claims to have overheard one of the men describing him to the farmer as "a blacksmith" and nothing else (36). Later, when he has established himself in the North, he asks a friend to inquire after the purchase of his family from his former master. In the response reprinted in the narrative, which was a decisive refusal, his master adds, "Jim was a first-rate mechanic, (blacksmith) and was worth to me one thousand dollars" (62). Even after he has physically escaped bondage, Pennington cannot escape his worth in the slave trade and the skills that confer that worth.

Pennington's text builds upon the consciousness of the market that pervades all of the slave narratives but expands on that economic awareness through its adjustments to the slave narrative tradition. *The Fugitive Blacksmith* becomes a road narrative, telling the tale of a traveling journeyman from a line of tradespeople, who uses his ingenuity and talent to free himself and become literally and socioeconomically mobile. Yet it also highlights the tension that came with the constant market presence that defined the lives of slaves and former slaves. While Pennington's narrative may present him as an autonomous individual due to his skilled labor, that labor also shaped his identity even beyond enslavement, when he is forever the "Fugitive Blacksmith." In short, Pennington's narrative models a paradigm of the free market but does so within the limited structures of mid-nineteenth-century labor discourse and the rhetoric of debates over slavery.

Although it may do well for men to portray their labor as slaves in the framework of the skilled-unskilled divide, the same portrayal for women during the nineteenth century would be much more difficult. For the most part, women during that time were excluded from any forms of labor but unskilled or domestic labor. As a result, women's labor, especially black women's labor, was often automatically associated with the degrading drudgery of slave labor. Female slaves were either field hands or house servants; few could learn trades. And for many enslaved women, breeding was also a key component of their "labor" in the South. As a result, critics often read women's narratives of slavery and work in the nineteenth century through the lens of domesticity, the home, and the disruption of the biological family.[43]

In the case of Harriet Jacobs's 1861 *Incidents in the Life of a Slave Girl,* the narrative style of the text, rather than her labor as a slave, becomes a focus in critical discussions, which overlooks the narrative's rhetorical connections to the labor debates of the era. Often cited for its frequent evocation of the sentimental and domestic traditions, *Incidents* is interpreted as Jacobs's attempt to bring herself to the level of her white middle-class readers who were also mothers.[44] Like the narratives written by Douglass, Bibb, Brown, and Pennington, however, Jacobs begins *Incidents* with her parentage and characterizes herself as a tradesman's daughter. According to Jacobs, her father was "a carpenter, and considered so intelligent and skilful in his trade, that, when buildings out of the common line were to be erected, he was sent for from long distances, to be head workman. On condition of paying his mistress two hundred dollars a year, and supporting himself, he was allowed to work at his trade, and manage his own affairs" (11). Immediately, the description conjures the image of an independent, skilled laborer as a way to distinguish Jacobs by proxy from the unskilled laborers in the slave system.[45]

Jacobs's grandmother is the other skilled worker in *Incidents,* and she presents another, equally important way in which Jacobs can characterize herself as part of the skilled labor force. As with her father, Jacobs represents her grandmother as a businesswoman and skilled domestic laborer: "She was much praised for her cooking; and her nice crackers became so famous in the neighborhood that many people were desirous of obtaining them. . . . The business proved profitable; and each year she laid by a little" (13). Through her business, Jacobs's grandmother eventually gains her freedom. This successful business also supplies the wants of the young Jacobs, even when she is owned by a master: "I was indebted to *her* for all my comforts, spiritual or temporal. It was *her* labor that supplied my scanty wardrobe" (19–20). By repeatedly emphasizing that her grandmother's labor provided her necessities and defined her identity, Jacobs creates an image of a slave family that is somewhat independent financially and emotionally from their owners. Further, the depiction of her grandmother's productive labor gestures to a more radical reclamation of women's labor. Rather than simply focusing on the more male-centered figure of the artisan, Jacobs refashions domestic labor to claim it as skilled and autonomous. Her family, then, resembles a maternally defined version of Pennington's family, a family of "artisans"—male and female—whose skilled labor marks them as unique in the context of nineteenth-century labor discourse.

But significantly, Jacobs's grandmother does not fulfill the promises of free labor in the manner offered up by abolitionist and labor reform advocates. Although she is independent, she remains in the South her entire life, working for slave owners and, after gaining her freedom, her former owners. Jacobs, in contrast, presents herself as an autonomous individual, but by dint of her exclusion from the sphere of free labor, she must harness other traits identified with laborers on the free market. In this case, the key characteristic is mobility, the common attribute for all of the narratives by men, in which their physical mobility eventually translates to their escape from slavery and their eventual socioeconomic mobility (at least within the confines of the racialized structures of the nineteenth-century

United States). While Jacobs's grandmother never achieves that mobility, Jacobs and the other, younger members of her family do. To illustrate the importance Jacobs places on mobility (and thus escape from slavery) in the narrative, she tells the story of her uncles Phillip and Benjamin, who both escape from North Carolina to New York. However, Phillip returns to be with his mother, who then works to earn his liberty: "After a while she succeeded in buying Phillip. She paid eight hundred dollars, and came home with the precious document that secured his freedom. The happy mother and son sat together by the old hearthstone that night, telling how proud they were of each other, and how they would prove to the world that they could take care of themselves. . . . We all concluded by saying, 'He that is *willing* to be a slave, let him be a slave.'" (43). Although Jacobs praises her grandmother's bravery and hard work, the tone of this passage is unmistakable: that of bewilderment, tinged with disapproval. Jacobs's grandmother represents the skilled, hardworking industry of the middle class, but her purchase of Phillip after his return to the South signals a form of immobility more in line with the unskilled drudgery of the slave. In contrast, Jacobs, her uncle Benjamin, and eventually her brother, William—all tradesman's children—adopt the mobility needed in a free market to first achieve their freedom, then to adapt to life in the North.

Mobility as a qualifying trait merges the demand for skilled labor with the patterns of women's labor and the domestic sphere in Jacobs's *Incidents.* In doing so, the narrative imagines a new paradigm for gendered labor in the context of the southern slave economy. According to the narrative of her life in slavery and her eventual escape, Jacobs's experience as a daughter of tradespeople makes her an active participant in the modern global economy, just as much as Bibb, Brown, Douglass, and Pennington or the wage workers in the North and abroad.

Thus, the canonical slave narratives published in the decades leading up to the Civil War demonstrate a rhetorical pattern that consistently represents the lives of their authors as part of the free labor that formed the core of an emerging economic order during the mid-nineteenth century. By presenting themselves as skilled and mobile laborers, these authors shifted discussions of slave and free labor by black Americans to the center of debates over labor reform and economic policies in an industrializing Atlantic world. In this sense, the authors affirm the values upheld by proponents of free market capitalism while also undercutting the racist and binary logic that pervaded the abolitionist and labor reform discourses during these decades.

In the examples of the popular slave narratives from the 1830s, 1840s, and 1850s, black authors from the antebellum period represent the central role of black Americans in the nineteenth-century global economy and, specifically, the regional economy of the southern United States. In the language of literary studies, this also places the work of former slaves squarely in the antebellum southern literary tradition. To return to the southern planter image that began this book (see again fig. 1, p. 2), the narratives reposition slave labor and the stories of enslaved individuals directly in the foreground, contradicting the representations of white proslavery advocates who, in their fiction, would ignore enslaved bodies entirely through their revisions and repurposing of regional identity. For the slave narratives, this meant presenting the labor of slaves as viable embodiments of the skilled labor demanded by the mid-nineteenth-century debates over free labor. Rather than nameless tools of racialized capitalism, these representations adapt the rhetoric of the nineteenth-century political economy to envision and promote black Americans as autonomous and active participants in the rapidly changing modern economic landscape. The obscured middle ground of the antebellum South—the always present yet willfully ignored slave labor force that drove the regional and national economy up to the Civil War—is thus represented as the nexus of nineteenth-century global capitalism.

EPILOGUE

How Did We Get Here?

> On this deluge the whole Southern social world, with its two distinct divisions—the shining upper—the dark nether—was reeling and careening, threatening, each moment, to turn once and forever wrong side up, a hope-forsaken wreck.
>
> —George Washington Cable, *John March, Southerner* (1894)

I began this book with two Souths: one, a pastoral agrarian space dotted with plantations; the other, a highly modernized, profitable area driven by global capitalism. Both were undergirded by the labor of enslaved men, women, and children. The reconciliation of these two Souths and their reliance on slave labor occupied the creative energy of the proslavery white authors who made up the southern literary world. And for the men and women who were enslaved in the region, the southern economy shaped the literary representations of their lives and identities.

For most modern readers and audiences, however, one of those Souths dominates the imaginary surrounding the region: the pastoral vision, the one held up by texts such as *I'll Take My Stand* (1930)—and the constant critical reevaluations of the book—as well as the endless "Lost Cause" simulacra that permeate popular discourse.[1] The economic underpinnings and racial violence that sustained the plantation economy often are bypassed in mainstream discussions of the South, in favor of what Tara McPherson calls a "boutique" South that focuses on "the unique and or colorful elements" (9). This "boutiquing" and the resulting popular images of the region maintain the primacy of the foreground illustration that begins this book: the white plantation South (see again fig. 1, p. 2).[2] Although a reexamination of the boutique representations has been ongoing for decades —with many activists, southern studies scholars, and historians being at the forefront of these conversations—the inevitable contentiousness of these discussions indicates the persistence of an agrarian ideal represented by the white planter lounging on a bale of cotton.[3]

Yet after the Civil War, the South was driven by the same dual impulses that structured the region during the antebellum period. In fact, emancipation forced the South to examine its cultural identity and economic networks even more thoroughly in the context of national development. The two Souths continued to exist in tandem, with the antebellum plantation economy laying the foundation for later social and economic patterns during the twentieth and twenty-first centuries: Jim Crow, sharecropping, the prison industrial complex, just to name a few.[4] Not only do these continuities indicate the ideological residue from the antebellum period, but their national prevalence points to the South's centrality in U.S. development over time. As the nation negotiated its recovery from war and its role as a growing world power, the South during the postbellum era—and more important for this study, *representations* of the South—is a case study for how the nation positioned itself in emerging global networks. As a result, the image of the southern planter reclining in front of slave laborers and the apparatuses of manufacturing is not just a nostalgic emblem of an extinct society but a way to understand the nation's place in a global economic system long after the Civil War.[5]

Rather than covering up the violence that stemmed from the history of U.S. slavery and the plantation in the global economy, some postbellum authors highlighted the continuing damage it wrought on a national level. These representations expose the process of simultaneous representation that defined antebellum literature, then move those processes into depictions of the United States as a whole. One of the foremost was George Washington Cable, specifically his 1894–5 novel, *John March, Southerner*.[6] Set in a fictionalized version of southeastern Tennessee and northern Georgia, the novel opens at the end of the Civil War and traces the progress of a small southern town, Suez, through Reconstruction and the 1880s. Cable's novel—as with the antebellum fiction by white southerners—represents an attempt to resolve and reconcile conflicting social and economic ideologies. Yet in a crucial divergence from the earlier representations, *John March, Southerner* indicates how that resolution consistently fails.

George Washington Cable is often held up as the "first modern southern writer," decades before authors such as Ellen Glasgow, William Faulkner, Eudora Welty, or Flannery O'Connor appeared on the literary scene.[7] Both in his biography and his writing, Cable straddles the generational line between antebellum and postbellum southern society. His family moved to New Orleans when numerous families of German descent settled there in the early nineteenth century, and he fought for the Confederacy during the Civil War. Many critics have noted his ambivalence toward slavery and the racialized social system that governed New Orleans and the plantation South generally—a system from which he benefited as a white, upper-class southerner.[8] In his nonfiction, Cable was a caustic critic of past southern institutions and their effects on later generations, and his conflicted attitude toward southern history and society appears in his fictional work, most of which is set in the antebellum South.[9] For instance, his most well-known novel, *The Grandissimes* (1880), relates the story of a New Orleans Creole family during the antebellum period. Through the family members, both black and white, the novel portrays the deleterious effects of slavery and reinforces criticisms Cable voiced throughout his life of the racialized discrimination and oppression that stemmed from the antebellum plantation system and slavery.[10] Given its frank representation of Louisiana history, the violence of slavery, and the racially based social codes in New Orleans, many critics have read the novel as an allegory for postbellum politics and the racism that pervaded the Reconstruction era.[11]

While *John March, Southerner* is not Cable's most popular or critically acclaimed novel, it nonetheless engages with the complexities of the southern economic system and artistic representation in a manner that parallels the antebellum authors of previous decades.[12] Rather than using capitalist ideologies to conceal the central role of racialized slavery in the region's development, however, Cable's representation of the South highlights the history of the institution in modern economic systems, both regionally and nationally. Further, his novel demonstrates that as much as white southerners—or Americans more generally—might want to create a unified, nostalgic version of the region and its role in the nation's history, the realities of that history will always resurface in violent and dramatic ways. While many authors (southern or not) wanted to uphold the "shining upper" of the South, the other South, the "dark nether" of the region's history of violence, would always threaten to overturn those fabricated visions.

Like most works of early southern literature, *John March, Southerner* begins with horrific violence that is quickly subsumed under discussions of economics and politics. The encounter occurs first between Major Garnet, a white former plantation owner and slaveholder, and Cornelius Leggett, his former slave. In response to a perceived affront, Garnet beats Leggett savagely, first with his fists, then with a whip. All of this takes place in front of Garnet's family and servants (other former slaves), who look on, horrified. After the beating, Cornelius snatches up the whip and runs off, only to discover the novel's titular character, a young John March, the eight-year-old son of another local plantation owner. Having also witnessed the beating, John is hiding, terrified. Out of anger and perhaps retaliation, Cornelius turns the whip on John and reenacts the thrashing he just received.

The beating of Cornelius Leggett is described in detail, but the violence to the young John March is only alluded to indirectly. In fact, without careful reading, it is easy to miss. After the encounter with Garnet, Cornelius grabs the whip and flees to the springhouse—where the reader knows John is hiding. Only later is the violence confirmed, when Cornelius brings the child home and John is put to bed by servants: "The child lay chest downward. She lifted his gown, and exposed his back. 'Good Gawd!' whispered the other [servant]" (36). The effect is chilling.

The moment's obvious symbolism is the clash between old and new, in which Garnet represents the Old South and its desperate and violent clinging to the racialized hierarchies represented by the destroyed plantation system. But the violence enacted on young John is what permeates the novel. Just as the postbellum United States is marked by consequences of institutionalized human bondage and the war fought to end that bondage, at least in its obvious forms, the character of John March carries this trauma throughout his life. For the rest of the novel, the event consistently invades discussions of economic development, Reconstruction era politics, and John March's own love story. The violence that is never addressed thus forms the core of the novel and assumes a pervasive role to the end.[13]

Although we could read the beating as a sort of "sins of the fathers visited upon the sons," *John March, Southerner* deliberately turns away from discussions of slavery and the South during the antebellum period to a concentrated focus on the "New South" and national politics. The term *New South* is typically credited to Henry Grady, a southerner and editor for the *Atlanta Constitution.* In a famous series of speeches given in the 1880s, he called for industrialization and economic modernization to revive the postwar New South. These revivals would always place the South firmly in the context of national economic development, for as Grady puts it in one 1886 speech: "We . . . have smoothed the path to southward, wiped out the place where Mason and Dixon's line used to be, and hung our latch-string out to you and yours" (14–15)—"you and yours" in this case being the rest of the country.[14] In this sense, Grady represented a sort of postbellum De Bow, and his New South policies repeatedly advocated free market capitalism as a remedy for all of the South's ills—and by extension, the entire nation's recovery after the Civil War.

Cable's novel, then, balances the two Souths of the postbellum era with the development of the nation as a whole. Rather than mitigating the presence of slavery and violence, *John March* points to the ways in which the region's history and economy are the foundations of broader national development—where the "shining upper" of the United States is always reliant on the "dark nether" of slavery and racial oppression. Cable uses the opening moment of trauma as a way to frame a critique of more contemporary social and economic policies. John March's present-day trauma, rooted in the region's history of violence and racism, comes to represent the perpetuation of corrupt political and economic policies from the antebellum period that shaped later generations during the postbellum era.

The rest of the novel is a complicated portrait of the Reconstruction South that depicts the racial tensions and financial intricacies occupying the entire nation at the end of the nineteenth century. Indicated by his choice of setting and the original proposed title, *Johnny Reb,* Cable wanted to illustrate the entire nation's experience after the war through the specific events surrounding a single, fictional southern community.[15]

With the opening moment of violence, however, the region's present-day development is always focalized through individual, past trauma. In many ways, *John March, Southerner* is a basic Bildungsroman and follows John March's life from the moment of childhood trauma to manhood (including the standard marriage plot typical of nineteenth-century novels). As John matures and attempts to create a new land company from his family's former plantation, the novel narrates the efforts to pull Suez—and by extension the entire South—into the modern era according to New South policies.

The novel sets up its focus on the emergence of the New South from the vestiges of the past in the first few paragraphs, which depict an idyllic landscape but one shaped by industry and commerce: "In the State of Dixie, County of Clearwater, and therefore in the very heart of what was once the 'Southern Confederacy,' lies that noted seat of government of one county and shipping point for three, Suez. The pamphlet of a certain land company . . . mentions the battle of Turkey Creek as having been fought only a mile or so north of the town . . . It also strongly recommends to the attention of both the capitalist and tourist the beautiful mountain scenery" (1). The opening pointedly shifts the focus of the novel from old associations (the southern Confederacy) to new. Instead of the isolated plantation of the antebellum pastoral, the town of Suez is a bustling commercial and political center described by a promotional land pamphlet encouraging investors and potential settlers. The implication is that the New South policies of the postwar era are harbingers for change. Yet the references to the "Southern Confederacy" and "Dixie" indicate that the foundations for such change are the very structures that New South advocates wished to place behind them: slavery and the plantation system.

The indivisible nature of the South's past from the nation's future is clearest in the attempts at reform orchestrated by John March, the character who bears the unseen markers of past trauma. John's land company ultimately fails, and it fails because John is cheated by the men who agree to invest in the project. The group is made up of an equal mix of northern capitalists and southern landowners as well as black businessmen from the area. Notably, two of the potential investors are Major Garnet and Cornelius Leggett. Whenever John is swindled or undercut by a shady business deal in the novel (which happens frequently), the agents of his early trauma always reappear. In these moments, they are in the background, or in brief mentions and asides by the narrator. Over time—and according to the pattern set up in the opening paragraphs of the novel—the two men shift from being representatives of the Old South to being associated with the New South policies espoused by northerners and southerners alike. These figures of early trauma orbit John, and their presence is built into the economic machinations implemented on a national scale. As the narrator puts it, that move from old to new put forth by New South proponents was desired by investors and businessmen throughout the country: "The lighting of every new coke furnace, the setting fire to any local rubbish-heap of dead traditions, seemed just then to Northern longings the blush of a new economic and political dawn over the whole South" (458). Therefore, the inherent social and economic inequalities that lie under the surface of the U.S. political and economic system push into the story, causing the same sort of disruption or uncanny dissonance represented by John's trauma at the beginning of the novel. As a result, the opening moment of violence against John becomes indistinguishable from the novel's representation of modern economic policies and the corruption they encourage.

John March concludes with the revelation of a secret that had been lurking in the background throughout the novel. It involves, of course, Major Garnet and Cornelius Leggett. And in good nineteenth-century literary tradition, there are secret midnight meetings between the two, hints of evil misdeeds by both men, and misplaced or hidden documents scattered throughout the plot that allude to the secret. Normally we would assume this mystery has something to do with Garnet's past, especially for a novel set in the South: a secret mistress, for example, or that Cornelius Leggett is actually Garnet's son.

But in reality, it is the most boring secret to ever drive a novel: John discovers through a miraculously recovered, long lost letter that Garnet had tampered with land records after the war and kept John from inheriting his family's entire estate adjoining the Garnet plantation. Leggett discovered this fact shortly after the war and agreed to keep Garnet's secret—but for a price. The act again follows the pattern of past southern structures shaping, or tainting, future national development. Garnet altered the records during the initial chaos of the postwar period, but he was allowed to continue by the "northern longings" that, as Grady put it, "smoothed the path to southward" and created the New South. Garnet's schemes made everyone rich—except, of course, John, the initial, inadvertent victim of the earlier, more explicit rage and violence.

Adapting the language of economics in this way allows Cable to build a critique of the past into an examination of the present moment—and further, to bring the issues of the Reconstruction era into the national arena, rather than relegating them to an isolated "southern problem." And given the United States' increased role as a global economic and imperial power, this places the region's postwar development firmly in an international context. In the same way that the significance of John's early trauma shifts from a representation of the violence perpetuated in the antebellum South to a larger-scale, more metaphorical violence perpetuated in the U.S. economy and political arena, the novel's focus goes from the sins of the South to the sins of the entire nation and possibly the globe. In this sense, although Cable titled the novel *John March, Southerner* (with the emphasis on *Southerner*), it is a tale of the faults and problems confronted by the entire nation during a moment of turmoil and drastic change occurring internationally. No one escapes the novel's criticisms, not even the former slave Cornelius Leggett.[16] As the novel presents it, the problems that made the South "a thing apart" during the antebellum period were always in mainstream national discourse. And those issues, as Cable presents them, could only be addressed by looking at the evils of the past in light of the corruption of the present and the future.

Cavaliers and Economists is an attempt to answer the question posed by the title of this epilogue: "How did we get here?" Postbellum texts such as *John March* maintain the dynamic of the two Souths from the antebellum period. As the novel reveals, despite the popularity of a certain image of the South, a blend of liberal capitalist principles and the adherence to racially and socially oppressive institutions would continue to shape both the region and the nation after the Civil War.

In short, the boutique South of the twentieth and twenty-first centuries only tells half of the story, and recognizing continuities between antebellum representations and modern conceptions of the region is necessary to understanding the evolution of the United States and the transatlantic world as a whole. Antebellum southern literature, in its form, developed in response to the context of global economics and political debates of the era, but the literature emerging from the U.S. South also played a role in how those debates evolved over the course of the century and after it. Antebellum southerners' representations of the region shed light on why an entire nation encouraged the continuance—nay, the impassioned defense—of what was a blatant violation of humane and human values until the nation was forced to confront those wrongs in 1861. These representations also reveal how southerners and all Americans long after the Civil War could fashion themselves as self-made individuals and progressives while also advocating for archaic social systems and racism. It is easy to say why slavery continued—it was profitable—but it is more difficult to understand why so many Americans (and even those outside of the United States) could continue to uphold the Old South as an aspirational ideal.

The fictions of the region created by antebellum southern authors are the stories that told the idea of the South into existence. In these texts, and nowhere else, the authors could act out a version of regional identity that was at once modern, traditional, progressive, and inhumane. For formerly enslaved black men and women, their narratives created a space of autonomy and agency in a system that deliberately stripped away individual power. For the white proslavery authors, the narratives mitigated the realities of the system and made it easier to represent slavery and southern society as contributing positively to a modernizing world order. The uneasy tension between liberal capitalism and the slavery-based plantation economy that emerges in these texts shapes the idea of the South that continues to hold sway over the public imagination, the idea that continues to be passed between popular films and television shows, books and critical academic studies. Returning to the texts of the antebellum period exposes the interconnected nature of literary form and economic change and lays bare the centrality of slavery and regional identity in global capitalism and the growth of the modern United States.

NOTES

Introduction: Two Souths

1. The image is unattributed and part of the Library Company of Philadelphia's print and digital collections. Many thanks to John Stromski for bringing the image to my attention.

2. For more on De Bow and the periodical, see Kvach. De Bow served as the primary editor—and often the primary contributor—for the periodical until 1867.

3. For more on the intellectual and philosophical influences circulating in the antebellum South, see O'Brien, *Conjectures of Order.*

4. For more on the effects of slavery on non-slave-owning whites, see Merritt, *Masterless Men.*

5. Genovese, among others, has outlined another rationale that proslavery southerners used to justify slavery: paternalism. According to paternalistic logic, black men and women were incapable of caring for themselves, and thus required the oversight of whites. See Genovese; Ford; Fox-Genovese and Genovese, *Mind of the Master Class;* and Faust, *Ideology of Slavery* and *Sacred Circle.* Although I do not directly address paternalism, it appears in many of the texts discussed in the following chapters, particularly in the stereotypical representations of black men and women. See, in particular, the discussions of the historical romances in chap. 1, the discussion of Hooper in chap. 2, the idea of a benevolent slaveholding empire in chap. 3, and the reading of *The Lofty and the Lowly* in chap. 4. Paternalism was a dominant mode of thought for whites, proslavery or not, and abolitionists and progressives were not immune to it.

6. Recent texts that buck this trend are excellent studies such as Paul Jones; Greeson, *Our South;* Hanlon; Hutchison; and Caison, to name just a few. Prior to these efforts was a smattering of texts by bastions of southern literary studies such Ridgley, *Nineteenth-Century Southern Literature;* and Rubin, *Edge of the Swamp.* See also Simpson; Watson, *Cavalier in Virginia Fiction;* Kreyling, *Figures of the Hero;* Tracy; Grammer; Goodwyn Jones and Donaldson; Romine, *Narrative Forms*; and Hare.

7. See, e.g., Wells; and Hardwig.

8. See Duck; Bone; Kreyling, *South That Wasn't There;* Romine, *Real South;* and Jon Smith. These texts are often included as part of the "New Southern Studies" movement, an attempt on the part of southern studies scholars in the twenty-first century to break down the regional exceptionalism that characterized the field for decades.

9. These include studies such as Weisbuch; Tennenhouse; Tamarkin; and also the essay collections by Beer and Bennett; and Peel and Maudlin. Even Levine in *Race, Transnationalism,* despite his focus on race and slavery, entirely bypasses southern texts in favor of authors such as Cooper, Hawthorne, and Melville. Studies that deviate from this trend are Hutchison; and Hanlon. For the connections between the South and African American literature in Victorian fiction, see Hack; and Lee.

10. In their introduction to a special issue of *American Literature* in 2006, "Global Contexts, Local Literatures: The New Southern Studies," McKee and Trefzer write that the aim of the Global South movement is "to refer to a two-way process: the dimensions of the global refer simultaneously to the importation of the world into the South and to the exportation of the South into the world" (679). In line with this global emphasis, subsequent studies of the region and its literature have taken pains to situate the South in transnational networks and global patterns of cultural circulation. See the collections by Smith and Cohn; and Jones and Gray.

11. Melanie Benson Taylor discusses twentieth-century southern literature in light of the South's historical involvement in slavery, colonialism, and globalization. More recent works have included nineteenth-century texts in these geographic reconsiderations. Greeson, e.g., takes up these questions and applies them specifically to representations of the early South and its function in early U.S. nationalist literature, while Clymer addresses the role of slavery, family, and property rights in nineteenth-century American literature. See also Gray and Zacharasiewicz.

12. Manning traces the legacy of Twain's criticism by examining Scott's role in American literature and in Twain's own writing.

13. Of course, here Anderson is specifically referring to nation formation, while I am talking more generally about communal cultural formation. However, a specific version of southern nationalism takes shape in antebellum literature, as I discuss in chap. 3.

14. The most frequently discussed is Henry Timrod, whose "Ethnogenesis" (1861) is often considered the poetic manifesto for the Confederacy. William Gilmore Simms also wrote plenty of poetry, as did Paul Hamilton Hayne and Sidney Lanier. During and after the Civil War, poetry by Confederate sympathizers and "Lost Cause" adherents was incredibly popular. For an interpretation of Timrod, see Hanlon; and Hutchison. For poetry during and after the Civil War, see Hutchison; and Fahs.

15. Tamarkin similarly points out that a study of American Anglophilia in the nineteenth century is more a study of how Americans understood themselves (xxiv).

16. Nineteenth-century Americanists have reclaimed the value of literary copying. In *Sensational Designs* (1985), Tompkins refers to "the power of copy as opposed to the original" (xvi), while Howell's *Against Self-Reliance* (2015) argues for the power of imitation in the early American literary sphere.

17. Forerunners of the movement include Shell, *Economy of Literature; Money, Language, and Thought;* and *Art and Money* (1995); as well as Michaels. The movement was officially heralded by the publication of the essay collection *The New Economic Criticism* in 1999, and since then, more literary studies have emphasized economics and finance as their primary modes of interpretation. See Poovey; Henry and Schmitt; Çelikkol; and Armstrong.

18. For a study of the 1837 Panic and the circumstances surrounding it, see Lepler. And for more on "panic fiction," see Templin; and Zimmerman.

19. I am pointedly not covering what is called "domestic fiction," or novels typically written by women that feature the home and familial drama. While some of the texts I discuss would fall into the category of domestic fiction (especially the Tucker and McIntosh novels featured in chap. 4), many scholars have covered this element in antebellum southern literature much more thoroughly. In addition, it is one of the few genres of antebellum southern literature that is regularly included in studies of nineteenth-century literature or studies of fiction written by women. Instead, I am much more interested in a broader range of genres as a way of understanding how southerners throughout the antebellum period, from a number of different angles, attempted to refashion a vision of the South that corresponded with liberal capitalist ideals and effectively erased the brutality that lay at the heart of southern society. See Moss's excellent study; as well as Paul Jones; and Homestead.

1. The Cavalier and the Economist: Southern Historical Romance

1. Of course, another South Carolinian would set the record straight in a much more direct and infamous fashion: several days after the speech, Representative Preston Brooks beat Sumner with a cane in the Senate chamber.

2. The lecture reiterates many of the points made in Simms's earlier histories of South Carolina, *The History of South Carolina* (1840) and *South Carolina in the Revolutionary War* (1853).

3. Edgar Allan Poe and Frederick Douglass could also be included in this list. However, both men are treated as though they operated outside of the dominant structures of white, southern society: Poe as a Gothic, somewhat antiestablishment figure, Douglass as an abolitionist and former slave. Yet as I argue in my final chapter, Douglass's writing developed in response to—and in conjunction with—dominant economic structures. Coleman Hutchison also reads Poe, and specifically his work with the *Southern Literary Messenger*, as upholding an early form of southern nationalist discourse (chap. 1).

4. *Swallow Barn* was also Kennedy's most successful novel. Set in a rural area outside of Richmond, Virginia, the novel presents the antebellum South through a series of sketches. With its realistic depiction of life on a Virginia plantation and its somewhat complicated representations of slavery and the southern plantation elite, *Swallow Barn* has become a popular text to study in southern literary circles. For just a few examples of the "first plantation novel" label, see Gaines; Bohner; MacKethan, "Plantation Fiction"; Cassuto; Cowan; and Hanlon. George Tucker's *The Valley of Shenandoah* (1824) might actually be the first plantation novel, but because it is a less romanticized version of plantation life, it rarely earns the "first" designation. See chap. 4 for more on Tucker and *Valley*.

5. For a few examples, see Osterweis; Hubbell; Taylor, *Cavalier and Yankee;* Ridgely, *Nineteenth-Century Southern Literature;* Werner; Watson, *Yeoman versus Cavalier;* Tracy.

6. "The style," Michael Kreyling points out in *Figures of the Hero in Southern Narrative,* "was [viewed as] simply and lazily borrowed from Scott with a few unimaginative changes to fit the American locale" (9). To counteract that critical trend, critics such as Kreyling and Paul C. Jones have made efforts in the past few decades to examine antebellum southern fiction in more depth, while in their studies, C. Hugh Holman and Mary Ann Wimsatt reach beyond the dismissive labels, especially in reference to Simms. See Holman; Wimsatt; and Jones, *Unwelcome Voices.* See also Ackermann on antebellum southern romances.

7. In *Rethinking the South,* Michael O'Brien observes that "in the South, the grievances of politics, slavery, and trade, the flux that preconditioned Romanticism, created the case for provincial self-justification" (51). And often the southern historical romances portray the South as "a provincial culture anxious to invent and legitimate itself" through their defense of slavery and plantation social organization (50).

8. These patterns are similar to those outlined by Northrop Frye in his 1957 study of the romance archetype in *Anatomy of Criticism.* However, I am not incorporating Frye into my discussion for the same reasons Fredric Jameson modifies Frye's theory of romance in *Political Unconscious*—namely, viewing romance as archetype "also amounts to the rewriting of a body of varied texts in the form of a single master narrative" (122). As I hope my discussion of southern historical romance demonstrates, although southern authors adapted the romance genre as a mode of reframing southern history, their novels are a particular response to a particular political, social, and economic moment that cannot be accounted for in an overarching myth narrative.

9. In her book-length study of Simms's fiction, e.g., Mary Ann Wimsatt points out critics' tendency to read Simms as a "failed realist," rather than a nuanced practitioner of the romance genre (8–9). See, e.g., Holman.

10. Similarly, Susan Tracy's study, *In the Master's Eye,* while an insightful overview of the antebellum novels, ends with the assertion that perhaps it is best that these novels are not read on account of the ethical and moral problems they raise for contemporary readers.

11. Michael O'Brien points out that for antebellum southerners, "the attraction of Romanticism was precisely the dignity it gave to the local" (*Rethinking the South* 50–1). In turn, it follows that southerners would adapt the romance—particularly that of Scott—to their own ends "because his standpoint so matched their own situation, buckling down to modernity while shedding a tear for the old ways. . . . [and] Southerners knew when Scott spoke to real issues, when he permitted himself nostalgia" (53–4). Likewise, Wimsatt observes that "Simms's works employ the central conventions of popular fiction; they show a keen awareness of romance traditions; and they convey a statement about history through literary terms" (38). In many ways, my analysis of southern historical romances takes up O'Brien's critique of the standard scholarly attention paid to southern romances, or as he puts it, southern Romanticism (see chap. 2, *Rethinking the South*).

12. For similar explorations of the romance genre and economic systems, see Çelikkol; and Freedgood.

13. Emily M. Budick also describes the "duality" of historical romance in her study: "American historical romance . . . renders a double consciousness of interpretative processes. Its symbols and allegories enforce an awareness of the unknowability of material reality. Simultaneously, it presents a world that, however, defamiliarized, is still intensely recognizable" (ix).

14. A comparison could be drawn between antebellum historical romances and postbellum regional or local color writing: both genres work to establish their cultural and historical authenticity, and both have a history of being similarly denigrated by critics.

15. Or in White's terms, history is "a verbal structure in the form of a narrative prose discourse that purports to be a model, or icon, of past structures and processes in the interest of *explaining what they were by representing* them" (2).

16. However, in his critique of southern novels given in the epigraph to this section, Twain is referencing *Ivanhoe.*

17. In *The Historical Novel* (1955), Georg Lukács makes a similar argument, yet his emphasis is on the interactions between social and political groups, rather than the interiority of an individual. Lukács describes the genre as a fictional mediation of radical social and historical change. In this interpretation, the historical novel depicts a moment of "great crisis" in the history of a nation, and the task of the hero is "to bring the extremes whose struggle fills the novel, whose clash expresses artistically a great crisis in society, into contact with one another. Through the plot, at whose centre stands this hero, a neutral ground is sought and found upon which the extreme, opposing social forces can be brought into a human relationship with one another" (36). Similarly, Ian Duncan writes in *Modern Romance and Transformations of the Novel* (1992) that the Waverley novels "represent the historical formation of the modern imperial nation-state in relation to the sentimental formation of the private individual" (15). The implication with both readings is that the individual's position in a historical moment is symbolic or allegorical. For more on *Waverley* as a Bildungsroman, see Duncan; Moretti; and Bour.

18. In his introductions to the 1823 and 1832 editions of *The Pioneers,* Cooper repeatedly asserts that the narrative is a "general picture," or "observation," of a moment in time, while the later introduction details particular points of history and changes that have occurred since the time represented in the novel (3–4 and 6–10, respectively). Likewise, the 1850 introduction to *The Last of the Mohicans* is almost entirely devoted to a brief history of the Mohican tribe, general characteristics of the North American Indian population, and the current state of the area depicted in the novel. For both, Cooper presents his novels as almost unbiased accounts of formative moments in American colonial and post-Revolutionary history—that just happen to be peopled with fictional characters.

19. As Dekker notes, the task of the author in the historical romance is to give "dramatic expression [to] and at the same time transcend history" (45).

20. Here I use the term *mediating figure* in the way Lukács would describe it in *Historical Novel.*

21. Wimsatt elaborates on Simms's use of what she calls the "framing action" and "time perspective" of his novels, both of which allow for a commentary on contemporary antebellum society and politics while relating a tale set during a more distant historical period (37–40).

22. The elegy for a departed moment and nostalgia for a past time as circumscribed in a specific place also recalls Oliver Goldsmith's poem "The Deserted Village" (1770), which implies that Kennedy's novel, to some extent, also draws from eighteenth-century literary models. In *America's England,* Christopher Hanlon discusses Kennedy's use of the picturesque—derived from British authors like Goldsmith—in his first novel, *Swallow Barn.*

23. John L. Hare argues that this political shift drastically influenced Kennedy's later fiction and reads *Horse Shoe Robinson* as an allegory for Whig politics during the 1830s. Andrew Black also reads Kennedy's literary and political career as closely aligned with the development of Whig politics and notes that *Swallow Barn*'s original publication in 1832 and its later revision in 1851 "closely bracketed the lifespan of the Whig party" (5). Similarly, he interprets both *Horse Shoe Robinson* and *Rob of the Bowl* almost exclusively in light of Whig political leanings. While I do agree that Kennedy's political views, particularly his position on economic growth and social mobility, emerge in his fiction, such readings of Kennedy's novels oversimplify their complicated representations of southern history.

24. Kennedy became involved in the Whig Party around the same time he composed *Horse Shoe Robinson,* beginning in 1832. He would later serve as a member of the party in the House of Representatives in 1838-9 and 1841–5 (Bohner 120–3, 143, 163–4, 172–3; Black 122–5, 132–3, 171–2, 186–7). In 1840, Kennedy published *Quodlibet,* a satire of Jacksonian politics, and in 1844 he published *The Defense of the Whigs,* which outlined the Whig political platform.

25. In *Cavalier and Yankee* (1961)—an influence for this book in both title and content—Taylor describes the "New Man" as the figure that emerged from the fading Virginia aristocracy of the Revolutionary era. That New Man would fit into what John Grammer calls, in *Pastoral and Politics in the Old South* (1996), the "pastoral republicanism" that shaped many southern intellectuals of the post-Revolutionary generation, including John Randolph and Nathaniel Beverley Tucker.

26. The phrase *singular genius* appears repeatedly in a biography Kennedy wrote in 1849, *Memoirs of the Life of William Wirt.* Wirt was a politician and author whose biographies of early American founding fathers and service as the U.S. attorney general (1817–29) earned him the admiration of many American authors and southerners, including Kennedy. Kennedy and Wirt developed a friendship while the younger man was first beginning his legal career in Baltimore in the 1820s; Kennedy even dedicated *Swallow Barn* to him.

27. Likewise, Black characterizes Kennedy as a "Border Whig," who "belonged to neither the North nor the South and shared a sense of insecurity regarding future sectional relations" (3). These social and political philosophies mirrored Kennedy's Whig economic policies. As Kennedy's biographer Charles Bohner notes, "Kennedy was irresistibly attracted to the idea of an industrial America, a self-sufficient nation doing sustenance from commerce and manufacturing" (118). The best way to ensure that success, Kennedy determined, was to limit free trade and impose tariffs on foreign commodities. Just as social and economic mobility was limited to certain (white) men, free trade would be limited to American goods.

28. See Moltke-Hansen.

29. Bizarrely, this philosophy is somewhat echoed in W. E. B. Du Bois's later "Talented Tenth" philosophy.

30. In an article published in the August 1834 issue of *American Monthly Magazine,* "The Philosophy of the Omnibus," Simms uses the image of the omnibus—or the form of public transportation common at the time—as a symbol for the contemporary age (and also cleverly nods to the literary omnibus). In part, this is a positive portrayal, for the omnibus represents the potential for egalitarian change: "The Omnibus marks that period in human economy when the barriers are to be overthrown—when the gross deference to authority must be done away with—when all men may stand upon the same level, and look fearlessly and freely upon one another." However, in the same passage, Simms cautions the need to temper that change: "Our prayer is, that something may be spared, in this general overthrow, to the spirit which was great and glorious in the history of the past" (159). Around this same time, Charles Dickens was writing literary sketches on the London omnibus that would later be published in *Sketches by Boz* (1836). For more on Dickens and the sketch, see chap. 2.

31. Likewise, in an 1832 review of another English novelist's observations of the United States, Frances Trollope's *Domestic Manners of the Americans* (1832), Simms refutes Trollope's criticism of Americans' lack of manners (especially in the Southwest states) and the nation's dearth of artistic production. Early-nineteenth-century America was still in development, according to Simms, when the material conditions of the nation's citizens carried more weight than good breeding and the arts. Yet he contends that the freedom found in democratic American institutions promoted individual advancement, for they "show no pampered and isolated classes, afford equal protection of the liberties of all, and strangle not their industry, and obstruct not their enterprise" ("Domestic Manners" 133). In this version of American development, each man labors in a free market for profit and without restrictions, with the ultimate goal of nurturing more refined cultural elements.

32. Dauntrees is also a Falstaffian, or better put, a Captain Porgy character. Porgy, who features prominently in Simms's *Woodcraft,* also appeared in his earlier Revolutionary romance, *The Partisan* (1835). Although there is no direct proof that Kennedy modeled Dauntrees after Simms's character, Porgy's popularity after the publication of the earlier novel could have had an influence.

33. These lines reflect what Ridgely calls Kennedy's "truth of fiction" philosophy, in which his historical romances "represented his *own* view of the realities of the past which could be truthfully celebrated only through the medium of fiction" (*John Pendleton Kennedy* 104).

34. Ridgely observes that this pair, a common trope for many antebellum historical romances, "are depicted as parts of a developing whole—the ideal southern leader" (*Nineteenth-Century Southern Literature* 56).

35. In his study of antebellum southern fiction, *The Edge of the Swamp* (1989), Louis D. Rubin Jr. notes this shift in the character. "Simms took the historical figure of an English-born royal governor," Rubin argues, "and converted him into what is essentially a *middle-class American,* a frontier hero" (115).

36. Bess, in fact, though well-bred and educated, is actually a middle-class figure who marries "up" in the novel. However, like the other middle-class heroes, she displays the "singular genius" and good breeding that make her social mobility acceptable. Simms's representations

of his heroines can often be more progressive than his male characters, his later Revolutionary novel, *Katherine Walton* (1851), being a perfect example.

37. Katherine is a recurring character in Simms's Revolutionary era novels, the titular character in his conclusion to the Revolutionary trilogy.

38. In fact, Lance's father is barely human. Before the beginning of the novel's action, the Framptons are raided by a group of British soldiers. Mrs. Frampton dies as a result of the attack, and Frampton is driven mad. Subsequently, all of the novel's descriptions of the man are in animalistic terms: he stalks the swamps and only enters the camp for food.

39. Rubin also describes Grayson's role as a representative middle-class figure in *The Edge of the Swamp,* but (rightly) points out that "Hugh Grayson is *not* the hero of the novel, and . . . it is Charles Craven, alias Gabriel Harrison, upon whom the author centers his attention" (120).

40. In *Nineteenth-Century Southern Literature,* Ridgely describes Robinson as a frontier scout figure, "an exemplar of the spirit of rebellion against unfairly imposed authority" (56).

41. William Taylor argues that this narrative emphasis allows Kennedy to project an image of southern history that incorporates elements of the aristocratic elite (Butler) with the social and economic progress represented by middle-class figures such as Robinson. By pairing the frontier scout with the southern gentleman cavalier, Kennedy could create "an expressive amalgam of the mixed cultural ingredients" that made up antebellum southern society (*Cavalier and Yankee* 199).

42. Contrary to the representation in *Horse Shoe Robinson,* several critics have pointed out Kennedy's relatively progressive position on slavery. In particular, Jones (*Unwelcome Voices*), Cowan, and MacKethan (*Swallow Barn,* intro.) describe his more complicated depictions of black characters and slavery in *Swallow Barn.*

43. In the 1852 edition of the novel, the epilogue was expanded and revised as an introduction.

44. According to a frequently repeated anecdote, at the 1856 Southern Convention in Savannah, Georgia, the convention members stipulated that "there be a Southern literature" and that William Gilmore Simms "be requested to write this literature" ("Southern Literature" 207–8). Although the story is a "pithy, pretty piece of apocrypha," as Coleman Hutchison puts it, it has become a touchstone for Simms scholars and critics of nineteenth-century southern literature as a way to understand the author's significance in championing and defining southern culture before the Civil War (18). See Holman; Wimsatt; and Hutchison.

45. Charles S. Watson argues, in *From Nationalism to Secessionism,* that Simms's novels after the 1840s are almost entirely focused on a polemical defense of the South. See also Wakelyn.

46. As Adam L. Tate observes, "Simms's thought did not so much shift as it adapted to the events of the 1850s to conservative principles he had long held" (239).

47. For this reading, I am focusing specifically on Simms's Revolutionary novels, not those of the frontier, such as *Guy Rivers* (1834), *Border Beagles* (1840), and *Southward Ho!* (1854).

48. In these later novels, Drew Gilpin Faust observes, the post-Revolutionary society of the South embodies "the one [Simms] sought to create in the Old South" (*Sacred Circle*

75). Or as David Moltke-Hansen puts it, in Simms's novels, "history favors progress, or, in other words, progressives deservedly are winners" (131). Moltke-Hansen goes on to argue that this sort of historical vision manifests itself in Simms's earlier novels as a justification for the eventual extinction of American Indian tribes and the defeat of British Loyalists in the Revolutionary War. The epigraph to chap. 1 of *The Yemassee,* presumably written by Simms himself, is equal parts eulogy for vanished Native American tribes and laconic explanation for their inevitable disappearance:

> A scatter'd race—a wild, unfetter'd tribe,
> That in the forests dwell—that send no ships
> For commerce on the waters—rear no walls
> To shelter from the storm, or shield from strife;—
> And leave behind, in memory of their name,
> No monument (9)

The reason for the tribe's disappearance, in Simms's poetic estimation, is their lack of modernization: they engage in no *commerce* and do not build cities, as any thriving civilization should do. See Moltke-Hansen. For more on Simms and representations of American Indian tribes, see Caison.

49. In *Apples and Ashes,* Hutchison describes Confederate literature as "future oriented." He extends that reading to include interpretations of antebellum literature in which southern authors engage with potential ideas of southern nationalism (8). I will discuss the formation of southern nationalism in more detail in chap. 3.

50. Historian David Donald observes, "In poverty [Simms] yearned for the place in society which his ancestors had occupied" ("Proslavery Argument" 11). Louis D. Rubin also argues that Simms's work is shaped by what he calls the "planter ideal" and equates the middle-class Hugh Grayson in *The Yemassee* with a young Simms (*Edge of the Swamp* 119–20).

51. John C. Guilds, Simms's biographer, writes, "The Panic of 1837, with which a gradual collapse of the national economy began, had devastated the book market by 1843" (*Simms* 166).

52. The Panic was the result of a combination of factors, including rampant speculation on government lands in the West and banks overissuing paper money or unbacked loans. When the secretary of Treasury issued an order at the end of 1836 that demanded payment for land in gold or silver, banks began to restrict credit and recall their loans. The result was a dramatic contraction of the markets. For more on the Panic of 1837, see Roberts.

53. Simms did, however, revise many of his early novels during the 1850s to incorporate more overt defenses of slavery. See Watson, *From Nationalism to Secessionism.* Interestingly, so did Kennedy: the 1851 edition of *Swallow Barn* incorporated a lengthier discussion, and defense, of slavery.

54. Drew Gilpin Faust observes that beginning in the 1840s, southern intellectuals more frequently noted the need for the South to improve in its agricultural technology and methods. In turn, she writes, "the intellectual's perception of the agricultural problem could not be separated from his dedication to regional autonomy" (*Sacred Circle* 98). That consciousness

emerges again on more nationalistic terms in Henry Timrod's poem "Ethnogenesis" (1861), which many scholars consider a defining literary work for the Confederacy and southern nationalism in general. For more on Timrod and the poem, see Hutchison, intro.; and Hanlon.

55. Hammond's passage is an example of what Walter Johnson terms the "statistic." Beginning shortly after the Panic of 1837 and repeating every few years up to the Civil War, political economists observed that the South routinely exported more goods than it imported, creating a disparity in profit between the region and the rest of the world, especially the North. This made the South less self-sustaining and economically regressive. According to Johnson, "For those who employed it, this statistic held the key to understanding the history of Southern commercial 'decline'" (*River* 283). In their writings, Hammond and other proslavery economists attempted to counteract this "Statistic" with a utopian vision of a southern economic future.

56. In what seems to contradict his position in 1841, Hammond also famously used the phrase "Cotton is King" during a speech in the Senate in 1858. This apparent reversal most likely is due to the political climate of the 1850s, in which southerners more rabidly came to the defense of their established institutions, peculiar or not. However, I would also offer that we can read Hammond's famous phrase as an attempt to recognize the prominence of the cotton trade in the contemporary global economy but doing so within a vision of the South that upholds slavery and "traditional" southern values.

57. As Adam Tate has observed, Adam Smith was an influence on Simms, and his interpretation of the effects of cities and manufacturing in promoting cultural development reflects that influence (172). Simms, Tate notes, "believed that two issues provided a means of unity for the South: slavery and free trade" (241).

58. During the 1840s, Simms became involved with a cultural movement called the "Young America" group, which included writers such as William Cullen Bryant, E. A. Duyckinck (who became a close friend of Simms), Nathaniel Hawthorne, and Herman Melville. The group advocated for a national literature divorced from European traditions and standards. The movement correlates to the Young England movement, which occurred at roughly the same time. For more on Young England, see Faber.

59. *Views and Reviews* was designed to outline the tenets of the Young American position. When the book was released, however, it was not necessarily well received by other members of the movement. Nathaniel Hawthorne, as the passage at the beginning of this section demonstrates, found Simms's conception of American literature and history to be outdated. In a statement that prefigures Twain's dismissal of antebellum southern literature forty years later, Hawthorne proclaims that Simms's definition of exemplary American fiction relies entirely on the "worn-out mould" of the historical romance (Stewart, "Hawthorne's Contributions" 331–2).

60. In using the term *renaissance*, I deliberately conjure a phrase common in southern studies circles in the twentieth century, primarily due to Rubin's *Southern Renascence: The Literature of the Modern South* (1953). More than a century after Simms was publishing his historical novels, authors such as William Faulkner and Eudora Welty were credited with

reviving southern letters in a "renascence" that became representative of the southern literary tradition as a whole.

61. There are no substantial differences between the two versions of the novel, other than the title. I refer to *Woodcraft* simply because it is the more familiar and recognized title.

62. While Wimsatt interprets these comedic moments as Simms's adaptation of the Southwest humor stories that gained popularity in the 1840s and 1850s, Kreyling reads Porgy as an emblem of the fading plantation order, which he claims Simms ultimately casts into history and memory (*Figures* 50–1). For more on Simms and southwestern humor, see Wimsatt.

63. William Taylor calls the exchange "the central debate of the novel" (290).

64. See, e.g., Ridgely, *William Gilmore Simms* 97.

65. On this point, Lewis Simpson argues that the novel is "an effort to authenticate the historical existence of the South as a special historical case—a chosen nation" (54). Simpson then characterizes *Woodcraft* as a "plantation pastoral" that remains "vexed" in its simultaneous defense of slavery and opposition to modernity.

66. Following these patterns, Wimsatt observes the "disdain" Porgy shows for Millhouse in all of their exchanges, which clearly demonstrates his role as a social superior that the utilitarian could never achieve (169). Likewise, William Taylor notes that Porgy "has the last word" in defense of the more gentlemanly arts to which he is privy (291). And in a long, comedic scene, Millhouse makes a fool of himself and Porgy by presuming himself the equal with the genteel Mrs. Eveleigh and her aristocratic son.

67. In terms of gender, this ending also maintains the separate spheres within the nineteenth-century economy, with Mrs. Eveleigh representing a continued aristocracy confined to the domestic space and the male figures accessing the realm of economic and social mobility on the free market. However, the fact that Mrs. Eveleigh remains independent at the end implies a future autonomy on the part of upper-class women in the South. Like Katherine Walton, it reveals Simms's mildly progressive representation of his female characters.

2. Sketching the 1830s Cotton Boom: Southwestern Humor

1. Or *Watkins Tottle and Other Sketches,* as Poe identifies it in his review.

2. And in a clever connection between written and visual "sketches."

3. Sketches representing other western regions were also popular during this time. Caroline Kirkland's *A New Home—Who'll Follow? or, Glimpses of Western Life* (1839), depicts the northern Michigan territories.

4. When he wrote the sketch, Willis had been traveling in Britain for several months and sending back his impressions of the countryside, culture, and people. Willis, who would become famous in the United States and Europe for his travel sketches, eventually lived in London briefly. During the mid-nineteenth century, he was known for being the highest-paid periodical writer in America. On a more inglorious note, he was also brother to author Fanny Fern, and he appears as an egotistical dilettante in her autobiographical novel, *Ruth Hall* (1854). For more information on Willis, see Baker, *Sentiment and Celebrity.*

5. For an overview of the technological innovations in the cotton industry, see Chapman.

6. See, for one example, *The Spectator* papers published by Joseph Addison and Richard Steele between 1711 and 1712.

7. For more on the shift in print culture and its effects on cultural and social development in the transatlantic world, see Anderson, *Imagined Communities;* and Habermas, *Structural Transformation.* And for more on the sketch form, see Garcha.

8. Patton uses Dickens as an example—the foremost example—of the publishing industry's evolution during the 1830s and its subsequent impact on Victorian novelists' construction of their identities as authors. According to Patton, the Victorian era was a moment when "authorial power . . . would both fuel and stand up to capitalist material and cultural production during the heyday of British industrialism, and that would eventually extend its powers and benefits to writers around the rest of the world" (19–20).

9. Dickens was an author who consistently returned to London in his fiction and frequently returned to the 1820s and 1830s for the temporal setting of his work. Many of his later novels are set during this time, including *Little Dorrit* (1855/7) and *Great Expectations* (1860), to name just two.

10. As the capital of England's growing commercial and colonial empire, London was the embodiment of the changes occurring throughout the world. For more on how nineteenth-century authors capture the simultaneously global and local nature of the city through the use of the panorama and sketch forms, see Agathocleous. By shifting between the two in their work, Victorian authors imagine the details of an urban space (London) and at the same time view that space "as a way to conceptualize the totality of human society in a global age" (Agathocleous 15).

11. In the collected manuscripts, *Sketches* is always organized with shorter sketches of London as the first section and longer stories, or "Tales," as the second. The sketches and tales were originally published at varying times in London newspapers and periodicals, then collected into several editions; I will be referring to the 1839 edition, which combined all of the published sketches up until that point. For a more thorough account of the publication history and the revision process, see Butt and Tillotson; and Grillo.

12. See Benjamin. And for criticism that argues for the reassuring function of nineteenth-century British urban sketches, see Byerly; and Garcha.

13. Garcha notes, regarding the British sketches: "Broadly put, in these decades, sketches embodied contradictory, somewhat paradoxical, features of modern life. They accentuated the ideological value placed on newness, disconnection, and detachment—including the processes of 'progress,' temporal rush, capitalistic appropriation, and market differentiation; at the same time, they emphasized the ideological value Britain placed on opposite ideas of cultural homogeneity, unity, and stasis, which helped produce the image of England as a stable, single 'social body.'" (25). This description easily fits the space of the Southwest, which was undergoing a similar and equally drastic economic and social shift.

14. Payne also comments on Dickens's fascination with the cabdrivers and observes that they are affiliated with modernization and progress.

15. George Cruikshank, who at the time was one of the most popular British periodical illustrators, was commissioned to produce a series of images to accompany the sketches and tales. Apparently, he and Dickens collaborated well, and the illustrations are funny, detailed reflections of Dickens's scenes. See Dennis Walder's introduction to the 1995 edition of *Sketches* (xli).

16. In his chapter on *Sketches by Boz,* Garcha also situates the collection in the context of contemporary economic structures and market culture. However, he seems to take for granted that the "static" nature of the sketches is equivalent to the static nature of the socioeconomic position of the lower classes featured in the sketches. According to Garcha, the lower-class figures of the sketches are not able to participate in commercial transactions in the same way as the middle-class characters of the longer tales. Yet this sort of interpretation discounts the autonomy exhibited by the confidence men characters. See also Chittick for the class dimensions of the sketches versus the tales. She points out that the tales (especially those published earlier in the periodicals) "project a more elevated social scene than any [Dickens] was actually familiar with on a daily basis" (45).

17. Halttunen situates the confidence man in the context of antebellum urbanization, another space of increased openness in terms of economic mobility.

18. In *American Humor* (1931), Constance Rourke virtually dismisses the stories: "They were rough fantasies cast into the habitual large outline . . . their odd local figures were generic, the events preposterous" (70). By this description, the stories have no basis in reality and may as well be mere tall tales. Later critics have credited the stories with more realism, situating them more firmly in their social and historical context. However, the humor still functions as a means of distancing readers from the characters and scenes. In their introduction to the collection *Humor of the Old Southwest* (1964/94), Hennig Cohen and William B. Dillingham write that the Southwest humorists were conscious of the dangers existent (physical or otherwise) in the Old Southwest, and "they sought through humor to reduce this fearful spectre to less awful proportions" (xxxvi). Lenz echoes this assessment; writing specifically of Hooper's confidence man, Simon Suggs, he argues, "To participate imaginatively in such humorous confidence games allows the reader to envision the worst image of Americans within the safe confines of comic fiction and to discharge the anxieties this image creates through laughter at the apparent poetic justice dispensed by the confidence man in Hooper's narrow focus on a highly exaggerated, stylized, corrupt new country" (21).

19. Walter Blair, another formative critic for southwestern humor, also adopts the "Whiggish" mantra in his introduction to the collection *Native American Humor* (1937), and Cohen and Dillingham take up the phrase to again characterize the whole of Old Southwest humor writers as "Whig gentlemen" (xx).

20. In his discussion of postbellum politics in *Origins of the New South, 1877–1913* (1951), C. Vann Woodward observes that though they were seen as allied with the planter class, antebellum southern Whigs often endorsed the very interests that led to its downfall: "They spoke for much the same type of railroad and industrial interests as did the Republicans and took a 'practical' view of things" (28). Similarly, John Pendleton Kennedy was a staunch "southern

Whig," yet he also championed the "New Man" of the mid-nineteenth century, a figure shaped by the free market.

21. For more on the relationship between the Whig Party and individualism, see Kohl.

22. Arlin Turner and William Thorp have pointed out this iconoclastic trend in Southwest humor toward the aristocracy or traditional American institutions, and David S. Reynolds argues in *Beneath the American Renaissance* (1988) that often the humorists highlighted the hypocrisy of the American elite. See Turner, "Seeds of Literary Revolt"; and Thorp.

23. For more on Hooper's shifting political allegiances, see Hoole.

24. With the exception of "Taking the Census" and the illustrations discussed, all citations and references to *Some Adventures* are to the 1969 edition, which is identical to the 1845 edition outside of the exceptions noted.

25. The term *chicken man* comes from the idea held by inhabitants of the newly settled states that the federal census taker would literally count the number of chickens one possessed so that he could take more money and property on behalf of the federal government. Hooper actually worked as a census taker when he first moved to Alabama, and the story is based on his experiences.

26. The illustrator for *Some Adventures* was F. O. C. Darley, who did many of the Southwest humor illustrations (Barnhill 47–50).

27. Several critics have observed the complicated treatment of black characters in Southwest humor. See, e.g., Shields, "Sadder Simon Suggs."

28. In 1966, a full edition of the book was collected and published by Richard E. Amacher and George W. Polhemus.

29. Similarly, in his chapter on Baldwin in *Pastoral and Politics in the Old South* (1996), John M. Grammer observes that Baldwin's political biography, *Party Leaders,* is "a narrative of decline," tracing the gradual dissipation of "virtue" in American culture and politics (150). Grammer also notes the seeming contradiction between the ostensible message of Baldwin's works, a critique of the frontier and American society, and the playfulness and humor of his writing, particularly *Flush Times.* However, he never connects the two, focusing instead on the message rather than the way in which is presented.

30. Grammer also points out that Baldwin relegates the typical figures of the Southwest and Southwest humor (e.g., farmers and hunters) to the margins of his sketches and focuses, instead, on the legal system and questions of property ownership. Yet he also emphasizes that Baldwin saw "republican virtue" and "civilization" as "besieged" by the unethical practices of the frontier (137). As my earlier reading of Baldwin's politics and the following discussion of his fiction reveals, I find that this reading ignores *Flush Times*'s more complicated representation of the region's social and economic system.

31. All references to *Flush Times,* with the exception of the illustrations, are to the 1957 edition, which is essentially a reproduction of the first edition.

32. See *Pudd'nhead Wilson* (1892).

33. The illustrator for *Flush Times* was John McLenan (Hoffheimer 751).

34. Shields also reads the sketch this way in "Writers in the Old Southwest."

3. The Southern Imperial Dream: Novels of Adventure

1. Robert May observes in his historical study *The Southern Dream of a Caribbean Empire* (1973), "The dispute over Caribbean expansion became an important element in the matrix of events that led to the American Civil War" (21).

2. The novel was expanded from a short story Ingraham originally published in the *Southern Literary Messenger* in 1839.

3. Most critics who write of the U.S.-Mexican War novels barely mention texts by southerners, or they do not distinguish their differences. John Lowe notes this absence, and his sweeping study, *Calypso Magnolia,* includes a discussion of several southern texts, including William Clark Falkner's *The Spanish Heroine* and Pickens's *Free Flag of Cuba* (see chaps. 1 and 2). In *Apples and Ashes,* Hutchison highlights that southern authors such as Edgar Allan Poe, William Gilmore Simms, and Nathaniel Beverley Tucker engaged with regionally centered nationalism in their writings. However, his overview ultimately concludes that the discussions of nationalism are varied and disparate, a series of "possible histories of the future" rather than a unified sense of national identity (Hutchison 62).

4. Shelley Streeby describes these imperial adventure novels as both "sensational literature," in the sense that they were "low," popular fiction playing on the reader's desire for melodrama and extreme emotion, and as participating in the culture of sensation that was popular at the time, in the sense that they developed alongside other forms of popular culture and arts such as journalism, music, and theater (27).

5. Of course, William Clark Falkner's descendant, William Faulkner, would reach much wider acclaim.

6. Denning's phrase comes from his book *Mechanic Accents: Dime Novels and Working-Class Culture in America* (1987). See also Rodriguez; Johannsen.

7. See also Lowe 41. Meg Wesling argues that formal education—specifically the discipline of English—would play a similar role in later imperialist discourse. As Wesling argues, in the late nineteenth and early twentieth centuries, "the literary object functioned, in the context of overseas empire, as a kind of proxy; a substitute or stand-in for the colonizing subject" (6).

8. Rodriguez highlights the documentary nature of the fiction. Calling them "interstitial," he writes that the novels and novelettes were "a pulp medium that evolved from the rapid expansion of penny press newspapers . . . a fictive form in the moment of breaking free from its journalistic origins." What results, he claims, is "an intricate blend of romance, fantasy, history, and reportage" (18).

9. See also Streeby 11, 12, 220.

10. According to Streeby, imperial adventure fiction "both reveals and struggles to conceal the role of U.S. imperialism in the Americans in the mid-nineteenth century" (7). For more on the diversity of responses to the war, see Streeby 39–40.

11. I borrow the term *watershed* from Streeby, who references Martínez-Fernández. The year 1848 was pivotal in global reconfigurations of national identity: in 1848, Europe expe-

rienced a series of political revolutions wherein liberal factions attempted to overthrow the monarchies in power. See Sperber. The *Communist Manifesto* was also published that year.

12. See May, *Southern Dream;* Potter; Johnson, *River of Dark Dreams;* Baptist; Chance; and Lang, "Memory" and "'Upon the Altar.'"

13. See Onuf.

14. An article reprinted in the *Columbus (MS) Democrat* in December 1836 also argued for the annexation of Texas into the United States, claiming, "The people of the Southern slave States have also a strong motive for an alliance with Texas, independent of any political considerations. Texas is the greatest cotton region in the world" ("Texas").

15. For more on proslavery southerners' complicated relationship to the war, see Lander.

16. In doing so, Edward Baptist remarks in *The Half Has Never Been Told,* "this vision of perpetually expanding slavery as an alternative but still modern economy was once again becoming plausible" (331).

17. I borrow the term *continuity* from philosopher Étienne Balibar in *Race, Nation, Class.* According to Balibar, "The history of nations . . . is always already presented to us in the form of a narrative which attributes to these entities the continuity of a subject" (Balibar and Wallerstein 86). In *Belated Modernity and Aesthetic Culture* (1991), Gregory Jusdanis also describes literature (specifically canonical literature) as a form of "continuous textuality" for a national culture (59). He writes, "At its inception national culture is really literary in nature, for literature, in the extended sense of stories and specific meaning as fiction, is thought to mirror the nation" (xi).

18. In *Mapping Men and Empire* (1997), Richard Phillips describes the British adventure narratives as imaginative "maps" that are "part of the process of colonisation, of making imperial geographies" (18). "Like other modern maps," Phillips argues, "realistic adventure stories naturalize the geographies they represent, and normalise constructions of race, gender, class and empire those geographies inscribe" (15). As an example, Phillips points to *Robinson Crusoe*—the ur-text of imperial adventure novels—and argues that "through its narrative of colonisation and transformation on and of an island, [the novel] represents, promotes, and legitimates a form of colonisation" (34).

19. Many critics (Streeby, e.g.) cite Calhoun as a representative for the South and proslavery southerners' general reluctance to enter the war, when in reality he was one of many voices in the debate. For more on the intraregional debates over annexation, see Ashworth 1:452–3.

20. Graham Dawson, in *Soldier Heroes* (1987), explains, "As energizing myth, adventure helped to bring into being the emerging imaginaries of empire and the new historical forms of 'English' national identity and masculinity figured in them. These in turn charged the adventure quest with a specific imaginative quality which sedimented into its structure" (60).

21. Marx observes this pattern in the *Communist Manifesto:* "The need for a constantly expanding market for its products chases the bourgeoisie over the entire surface of the globe. It must nestle everywhere, settle everywhere, establish connections everywhere" (Marx and Engels 55). This is doubly true for a plantation-based economy reliant on an enslaved labor force, which requires actual, literal space for expansion and growth.

22. Çelikkol observes that "during the rise of free trade, literary works played a special role in scrutinizing the tension between circulation and enclosure, with numerous novelists, playwrights, and poets . . . mapping abstract economic principles onto subjective experiences of community and space" (4). Çelikkol refers to the novels primarily as "romances," although the majority of the texts she analyzes in her book would fall into the imperial adventure genre. I choose to maintain the term *imperial adventure novel* because it best characterizes the qualities that overlap between the British novels and those published by southern authors.

23. The characterization of the hunchbacked man as "evil" falls in line with standard cultural representations of disability at the time. See, e.g., Thomson.

24. Cartwright's theories were published as an essay in *De Bow's Review* in 1851, but the ideas were in circulation before that. In *Notes on the State of Virginia,* e.g., Thomas Jefferson refers to the "natural" inferiority of the black race.

25. The few critics who study the novel mention this trend. Jaime Rodriguez categorizes the novel as a "chivalric tale," or novelette, wherein Mexican characters are heroic and the contemporaneous historical debates over empire are relocated in a romanticized setting and plot (28). These novels, Rodriguez argues, "deploy a Mexican space that is simultaneously like the U.S. nation-state and different from it" (36–7). Mexico and Mexicans, in other words, are "like Americans, but also always proud Mexican nationals" (40).

26. Historian Reginald Horsman observes, "Most Americans realized that in practical terms the annexation of the whole of Mexico would mean either that eight million Mexicans would become American citizens or that they would be ruled as colonial subjects" (243).

27. Born in Maine in 1809, Ingraham moved to Mississippi during the southwestern land boom of the 1820s and 1830s. His most notable novels would have included *Lafitte: The Pirate of the Gulf* (1836) and *The Quadroone; or, St. Michael's Day* (1840). During his lifetime, he was almost as prolific as William Gilmore Simms, purportedly writing several hundred novels of dubious quality.

28. The remark was made by Mrs. Freeman, a niece of Ingraham's, in a letter to David H. Bishop, dated 3 March 1908, located in the Joseph Holt Ingraham records at the University of Mississippi Libraries Special Collections. Apparently, Henry Wadsworth Longfellow referred to Ingraham as "a tremendous ass!! really *tremendous!*" The comment appears in a letter Longfellow wrote to George Washington Greene on 22 October 1838 (Hilen 2:108).

29. The volume is cited frequently as a primary source for historians and scholars for its detailed descriptions of the Deep South and slavery. See, e.g., Justus.

30. The review appeared in the January 1836 issue. For more on Ingraham and Poe, see Hutchison 41–2; and Whalen.

31. Ingraham obtained a position as an instructor at Jefferson College and married a woman from Holly Springs, Mississippi, where he settled for several decades and ultimately died. The circumstances of his death, like much of Ingraham's work, were sensational. He died from a wound inflicted when he accidentally shot himself in the leg, although his family would later claim he was fending off a burglar. See the Joseph Holt Ingraham records in the Small Manuscripts Collection, 1976.5, Folder 4, located in the University of Mississippi Special Collections.

32. For a lengthier discussion of party politics at the time, see Ashworth, vol. 1.

33. Beyond the desire of southern expansionists, the cultures of the southern United States and Mexico did parallel each other in many ways. In *American Encounters* (1998), José E. Limón notes the interconnected nature of the U.S. South and what he calls "Greater Mexico."

34. In the novel, the Mexican characters make a point of using the term *Saxon* for the white American soldiers. In doing so, Ingraham claims all North Americans as Americans, with the only differentiation being racial.

35. Streeby observes that romances between very Anglicized Mexican heroines and white American men "try . . . to turn force into consent by reimagining the U.S. invasion as an international romance" (99). In his typical haphazard fashion, Ingraham sometimes spells her name *Margerita.*

36. Streeby observes that this is often accomplished in U.S.-Mexican War novels through "international race romances," in which "romantic and political discourses are mapped onto each other, [and] these scenarios also construct the Mexican government as despotic and the U.S. government as consensual, democratic, and 'free'" (130). But in the case of the adventure novels written by proslavery sympathizers such as Ingraham, the romance plot is secondary to the importance of the slave system and can only succeed if the slave system is firmly in place.

37. At the time, her family recently had moved from Texas to Mobile, Alabama. If we go by the story, Evans most likely witnessed some of the events of the war, at least distantly. The novel was published later, in 1855, by Harper & Brothers to poor reviews and low sales (Fidler 40–5).

38. Interestingly, *Inez* is never included in any of the scholarship on U.S.-Mexican War novels. Despite its subject matter, it is often characterized as a "domestic novel," largely due to Evans's body of work as a whole and the southern (white) female protagonists. In *Domestic Novelists in the Old South* (1992), e.g., Elizabeth Moss aligns the novel with other works of domestic fiction by authors such as Mary Virginia Terhune, even though Terhune's novels take place almost exclusively within the domestic realm. Although it doesn't strictly fall into the "literature of 1848" category defined by Streeby and others, its absence is nonetheless odd given the topic and publication date.

39. The act effectively dissolved the Missouri Compromise of 1820, which prohibited slavery above a certain latitude, and allowed the new states to decide their slaveholding status.

40. Robert May notes that southern defensiveness during this time was part and parcel of an attitude that viewed the defense of slavery as a defense of honor and republicanism in the face of northern or free-soil aggression (*Southern Dream* 269).

41. The circumstances of *Macaria*'s publishing history are fascinating enough to warrant a separate chapter. See Homestead; and Hutchison. Based on its unique representation of the Confederacy, Evans's role as an "arch rebel," as *Macaria*'s publisher J. C. Derby called her, was assuredly earned (qtd. in Homestead 192).

42. Her 1859 novel, *Beulah,* has been compared to Susan Warner's *The Wide, Wide World* (1850) as a female, domestic Bildungsroman. Although not a runaway success, it was popular enough to earn a reputation for Evans prior to the war.

43. The novel would give rise to a "St. Elmo craze," and its popularity created an obsession in mainstream culture similar to the fixation on Susanna Rowson's *Charlotte Temple* (1791) decades earlier.

44. The dichotomy also taps into a virulent anti-Catholic sentiment that was prevalent throughout the United States at the time, not just the South. Elizabeth Fenton interprets the novel, specifically Mary's frequent debates, as Evans's commentary on the power of a female Protestant belief system in the face of Catholic "seduction." Ingraham includes similar anti-Catholic tones in *The Texan Ranger,* although not as fiercely, when he aligns Catholicism with barbarity and Protestantism with humane behavior and civilization, especially on the battlefield (87–8).

45. Austin is considered to be the founder of Anglo-American Texas through his efforts to encourage white American settlement around San Antonio in the 1820s. However, by the 1830s, the time of the novel, the negotiations had gone sour, and the new U.S. colonists chafed under Mexican law. While Austin was, indeed, arrested by Mexican authorities in 1833 under suspicion of inciting a rebellion in Texas, Evans is very fuzzy with the timeline in *Inez,* which has the war taking place shortly after his arrest—not almost three years later. He was actually imprisoned for most of the war. Austin would die in 1836, shortly after the formation of the new Texas government. See Brands; and Haynes.

46. For more on the battles of the Revolution and conflicts with the Mexican military leader Santa Anna, see Hardin.

47. On March 27, 1836, the Mexican army executed more than three hundred Texan soldiers captured in battle, including their commander, James Fannin. The massacre fueled the Texas Revolution.

48. Tennessean William Walker, e.g., led an aborted attempt to seize Nicaragua in 1855. Walter Johnson includes an extensive discussion of the López and Walker expeditions in *River of Dark Dreams,* chaps. 11 and 13, respectively.

49. "Although Americans had previously expressed interest in annexing Mexico, parts of Central America, and some of the islands of the Caribbean," writes Robert May, "the urge to extend the national domain southward intensified significantly during the 1850s" (*Southern Dream* 3). Caroline Levander observes, "Cuba aligns U.S. imperialism with Southern separatism, revealing a complex, and often occluded, history of intervening sectional, regional, and national interests underpinning U.S.-Cuban relations throughout the nineteenth century" (824). See also Pérez.

50. In his discussion of the "Cuban imaginary," Lowe includes black authors such as Martin Delany, whose novel, *Blake* (1859–61) also depicts a Cuban American empire. *Blake,* however, frames that empire as part of the larger African diaspora engaged in combating slavery.

51. As Lowe takes care to underscore in *Calypso Magnolia,* the Deep South of the United States "is in many ways the northern rim of the Caribbean," and as such, the "circumCaribbean" is essential to understanding the development of the region (1).

52. For a brief summary of both events, see Burns.

53. See May, "Reconsidering Antebellum U.S. Women's History."

54. Pickens and Crittenden were engaged at the time he joined the López filibuster; he was executed with most of the men, supposedly leaving Pickens alone and heartbroken. For more details of Pickens's relationship with Crittenden in the context of the novel, see Orville Burton's introduction to the 2002 edition of *Free Flag.*

55. The passage also echoes John Pendleton Kennedy's discussion of history and fiction in "A Legend of Maryland" (1860). The similarities reveal how southern authors, regardless of topic, were hyperconscious of the ways in which their fiction shaped the image and story of the South and its history.

56. For most of the novel, however, the language centers around American nationalism, rather than a particular form of sectionalism. As a result, while most critics see the novel as a precursor to later Confederate nationalism, it often isn't recognized as espousing a distinctly southern imperialism. In a chapter on Pickens in *Calypso Magnolia,* e.g., Lowe focuses on Pickens's American patriotism, with slavery being a component of that, while Orville Burton, who edited the recovered 2002 edition of the novel, points to its blend of northern and southern characters as belying sectional affiliation.

4. Narratives of Reform: The Proslavery Social Problem Novel

1. The novel was officially registered by the publisher, D. Appleton, with the Library of Congress at the end of 1852. The publication announcements appeared early in 1853.

2. Such variant themes split the novel into two seemingly separate tales: a cautionary economic tale and a seduction romance. Many critics who discuss *The Valley* prefer to cite only specific sections, especially those not dealing with the romance. See Snavely, chap. 11; Noble; Ridgely, *Nineteenth-Century Southern Literature;* Kreyling, *Figures of the Hero;* and Ackermann. In her 1979 dissertation "The Virginia Historical Novel to 1835" (1979), Elizabeth S. Chamberlain probably comes closest to treating the novel's romantic plot and socioeconomic observations as two parts of a whole.

3. Noble briefly observes the generic borrowing, writing, "Tucker had read many of the eighteenth-century novels, and *The Valley* does display some of the conventions of the sentimental novel" (xviii).

4. Robert McLean mentions money and economics as being the primary theme of *The Valley.* According to McLean, however, *The Valley* is more of an elegy, nostalgic and mournful of the old Virginia gentry, rather than cautionary. See *George Tucker: Moral Philosopher and Man of Letters* (1961). Chamberlain also points out Tucker's emphasis on the poor financial practices of the Graysons.

5. The proposal, like many of the recolonization projects put forth throughout the antebellum period, rests on the premise that the prejudices of whites were too strong to allow for racial integration. In a later discussion with James Monroe on the subject, Jefferson would also propose relocating freed slaves to the West Indies (Jefferson to Monroe, 1801, *Selected Writings* 286–8).

6. For obvious reasons, the two are frequently confused, and often George Tucker's writings are attributed to St. George Tucker simply because he is more well-known.

7. *A Dissertation* also outlines the creation of a racialized slave system by enumerating laws put into place by the colonial and post-Revolutionary governments, in which the legal codes "create" the racial distinction. The argument presages critical race studies from the twentieth and twenty-first centuries. See, e.g., Allen; and Hartman. For histories of the profitability of slavery and its role in the development of global capitalism, see Williams; Johnson, *River of Dark Dreams;* Baptist; and Beckert.

8. Jefferson's abuse of the institution, especially the sexual violence toward his slave Sally Hemings, is now well-known. See Gordon-Reed, *Thomas Jefferson and Sally Hemings;* and *Hemingses of Monticello.*

9. As historian Robert McColley wryly observes, "With regard to slavery, Virginia statesmen were in the *peculiar* position of repeatedly describing an evil and then proceeding to insist that nothing could be done about it" (120, my emphasis). For more on the debates of early Virginian intellectuals on slavery, see Johnson, *River of Dark Dreams.*

10. Over the course of his lifetime, Tucker wrote three complete novels: *The Valley of Shenandoah* (1824) and two early science fiction novels, *A Voyage to the Moon* (1827) and *A Century Hence; or, A Romance of 1941* (written in 1841 but not published until 1977).

11. Tucker published almost twenty books of history and political economy, most of which were written while he was teaching at the university. For more on Tucker as an economist, see Helderman; Bernard; Popkin; Snavely; Dorfman, "George Tucker and Economic Growth"; and Huston.

12. The full title reads: *Letter to a Member of the General Assembly of Virginia, on the Subject of the Late Conspiracy of the Slaves; With a Proposal for Their Colonization* (1801). Often St. George Tucker is erroneously credited with having written the pamphlet.

13. He cites Prosser's rebellion as an example of the Virginia slave community's potential for organization and developed knowledge.

14. During the scene of the slave auction, Tucker describes a young girl going up for sale. When a trader attempts to bid on her, a local lawyer (appropriately named "Mr. Trueheart") buys her so that she can stay with her husband. After losing his bid to Trueheart, one of the traders assigns lascivious intent to the act and remarks snidely, "The old lawyer has taken a fancy to that mulatto girl" (*Valley of Shenandoah* 2:209).

15. Likewise, economic theorist Émile Durkheim asserts in *The Division of Labor in Society* (1896/1933), "The division of labor varies in direct ratio with the volume and density of societies, and, if it progresses in a continuous manner in the course of social development, it is because societies become regularly denser and generally more voluminous" (262).

16. Tucker's work was heavily influenced by the late-eighteenth–early-nineteenth-century British scholar T. R. Malthus. Malthus posited that population growth in any given society would be checked by the depletion of natural resources, which forces the society in question to adopt new economic practices. On Tucker's work in relationship to Malthus, see Huston; and Snavely.

17. In Tucker's next novel, *A Century Hence,* slavery has completely disappeared in many parts of the world, including areas in the southern United States. With that disappearance also comes a gradual acceptance of racial equality. As one character comments in a letter to

a friend, in London, "they walk arm in arm with a black man as soon as a white one, and some say sooner. Mr. Carlton's man James receives invitations to evening parties almost every day" (74).

18. In 1788, Elizabeth Whitman, the daughter of a respectable New England family, died in a tavern after giving birth to her child. She purportedly traveled to the tavern to meet her husband, the child's father, though the man never appeared. The story, which was printed and reprinted in local newspapers, caused a scandal and became fodder for gossip and other novels of seduction. William Hill Brown also adapted the story in his novel *The Power of Sympathy; or, The Triumph of Nature. Founded in Truth* (1789). Brown, too, presents the novel as "factual" (Davidson vii–ix).

19. Richardson's first novel, *Pamela* (1740), uses letters, as the subtitle proclaims, "In Order to Cultivate the Principles of Virtue and Religion in the Minds of the Youth of Both Sexes." Although Pamela is ultimately not a seduced woman, Richardson would employ the same epistolary form later in *Clarissa.*

20. Outside of the preface, all other references to the text of *The Valley of Shenandoah* are to the 1970 edition. Strangely, Noble does not include the preface in his edition, and his only reference to the "sentimental" tropes is to the romance plot. Few, if any, critics mention the preface in their discussions of the novel. See McLean; Kreyling, *Figures of the Hero;* and Chamberlain, among others.

21. The full title reads: *Progress of the United States in Population and Wealth in Fifty Years, as Exhibited by the Decennial Census.* Critics have noted Tucker's facility with statistical analysis. See Dorfman's introduction to the 1964 edition of Tucker's *Theory of Money and Banks* (originally published in 1839); and Snavely.

22. Snavely notes in his survey of Tucker's economic theories: "What [made] him unhappy . . . was the failure of the South to keep pace in the development of industry and in the growth of learning. . . . He never ceased to despair at what he regarded as the wasted opportunity of Virginia and the South. While he wanted to preserve its virtues and amenities, he sought for improvement and reform in the Southern way of life" (44). In Tucker's last novel, *A Century Hence,* that lopsided economic development ultimately drives the slaveholding states to consider a proposal for gradual emancipation.

23. The episode is nearly identical to the ending of *Charlotte Temple,* in which Charlotte's seducer marries another, less naive and dependent young lady from New York, leaving Charlotte alone to die.

24. Kreyling describes him as a romantic hero pitted against the "cash nexus" represented by New York businessmen, including Gildon's father (*Figures of the Hero* 16–17). Despite his use of the term *cash nexus,* Kreyling never explicitly connects Tucker's novel to Thomas Carlyle's later writings, specifically *Chartism* (1840) and *Past and Present* (1843).

25. In challenging Gildon, Edward utilizes what historian Bertram Wyatt-Brown describes as the tool held by every "man of honor" in the South to call for a "public recognition of a man's claim to power" (353).

26. The pamphlet was originally printed as a long letter and editorial in the *New York Observer* (*Letter* 11).

27. See, e.g., Sarah Josepha Hale's review in *Godey's Lady's Book* in Apr. 1853. For more on reviews of Stowe and proslavery fiction, see Peterson.

28. The line is actually a paraphrase; it summarizes key passages from his texts on British society and economics, *Chartism* (1840) and *Past and Present* (1843). U.S. authors in the nineteenth century, especially southerners, frequently referenced the phrase without attributing it to a specific written work or speech.

29. The quotation comes from a speech Hammond delivered to the U.S. Senate on the admission of Kansas under the Lecompton Constitution in Mar. 1858. See "On the Admission of Kansas," *Selections from Letters and Speeches.*

30. See Potter; Morrison, *Slavery and the American West;* Freehling, *Road to Disunion,* vols. 1 and 2.

31. As early as 1815, Virginia congressman John Randolph (who was, incidentally, St. George Tucker's stepson) frequently denounced "Yankee manufacturers" and "waxed nostalgic about the great Virginia planters of old whose principles, character, and wealth were largely responsible for the Old Dominion's onetime power and greatness" (Hamilton 164). See also Faust, *Ideology of Slavery;* Fox-Genovese and Genovese, *Mind of the Master Class;* and Ford.

32. See Goodloe's pamphlet, *Inquiry into the Causes Which Have Retarded the Accumulation of Wealth and Increase of Population in the Southern States* (1846).

33. In general, Helper was more interested in slavery's negative consequences for middle- and lower-class white southerners. His proposals for emancipation in *The Impending Crisis,* which also involved colonization in Africa, were all predicated on his extreme racism.

34. In June 1850, *De Bow's Review* reprinted Carlyle's highly racist and controversial essay, "Occasional Discourse on the Negro Question" (originally published in 1849), in which he uses the example of the West Indies as an argument against emancipation (527–38). George Fitzhugh also cites Carlyle's essay collection, *Latter-Day Pamphlets* (1850), in *Cannibals All!* and claims that his full title, *Cannibals All! or, Slaves without Masters,* came from his readings of the British author (108–9). For more on Carlyle's influence in the U.S. slavery debates, see "'At Least Half Right'"; and Straka.

35. Donald notes that like Helper, De Bow was one of the few proslavery advocates who addressed his arguments to the poorer whites in the South ("Proslavery Argument" 6). See De Bow, *Interest in Slavery.*

36. In *The American Slave Narrative and the Victorian Novel* (2010), Julia Sun-Joo Lee writes: "By resituating *North and South* to account for its cosmopolitan dimension, we have seen how slavery impacts the novel. In this alternate 'North and South,' England is reimagined as part of a global community that links Lancashire to the American South" (105).

37. For a more thorough definition of the genre, see Cazamian; Tillotson; Kestner; Gallagher; and Bizup.

38. Rebecca Harding Davis's "Life in the Iron Mills" (1861) is the most cited example of the genre in the United States.

39. The characterization of the narratives varies depending upon the critic. Cazamian uses "interventionism"; Bodenheimer calls it "reconciliation"; and Gallagher refers to the

novels' "mediation." I prefer *reconciliation* because the term better applies to the American proslavery novels and would later describe postbellum novels that promoted communication between northerners and southerners. For more on the function of reconciliation narratives in the postbellum era, see Blight; and Cowan.

40. Trollope was the mother of the popular Victorian novelist Anthony Trollope.

41. Both Trollope and Gaskell, like proslavery southerners, drew inspiration from Thomas Carlyle. Gaskell, whose *Mary Barton* (1845–7) and *North and South* (1854–5) became two of the better-known industrial social problem novels, was partially inspired by her own experiences with working-class families in Manchester but also from her readings of *Past and Present* (Vanden Bossche lv–lvi). Trollope's *Life and Adventures of Michael Armstrong, the Factory Boy* also takes up ideas communicated in Carlyle's earlier observations of English political economy and social life (Joshi 37–8).

42. Critics such as Mary Poovey and Elaine Freedgood have observed that Harriet Martineau's series of novellas and sketches, *Illustrations of Political Economy* (1832), served a similar purpose for British readers. Likewise, in *Panic Fiction,* Mary Templin discusses a series of novels written by American women in the decades surrounding the 1837 Panic whose plots were designed to introduce complicated financial matters to the female reading public.

43. Templin points out that in McIntosh's fiction, the female characters are not allowed true agency in their dealings with the market. Instead, she argues, the novels leave it to the male characters to "fix" the financial disasters and "save" the women (chap. 4).

44. The only extended biographical study of McIntosh is an unpublished dissertation written by Bashar Akili at the Loughborough University of Technology in 1990.

45. By the time *The Lofty and the Lowly* was published, McIntosh was well-known internationally as the author of popular children's morality tales and domestic fiction. Her "Aunt Kitty's tales" were immensely successful, and between 1839 and 1845, she published nine short story collections and novels mostly for juvenile readers. Her first two adult novels, *Woman an Enigma; or, Life and Its Revealings* (1843) and *Two Lives* (1846), appeared under her real name. Both were best sellers, and *Two Lives* went through seven editions in less than four years.

46. See also Templin.

47. Works such as *Aunt Phillis' Cabin* (1852) by Mary H. Eastman and *The Planter's Northern Bride* (1854) by Caroline Lee Hentz typically pit the southern plantation system and the institution of slavery against the space of free trade and competition in the North. In these portrayals, slavery and the space of the plantation provide the counterpoints to the social evils of free market capitalism.

48. Most of the proslavery authors of "anti-Tom" novels had few direct dealings with the running of a plantation or the institution of slavery. Mary H. Eastman, e.g., came from a prominent Virginia family, but she primarily lived in Washington, DC, with her husband, a captain in the U.S. Army. Caroline Lee Hentz was born in Massachusetts and moved south with her husband in 1826. She spent the rest of her life living in various southern states and supporting her family with her writing.

49. As Sarah Mesle points out in her study of McIntosh's novel, the anti-Tom designation limits the understanding of works such as *The Lofty and the Lowly* and downplays their

nationalist aims, in which "critics often mischaracterize national attitudes about race and slavery by minimizing the purchase of proslavery attitudes in national debates" (205). Mary Templin also points out that *The Lofty and the Lowly* specifically "speaks out in favor of making the plantation *more* of a capitalist enterprise" (178).

50. That quality also makes the passage reminiscent of McIntosh's invectives against aristocracy in *Woman in America* and the reconciliation tale that encourages financial literacy in *Two Lives*.

51. Several critics, including Templin, Mesle, and Moss, point out that despite the attempts at regional interaction and understanding, McIntosh consistently presents northern stereotypes as far more abhorrent than the southern plantation ideal. See also Jordan-Lake.

52. In *Michael Armstrong*, e.g., Mary Brotherton does not abolish child labor but adopts three factory children herself. And in *North and South*, Margaret Hale and John Thornton do not move south to run a farm but modify Thornton's existing factory so that the working conditions are improved.

53. In her reading of the novel, Mesle argues that McIntosh's aim is "to represent Southern society as the source of American morality" and that Alice and the changes she undergoes are key to creating this moral center (223). This is the way by which, Mesle argues, McIntosh could define a form of nationalism that nonetheless included slavery. Likewise, although Templin highlights McIntosh's critiques of southern economic practices, she nonetheless attributes the region's financial instability in the novel to "the contaminating and rapacious touch of Northern commerciality" (168).

54. The exact nature of the invention is, of course, left vague in the novel.

5. "Free Labor" and the Free Market: Slave Narratives

1. See Cowan.

2. Upon buying his freedom, Frank had his name officially listed in the 1820 federal census as "Free Frank" (Walker, *Free Frank* 48). He would later have it changed to Frank McWorter.

3. McWorter would also go on to found the town of New Philadelphia, Illinois. For a more thorough account of Frank's life, see Walker, *Free Frank*.

4. These include the historians whose work is essential to this book—Eric Williams, Walter Johnson, Edward Baptist, and Sven Beckert—as well as David Brion Davis and Thomas Haskell. Prior to Johnson and Beckert, historians such as Robert Fogel and Stanley Engerman evaluated slave systems as profitable in a capitalist economy, while Elizabeth Fox-Genovese and Eugene Genovese position slavery in certain economies as an integral part of the developing capitalist order. See Williams; Johnson, *River of Dark Dreams;* Baptist; Beckert; Fogel and Engerman; Fogel; Fox-Genovese and Genovese, *Fruits of Merchant Capital;* Davis, *Problem of Slavery;* and Haskell.

5. As critic Francis Smith Foster puts it, the authors of most narratives "divest themselves of any connection with the slave culture" (67).

6. See also Warren. Although Warren focuses on twentieth-century literature, he argues that the standard definition of African American literature—an engagement with civil rights

in a twentieth-century context—ceases to bear the same political weight in the late twentieth and twenty-first centuries. His basic premise suggests wider implications for the study of early African American literature. Building on existing scholarship, the discussion of early black American writing then shifts to include issues of class, gender, and sexuality as interacting with racial politics and racial identity.

7. For a general overview of the slave narrative genre and the number of narratives published in the eighteenth and nineteenth centuries, see Starling. Starling's study was originally a dissertation written in 1946; it took almost forty years for it to be published in book form.

8. See, e.g., Foster; and Levecq.

9. In his 1838 narrative, former slave Moses Roper even includes a diagram of the torture device.

10. For more on the role of women and marriage in the narratives, see Stanley.

11. See Andrews; Foster, *Witnessing Slavery,* for more on the specific conventions of the slave narrative.

12. In *Soul by Soul,* Walter Johnson also details the conjoined quality of the economic and the personal in Grandy's memory (64).

13. See Schlesinger; Dorfman, *Economic Mind;* and Comegna.

14. See Hobsbawm, "Making of the Working Class"; Glickstein, *Concepts of Free Labor;* Montgomery; and Foner, *Free Soil.*

15. For more on the slavery in the debates over labor, see Cunliffe. As Julia Sun-Joo Lee points out, popular British authors such as Charles Dickens and Charlotte Brontë were also influenced by the slave narratives. Elizabeth Gaskell, e.g., drew from the genre in her depiction of the British working class (see Lee chap. 4).

16. Garrison does, however, castigate the Chartists for their habit of usurping antislavery meetings for the cause of the working class. He calls it "dastardly," "criminal," and simply "rude."

17. For more on Douglass and Chartism, see McFeely; and Ostrowski.

18. See Davis, *Problem of Slavery;* and Ashworth, vol. 1.

19. Weld was one of the leading abolitionists in the 1830s and 1840s and wrote *American Slavery as It Is* (1839), a testimonial on the conditions of slavery that Harriet Beecher Stowe would use as a reference when writing *Uncle Tom's Cabin.* See also Ashworth, vol. 1.

20. See Cunliffe; and Walters.

21. This language is almost identical to Alexis de Tocqueville's observations of U.S. slavery in the first volume of *Democracy in America* (1835): "There is no African who has come freely to the shore of the New World, from which it follows that all those found there in our day are slaves or freedmen. Thus the Negro transmits to all his descendants, with their existence, the external sign of his ignominy. The law can destroy servitude; but God alone can make the trace of it disappear" (327). And Tocqueville observes the same effects: that the South has effectively abolished work for white men and women, creating a society in which "misery appeared preferable to industry" (335).

22. For more on the *Liberator's* relationship to the literary marketplace and commercial exchange—specifically its role in commercializing abolitionism—see Rohrbach.

23. Eric Foner notes that "whereas labor leaders tended to see abolition as a diversion from the grievances of northern labor and slavery as simply one example of more pervasive problems in American life, abolitionists considered the labor issue as artificial or secondary" ("Abolitionism" 261).

24. Brownson was also affiliated with the Transcendental writers, and the *Boston Quarterly Review*—the paper he edited—published work by George Bancroft, Margaret Fuller, and George Ripley.

25. Unlike Fitzhugh, however, Brownson advocates for the forces of free market capitalism; in suggesting that perhaps there will not always be a division between laborers and capitalists—or "proprietors"—he suggests the possibility and even probability of economic mobility within a capitalist system. This rhetoric was not uncommon in the discourse over free labor during the antebellum period. Jonathan Glickstein observes that antebellum reformers displayed a consistent faith in the notion of an American economic exceptionalism, which asserted that despite apparent inequalities, the United States furnished enough abundant material opportunities in a free market so as to enable *anyone* to achieve social and financial mobility (*American Exceptionalism* 4–5, 62–3).

26. Though in Fitzhugh's case, the defense of slavery was not inadvertent.

27. See Roediger.

28. See Boston.

29. See Voss. "It was not until the New Deal," according to Voss, "that less-skilled workers were successfully incorporated into the labor movement" (2).

30. Houston A. Baker argues in *Long Black Song* (1972) that "Douglass's work is a spiritual autobiography akin to the writings of such noted American authors such as Cotton Mather, Benjamin Franklin, and Henry Adams" (78). Robert Levine adopts a similar approach and interprets some of the narratives as writing in the "Revolutionary tradition" of Benjamin Franklin" (chap. 5). William Andrews also labels Douglass's *Narrative* an "American jeremiad" (124), and Valerie Smith argues that "the plot of [Douglass's] narrative offers a profound endorsement of the fundamental American plot, the myth of the self made man" (27). See also Dudley. For more on responses to capitalism, see Kazanjian. Similarly, in *Slavery and Sentiment,* Christine Levecq argues that the early-nineteenth-century narratives of William Grimes and Charles Ball "indirectly [build] an image of African Americans as particularly apt for survival in the budding liberal, capitalist system" (208).

31. See, e.g., the narratives of Josiah Henson (1849), Moses Grandy (1843), and Lunsford Lane (1842). See Andrews for more on the performance of the Protestant work ethic in slave narratives (chap. 4).

32. Many of the articles in the *North Star* that addressed skilled labor were written by Martin Delany, one of the strongest advocates of black economic autonomy. See Delany.

33. The article's tone reflects a general sentiment held by Douglass. Although he was sympathetic to the plight of the Irish workingmen and Chartists during his visit to Britain and Ireland in 1845, he was more critical of the Irish who were immigrating to the United States in the 1840s and 1850s. According to Paul Giles, "To some extent, this hostility emerged from what the African American community in general took to be the reactionary, proslavery ten-

dencies of Irish-American culture" ("Narrative Reversals" 798). For more on Douglass, the Irish, and transatlanticism, see Giles, "Narrative Reversals."

34. According to Santamarina, this posturing on the part of civil rights leaders such as Douglass erased any forms of labor that did not fall into the category of "skilled," including most labor available to workingwomen at the time. Santamarina writes, "Ironically, in advocating on behalf of black workers consigned to menial employments, reformers at times depicted black workers as acquiescent, and even complacent, in the face of discrimination" (15). She then goes on to cite Douglass repeatedly as the perpetrator of such trends and frequently contrasts his representation of field labor and the work of slaves as methods of oppression in his *Narrative* with the more positive representations in Truth's text (47).

35. Douglass only briefly describes northern racism in *Narrative*, but he goes into more detail in his later autobiography, *My Bondage, My Freedom* (1855).

36. Haskell writes that global economic shifts altered the "perception and cognitive style" in regard to abolitionist arguments as well as "a change in the perception of causal connection" between slavery and the global economy (111).

37. See, e.g., Stepto; Olney; and Barrett.

38. Quincy was a prominent Boston abolitionist who edited the *National Anti-Slavery Standard.*

39. See, e.g., Dance; and Byerman.

40. In another point of similarity between the slave narratives and the discourse of free labor, memoirs and autobiographies of former Chartists and working-class men in Britain evince the same qualities of the "road narrative." See, e.g., the 1845 autobiography of the Chartist and labor activist Allen Davenport.

41. Continuing the connections with Britain, like many texts by African American authors and former slaves, Pennington's narrative was first published in London.

42. Here I use the term *alienation* in the sense that Marx defines it in the *Economic and Philosophic Manuscripts of 1844* (1964). In describing alienation, Marx writes that "the worker is related to the *product of his labour* as to an *alien* object. For on this premise it is clear that the more the worker spends himself, the more powerful the alien objective world becomes which he creates over-against himself, the poorer he himself—his inner world—becomes, the less belongs to him as his own. . . . The *alienation* of the worker in his product means not only that his labour becomes an object, an *external* existence, but that it exists *outside him,* independently, as something alien to him, and that it becomes a power of its own confronting him; it means that the life which he has conferred on the object confronts him as something hostile and alien" (108).

43. See, e.g., Reid-Pharr; Stover; and Smith, "'Don't Be Too Careful.'" For more on gender and labor, see Santamarina; Glickstein, *Concepts of Free Labor;* and Merish.

44. For more on Jacobs and her appeals to motherhood, see Li. For examples of interpretations that account for Jacobs's representation of labor, see Santamarina; and Greeson, "'Mysteries and Miseries.'" While Santamarina recognizes that Jacobs depicts women's labor, she dismisses it as primarily "unpaid domestic labor" (21). In a unique take on Jacobs's narrative, Greeson argues that *Incidents* must be read as a hybrid of urban gothic fiction—to which

Jacobs would have been exposed while living in New York—and the earlier slave narratives. Greeson concludes, "Jacobs's blending of the conventions of these two genres in *Incidents* troubles equally the binary opposition of Northern industrial capitalism and Southern chattel slavery in antebellum discourse" (302).

45. Greeson also notes this self-definition and observes that it "deliberately invokes terms—'skillful,' 'trade,' 'mechanic,' 'freeman,'—explosively charged in the antebellum North" ("'Mysteries and Miseries'" 291).

Epilogue: How Did We Get Here?

1. *I'll Take My Stand* is the critical ur-text of twentieth- and twenty-first-century southern studies. It almost always warrants a mention or extended discussion in southern studies criticism, yet it is taught and read less and less. For examples of critical studies that examine *I'll Take My Stand's* influence, see Kreyling, *Inventing Southern Literature;* Bone; and Duck.

2. McPherson attributes this "boutiquing" of the region to the practices that dominated southern studies up through the end of the twentieth century, although popular imagination clearly has also played a role.

3. Debates over the presence of Confederate monuments throughout the United States are prime examples of this pattern. In 1978, for instance, a bust of Nathan Bedford Forrest was erected in the Tennessee State Capitol—more than one hundred years *after* the end of the Civil War. Yet when local groups, including the Nashville chapter of the NAACP, protested its original placement and when groups have repeated those protests every few years since, defenders always cite "tradition" and "history" as its reason for being. See Gervin.

4. Numerous historians and critics have identified how the racist institutions of the nineteenth century carried over into the twentieth and twenty-first centuries, including Ta-Nehisi Coates in his articles for the *Atlantic;* Carol Anderson; Kendi; and Alexander. Scholars have also traced the continuity of the plantation structure into the modern era: see Houston A. Baker, *Turning South Again* (2001); and the special issue of the *Global South* featuring "plantation modernity," edited by Amy Clukey and Jeremy Wells in 2016.

5. See Stecopoulos for more on the role of the South and southern literature in the context of postbellum and early-twentieth-century U.S. imperialism.

6. The novel was published serially in *Scribner's Magazine* in 1894, then in book form in 1895 (Turner, *George W. Cable* 292; Rubin, *George Washington Cable* 212).

7. See Rubin, *George Washington Cable;* and Bendixon.

8. See Rubin, "Division of the Heart."

9. Cable's 1885 essays for *Century* magazine, "The Freedman's Case in Equity" and "The Silent South," are both sharp critiques of southern racial codes and the effects of slavery in the postbellum era. The essays are frequently cited as evidence of Cable's engagement with discussions of race and civil rights.

10. Some critics have noted that his ambivalence causes Cable to hedge away from a direct refutation of the racialized southern social structures in his fiction. See Ladd, *Nationalism and the Color Line;* and Handley.

11. See Ladd, *Nationalism and the Color Line;* Greeson, "Expropriating *The Great South* and Exporting 'Local Color'"; and Peip.

12. By the time *John March* was published, in 1895, Cable was known through his work featuring antebellum New Orleans culture and his advocacy of civil rights for black Americans, specifically *Old Creole Days* (1879) and *The Grandissimes.* Compared with his previous work, the reception of *John March, Southerner* was tepid, ambivalent at best. While some reviewers saw the novel as "powerful" and "thoroughgoing" in its critique of Reconstruction, others bemoaned the lack of New Orleans local color that had made his writing popular (qtd. in Turner, *George W. Cable* 295; and "John March, Southerner"). Later biographers and critics have also written off the book as Cable's failed attempt at creating a romance not dependent on local color (Butcher 119; Rubin, *George Washington Cable* 237–8).

13. For more on the idea of pervasive literary haunting and "spectrality," especially in representations of racial violence, see Melanie Anderson.

14. "Speech Delivered at the Banquet of the New England Society, New York, December 21, 1886" in Shurter.

15. See the Turner and Rubin biographies for more on the book's publication history.

16. The representation of Leggett is truly odd. He is a former slave and the victim of incredible violence. Yet he is also represented as a villain throughout much of the novel; he participates and orchestrates some of the worst, morally dubious activities. It seems to contradict Cable's sympathetic portrayals of black southerners in his other fictional works, but it also fits the intent of *John March* to implicate the entire nation in the problems resulting from Reconstruction and Gilded Age era capitalism. In short, no one is safe in Cable's estimation.

WORKS CITED

Primary Sources

Baldwin, Joseph Glover. *The Flush Times of Alabama and Mississippi*. New York: D. Appleton & Co., 1853.

——. *The Flush Times of Alabama and Mississippi*. 1853. Edited by William A. Owens. Hill & Wang, 1957.

——. *The Flush Times of California*. Edited by Richard E. Amacher and George W. Polhemus. U of Georgia P, 1966.

——. *Party Leaders*. New York: D. Appleton & Co., 1855.

Bibb, Henry. *Narrative of the Life and Adventures of Henry Bibb, An American Slave, Written by Himself. With an Introduction by Lucius C. Matlack*. New York: Published by the author, 1849.

"Black Slavery!" *Northern Star*, 2 Dec. 1837.

Brown, William Wells. *Narrative of William W. Brown, A Fugitive Slave. Written by Himself.* Boston: Anti-Slavery Office, 1847.

Brownson, Orestes. *The Laboring Classes, an Article from the Boston Quarterly Review*. 3rd ed. Boston: Benjamin H. Greene, 1840.

Bulwer-Lytton, Edward. *England and the English*. 2 vols. New York: Harper, 1833.

Burton, Orville Vernon, and Georganne B. Burton, eds. *The Free Flag of Cuba: The Lost Novel of Lucy Holcombe Pickens*. Louisiana State UP, 2002.

Cable, George Washington. *John March, Southerner*. New York: Grosset & Dunlap/ Charles Scribner's Sons, 1894.

Calhoun, John C. "The Slavery Question." *Congressional Globe*, Senate, 29th Cong., 2nd Sess. 19 Feb. 1847: 453–5.

——. *The Works of John C. Calhoun.* Edited by Richard K. Crallé. Vol. 1. Charleston, SC: Walker & James, 1851.

——. *The Works of John C. Calhoun.* Edited by Richard K. Crallé. Vols. 2–6. New York: D. Appleton & Co., 1860–70.

Carlyle, Thomas. "Occasional Discourse on the Negro Question." 1849. *De Bow's Review* (June 1850): 527–38.

——. *Chartism.* Boston: Charles C. Little & James Brown, 1840.

——. *Past and Present.* 1843. Edited by Chris R. Vanden Bossche. U of California P, 2005.

Cartwright, Samuel. "Diseases and Peculiarities of the Negro Race." *De Bow's Review* (Jan. 1851): 64–9.

Cocke, James D. *A Glance at the Currency and Resources Generally of the Republic of Texas.* Houston: Niles & Co., Printers, 1838.

Cooper, James Fenimore. *The Last of the Mohicans.* 1826. Signet, 1962.

——. *The Pioneers.* 1823. Intro. Donald Ringe. Penguin Books, 1988.

Davenport, Allen. *The Life and Literary Pursuits of Allen Davenport.* 1845. Edited by Malcolm Chase. Scholar P, 1994.

Davis, Rebecca Harding. "Life in the Iron Mills." *Atlantic Monthly* (Apr. 1861): 430–51.

De Bow, James D. B. *The Interest in Slavery of the Southern Non-Slaveholder. The Right of Peaceful* Succession. *Slavery in the Bible.* Charleston, SC: Steam-Power Presses of Evans & Cogswell, 1860.

——. "Introduction: Carlyle on West India Emancipation." *De Bow's Review* (June 1850): 527.

——. "Mexico, Its Social and Political Condition." *De Bow's Review* 1.2 (Feb. 1846): 116–32.

——. "The Progress of American Commerce." *De Bow's Review* 2.6 (Dec. 1846): 368–426.

——. "Southern Industrial Revolution." *De Bow's Review* (July 1850).

Delany, Martin R. *The Condition, Elevation, Emigration, and Destiny of the Colored People of the United States.* Philadelphia: King & Baird, 1852.

Dickens, Charles. *Sketches by Boz.* 1836–9. Edited by Michael Slater. Illustrated by George Cruikshank. Ohio State UP, 1994.

——. *Sketches by Boz.* 1836–9. Edited by Dennis Walder. Penguin Books, 1995.

Douglass, Frederick. "Learn Trades or Starve!" *Frederick Douglass's Paper,* 4 Mar. 1853.

——. "Make Your Sons Mechanics and Farmers, Not Waiters, Porters, and Barbers." *Frederick Douglass's Paper,* 8 Apr. 1853.

——. *My Bondage, My Freedom.* 1855. Edited by John David Smith. Penguin Books, 2003.

——. *Narrative of the Life of Frederick Douglass, An American Slave. Written by Himself.* Boston: Anti-Slavery Office, 1845.

Emerson, Ralph Waldo. "The American Scholar." *Ralph Waldo Emerson: The Major Prose.* Edited by Ronald A. Bosco and Joel Myerson. Belknap P of Harvard UP, 2015. 91–109.

——. "The Poet." *Ralph Waldo Emerson: The Major Prose.* Edited by Ronald A. Bosco and Joel Myerson. Belknap P of Harvard UP, 2015. 202–25.

Evans, Augusta Jane. *Inez: A Tale of the Alamo.* New York: Harper & Brothers, 1855.

Fitzhugh, George. *Cannibals All! Or, Slaves without Masters.* 1857. *Ante-Bellum: Writings of George Fitzhugh and Hinton Rowan Helper on Slavery.* Edited by Harvey Wish. Capricorn Books, 1960. 97–156.

——. *Sociology for the South; or, The Failure of Free Society.* 1854. *Ante-Bellum: Writings of George Fitzhugh and Hinton Rowan Helper on Slavery.* Edited by Harvey Wish. Capricorn Books, 1960. 41–96.

Foster, Hannah W. *The Coquette; or, The History of Eliza Wharton.* 1797. Edited by Cathy N. Davidson. Oxford UP, 1986.

Freeman, Mrs. Letter to David H. Bishop. Small Manuscripts Collection. 1977.2. Folder 3. University of Mississippi Special Collections.

Garrison, William Lloyd. "Free Labor." *Liberator,* 26 Mar. 1847.

——. "Lecture in Wilmington, Delaware." *Liberator,* 12 June 1857.

——. "The Scottish Chartists." *Liberator,* 18 Dec. 1840.

Gaskell, Elizabeth. *North and South.* 1854–5. Edited by Angus Easson and Sally Shuttleworth. Oxford World's Classics. Oxford UP, 1998.

Goodloe, Daniel R. *Inquiry into the Causes Which Have Retarded the Accumulation of Wealth and Increase of Populations in the Southern States: In Which the Question of Slavery Is Considered in a Politico-Economical Point of View.* Washington, DC: W. Blanchard, 1846.

Grandy, Moses. *Narrative of the Life of Moses Grandy; Late a Slave in the United States of America.* London: C. Gilpin, 1843.

Hale, Sarah Josepha. "The Lofty and the Lowly." *Godey's Magazine and Lady's Book* (Apr. 1853): 378.

Hammond, James Henry. "Anniversary Oration of the State Agricultural Society." *Proceedings of the South Carolina State Agricultural Society at Their Annual Convention, Nov. 22 1841.* Columbia, SC: A. S. Johnston, 1841. 3–26.

——. "On the Admission of Kansas, under the Lecompton Constitution. Delivered in the Senate of the United States, March 4, 1858." *Selections from the Letters and Speeches of Hon. James Henry Hammond.* New York: John F. Trow & Co., 1866. 301–22.

Harper, William. *Memoir on Slavery.* 1838. *The Ideology of Slavery: Proslavery Thought in the Antebellum South, 1830–1860.* Edited by Drew Gilpin Faust. Louisiana State UP, 1981. 78–135.

Hawthorne, Nathaniel. "Simms's *Views and Reviews.*" *Salem Advertiser,* 2 May 1846. "Hawthorne's Contributions to *The Salem Advertiser,*" by Randall Stewart. *American Literature* 5.4 (1934): 327–41.

Helper, Hinton Rowan. *The Impending Crisis of the South: How to Meet It.* 1857. *Ante-Bellum: Writings of George Fitzhugh and Hinton Rowan Helper on Slavery.* Edited by Harvey Wish. Capricorn Books, 1960. 157–256.

Hilen, Andrew, ed. *The Letters of Henry Wadsworth Longfellow.* 6 vols. Belknap P of Harvard UP, 1966.

Hooper, Johnson Jones. *Adventures of Captain Simon Suggs, Late of the Tallapoosa Volunteers.* 1845. Edited by Manly Wade Wellman. U of North Carolina P, 1969.

———. "Cow Heel Aristocracy." Editorial. *Montgomery (AL) Daily Mail,* 27 Nov. 1855.

———. "The Morality of the Country." Editorial. *Montgomery (AL) Daily Mail,* 21 Nov. 1854.

———. "Railroads." Editorial. *Montgomery (AL) Daily Mail,* 17 Nov. 1854.

———. *Some Adventures of Captain Simon Suggs, Late of the Tallapoosa Volunteers; Together with "Taking the Census," and Other Alabama Sketches.* Philadelphia: Carey & Hart, 1845.

———. "Taking the Census in Alabama. By a Chicken Man of 1840." *Some Adventures of Captain Simon Suggs.* Philadelphia: Carey & Hart, 1845. 149–88.

Ingraham, Joseph Holt. *Montezuma, the Serf; or, The Revolt of the Mexitili. A Tale of the Last Days of the Aztec Dynasty.* 2 vols. Boston: H. L. Williams, 1845.

———. *The South-West, by a Yankee.* 2 vols. New York: Harper & Brothers, 1835.

———. *The Texan Ranger; or, The Maid of Matamoras. A Tale of the Mexican War.* Boston: H. L. Williams, 1846.

Jacobs, Harriet. *Incidents in the Life of a Slave Girl. Written by Herself.* Edited by L. Maria Child. Boston: Published for the author, 1861.

Jefferson, Thomas. *Notes on the State of Virginia.* 1887. *The Selected Writings of Thomas Jefferson.* Edited by Wayne Franklin. Norton, 2010.

"John March, Southerner." *New York Times,* 10 Dec. 1894.

Kennedy, John Pendleton. *Horse-Shoe Robinson; A Tale of the Tory Ascendency.* 2 vols. Philadelphia: Carey, Lea, & Blanchard, 1835.

———. "A Legend of Maryland." *Atlantic Monthly* 6.33–4 (July–Aug. 1860): 29–44, 141–52.

——. *Memoirs of the Life of William Wirt, Attorney General of the United States.* 2 vols. 1849. Philadelphia: Blanchard & Lea, 1852.

——. *Rob of the Bowl: A Legend of St. Inigoe's.* 2 vols. Philadelphia: Lea & Blanchard, 1838.

Kirkland, Caroline. *A New Home—Who'll Follow? Or, Glimpses of Western Life.* New York: C. S. Francis, 1839.

"Last Days of Rev. Dr. Ingraham." Small Manuscripts Collection. 1976.5. Folder 4. University of Mississippi Special Collections.

McCluskey, M. W., ed. *Speeches, Messages, and Other Writings of the Hon. Albert Gallatin Brown, a Senator in Congress from the State of Mississippi.* 2nd ed. Philadelphia: Jas. B. Smith, 1859.

McIntosh, Maria J. *Letter on the Address of the Women of England to Their Sisters of America in Relation to Slavery.* New York: T. J. Crowen, 1853.

——. *The Lofty and the Lowly; or, Good in All and None All-Good.* 2 vols. New York: D. Appleton & Co., 1852.

——. *Two Lives; or, To Seem and to Be.* New York: D. Appleton & Co., 1846.

——. *Woman an Enigma; or, Life and Its Revealings.* New York: Harper & Brothers, 1843.

——. *Woman in America: Her Work and Her Reward.* New York: D. Appleton & Co., 1850.

"Obituary Notice of Prof. George Tucker." *Proceedings of the American Philosophical Society* 9.68 (1862): 64–70.

Pennington, James W. C. *The Fugitive Blacksmith; or, Events in the History of James W. C. Pennington, Pastor of a Presbyterian Church, New York, Formerly a Slave in the State of Maryland, United States.* London: C. Gilpin, 1849.

Poe, Edgar Alan. "Watkins Tottle." *Southern Literary Messenger* (June 1836): 433–4.

Pollard, Edward. *Black Diamonds Gathered in the Darkey Homes of the South.* New York: Pudney & Russell, Publishers, 1859.

Richardson, Samuel. *Pamela; or, Virtue Rewarded.* 1740. Edited by Thomas Keymer and Alice Wakely. Oxford World's Classics. Oxford UP, 2008.

Roper, Moses. *A Narrative of the Adventures and Escape of Moses Roper, from American Slavery.* Philadelphia: Merrihew & Gunn, 1838.

Rowson, Susanna. *Charlotte Temple.* 1791. Edited by Ann Douglas. Penguin Books, 1991.

Scott, Walter. *Waverley; or, 'Tis Sixty Years Since.* 1814. Edited by Andrew Hook. Penguin Books, 1972.

Seymour, Almira. "Song of a Kansas Emigrant." *Liberator,* 13 Apr. 1855.

Shurter, Edwin DuBois, ed. *The Complete Orations and Speeches of Henry W. Grady.* Hinds, Noble & Eldredge, 1910.

Simms, William Gilmore. "Domestic Manners of the Americans by Mrs. Trollope." *American Quarterly Review* (Sept. 1832): 109–33.

——. *The History of South Carolina.* Charleston SC: S. Babcock, 1840.

——. *The Letters of William Gilmore Simms.* Edited by Mary C. Simms Oliphant, Alfred Taylor Odell, and T. S. Duncan Eaves. 4 vols. U of South Carolina P, 1954.

——. "Miss Martineau on Slavery." *Southern Literary Messenger* (Nov. 1837): 641–57.

——. *The Partisan: A Tale of the Revolution.* 2 vols. 1835. Gregg P, 1968.

——. "The Philosophy of the Omnibus." *American Monthly Magazine* 3 (Aug. 1834): 153–9.

——. *Poetry and the Practical.* 1851–4. Edited by James E. Kibler Jr. U of Arkansas P, 1996.

——. *South-Carolina in the Revolutionary War.* Charleston SC: Walker & James, 1853.

——. "South Carolina in the Revolution. A Lecture." 1856. *The Letters of William Gilmore Simms.* Edited by Mary C. Simms Oliphant, Alfred Taylor Odell, and T. S. Duncan Eaves. Vol. 3. U of South Carolina P, 1954. 521–50.

——. "Summer Travel in the South." *Southern Quarterly Review* (Sept. 1850): 24–63.

——. *The Sword and the Distaff; or, Fair, Fat, and Forty, A Story of the South at the Close of the Revolution.* Charleston, SC: Walker, Richards, & Co., 1852.

——. *Views and Reviews in American Literature, History, and Fiction, First Series.* 1845. Edited by C. Hugh Holman. Belknap P of Harvard UP, 1962.

——. *Woodcraft; or, Hawks about the Dovecote. A Story of the South at the Close of the Revolution.* 1854. Gregg Press, 1968.

——. *The Yemassee. A Romance of Carolina.* 1835. Edited by Alexander Cowie. American Book Co., 1937.

"Southern Literature." *Putnam's Monthly* 9 (Feb. 1857): 207–8.

Stowe, Harriet Beecher. *Uncle Tom's Cabin; or, Life among the Lowly.* Boston: John P. Jewett, 1852.

Sumner, Charles. *The Crime against Kansas. Speech of Hon. Charles Sumner of Massachusetts. In the Senate of the United States, May 19, 1856.* New York: Greeley & McElrath, 1856.

Ten Hour Day Circular. 1835. *A Documentary History of American Industrial Society.* Edited by John Commons, Ulrich B. Phillips, Eugene A. Gilmore, Helen Sumner, and John B. Andrews. Vol. 6. Arthur H. Clark Co., 1910. 94–9.

"Texas." *Columbus (MS) Democrat,* 17 Dec. 1836, 1. Chronicling America, Historical American Newspapers, Library of Congress.

Tocqueville, Alexis de. *Democracy in America.* 1835/40. Edited and translated by Harvey C. Mansfield and Delba Winthrop. U of Chicago P, 2000.

Trollope, Frances. *The Life and Adventures of Jonathan Jefferson Whitlaw; or Scenes on the Mississippi.* Paris: Baudry's European Library, 1836.

——. *The Life and Adventures of Michael Armstrong, the Factory Boy.* London: Henry Colburn, 1840.

Tucker, George. *A Century Hence; or, A Romance of 1941.* Edited by Donald R. Noble Jr. UP of Virginia, 1977.

——. *The Laws of Wages, Profits, and Rent, Investigated.* Philadelphia: E. L. Carey & A. Hart, 1837.

——. *Letter to a Member of the General Assembly of Virginia on the Subject of the Late Conspiracy of the Slave; With a Proposal for Their Colonization.* Baltimore: Bonsal & Niles, 1801.

——. *Progress of the United States in Population and Wealth in Fifty Years, as Exhibited by the Decennial Census.* Philadelphia: Carey & Hart, 1843.

——. *The Valley of Shenandoah; or, Memoirs of the Graysons.* 1824. Introduction by Donald R. Noble Jr. U of North Carolina P, 1970.

——. *A Voyage to the Moon: With Some Account of the Manners and Customs, Science and Philosophy, of the People of Morosofia and Other Lunarians. By Joseph Atterley.* New York: Elam Bliss, 1827.

Tucker, St. George. *A Dissertation on Slavery: With a Proposal for the Gradual Abolition of It, in the State of Virginia.* Philadelphia: Matthew Carey, 1796.

Twain, Mark. *Life on the Mississippi.* 1882. Introduction by Jonathan Raban. Library of America, 2009.

Walker, Samuel R. "Cuba and the South." *De Bow's Review* 17.5 (Nov. 1854): 519–25.

Whittier, John Greenleaf. "Whittier's Reply." *Liberator,* 10 Aug. 1833.

Willis, Nathaniel Parker. "Willis's Account of London." *Southern Literary Messenger* (Mar. 1835): 366–9.

Secondary Sources

Ackermann, Zeno. *Messing with Romance: American Poetics and Antebellum Southern Fiction.* Peter Lang, 2012.

Agathocleous, Tanya. *Urban Realism and the Cosmopolitan Imagination in the Nineteenth Century: Visible City, Invisible World.* Cambridge UP, 2011.

Akili, Bashar. "Maria Jane McIntosh, a Woman in Her Time: A Biographical and Critical Study." Diss. Loughborough U of Technology, 1990.

Alexander, Michelle. *The New Jim Crow: Incarceration in the Age of Color Blindness.* New Press, 2010.

Allen, Theodore. *The Invention of the White Race,* vol. 2: *The Origin of Racial Oppression in Anglo-America.* Verso, 1997.

Anderson, Benedict. *Imagined Communities: Reflections on the Origin and Spread of Nationalism.* 1983. Verso, 1991.

Anderson, Carol. *White Rage: The Unspoken Truth of Our Racial Divide.* Bloomsbury, 2016.

Anderson, Melanie R. *Spectrality in the Novels of Toni Morrison.* U of Tennessee P, 2013.

Andrews, William. *To Tell a Free Story: The First Century of Afro-American Autobiography, 1760–1865.* 1986. U of Illinois P, 1988.

Armstrong, Tim. *The Logic of Slavery: Debt, Technology, and Pain in American Literature.* Cambridge UP, 2012.

Ashworth, John. *Slavery, Capitalism, and Politics in the Antebellum Republic.* Vols. 1 and 2. Cambridge UP, 1995–2007.

"'At Least Half Right': Carlyle, Abolition, and the American Civil War." *Carlyle Society Papers* 16.1 (2003–4): 34–45.

Baker, Houston A., Jr. *Long Black Song: Essays in Black American Literature and Culture.* UP of Virginia, 1972.

——. *Turning South Again: Re-Thinking Modernism/Re-Reading Booker T.* Duke UP, 2001.

Baker, Thomas N. *Sentiment and Celebrity: Nathaniel Parker Willis and the Trials of Literary Fame.* Oxford UP, 2001.

Balibar, Étienne, and Immanuel Wallerstein. *Race, Nation, Class: Ambiguous Identities.* Translated by Chris Turner. 1988. Verso, 1991.

Baptist, Edward E. *The Half Has Never Been Told: Slavery and the Making of American Capitalism.* Basic Books, 2014.

Barnhill, Georgia B. "F.O.C. Darley's Illustrations for Southwestern Humor." *Graphic Arts and the South: Proceedings of the 1990 North American Print Conference.* Edited by Judy L. Larson. U of Arkansas P, 1993. 31–62.

Barrett, Lindon. "African-American Slave Narratives: Literacy, the Body, Authority." *American Literary History* 7.3 (1995): 415–43.

Beckert, Sven. *Empire of Cotton: A Global History.* Vintage Books, 2014.

Beer, Janet, and Bridget Bennett, eds. *Special Relationships: Anglo-American Affinities and Antagonisms, 1854–1936.* Manchester UP, 2002.

Beidler, Philip D. *First Books: The Printed Word and Cultural Formation in Early Alabama.* U of Alabama P, 1999.

Bell, Michael Davitt. *The Development of American Romance: The Sacrifice of Relation.* U of Chicago P, 1980.

Bendixon, Alfred. "Cable's *The Grandissimes:* A Literary Pioneer Confronts the Southern Tradition." *Southern Quarterly* 18.4 (1980): 23–33.

Benjamin, Walter. *Charles Baudelaire: A Lyric Poet in the Era of High Capitalism.* NLB, 1973.

Bernard, Jessie. "George Tucker: Liberal Southern Social Scientist." *Social Forces* 25.2 (1946): 131–45.

Bibler, Michael. "Introduction: Smash the Mason Dixon! Or, Manifesting the Southern United States." *PMLA* 131.1 (2016): 153–6.

Bizup, Joseph. *Manufacturing Culture: Vindications of Early Victorian Industry.* U of Virginia P, 2003.

Black, Andrew W. *John Pendleton Kennedy: Early American Novelist, Whig Statesman, and Ardent Nationalist.* Louisiana State UP, 2016.

Blair, Walter, ed. *Native American Humor.* American Book Co., 1937.

Blight, David W. *Race and Reunion: The Civil War in American Memory.* Harvard UP, 2001.

Bodenheimer, Rosemarie. *The Politics of Story in Victorian Social Fiction.* Cornell UP, 1988.

Bohner, Charles H. *John Pendleton Kennedy, A Gentleman from Baltimore.* John Hopkins P, 1961.

Bone, Martyn. *The Postsouthern Sense of Place in Contemporary Fiction.* Louisiana State UP, 2005.

Boston, Ray. *British Chartists in America, 1839–1900.* Manchester UP, 1971.

Bour, Isabelle. "Sensibility as Epistemology in *Caleb Williams, Waverley,* and *Frankenstein.*" *SEL* 45.4 (2005): 813–27.

Bourdieu, Pierre. *The Field of Cultural Production: Essays on Art and Literature.* Columbia UP, 1993.

Brands, H. W. *Lone Star Nation: The Epic Story of the Battle for Texas Statehood.* Doubleday, 2004.

Brooks, Van Wyck. *The World of Washington Irving.* World Publishing Co., 1944.

Budick, Emily. *Fiction and Historical Consciousness: The American Romance Tradition.* Yale UP, 1989.

Burns, Adam. *American Imperialism: The Territorial Expansion of the United States, 1783–2013.* Edinburgh UP, 2017.

Butcher, Philip. *George Washington Cable.* Twayne, 1962.

Butt, John, and Kathleen Tillotson. *Dickens at Work.* Methuen, 1957.

Byerly, Allison. "Effortless Art: The Sketch in Nineteenth-Century Painting and Literature." *Criticism* 41 (1999): 349–64.

Byerman, Keith. "We Wear the Mask: Deceit as Theme and Style in Slave Narratives." *The Art of Slave Narrative: Original Essays in Criticism and Theory.* Edited by John Sekora and Darwin T. Turner. Western Illinois UP, 1982. 70–82.

Caison, Gina. *Red States: Indigeneity, Settler Colonialism, and Southern Studies.* U of Georgia P, 2018.
Cassuto, Leonard. *The Inhuman Race: The Racial Grotesque in American Literature and Culture.* Columbia UP, 1997.
Cazamian, Louis. *The Social Novel in England, 1830–1850: Dickens, Disraeli, Mrs. Gaskell, Kingsley.* 1903. Translated by Martin Fido. Routledge, 1973.
Çelikkol, Ayşe. *Romances of Free Trade: British Literature, Laissez-Faire, and the Global Nineteenth Century.* Oxford UP, 2011.
Chamberlain, Elizabeth S. "The Virginia Historical Novel to 1835." Diss. U of North Carolina, Chapel Hill, 1979.
Chance, Joseph E. *Jefferson Davis's Mexican War Regiment.* UP of Mississippi, 1991.
Chapman, S. D. *The Cotton Industry in the Industrial Revolution.* 1972. 2nd ed. Macmillan, 1987.
Chittick, Kathryn. *Dickens and the 1830s.* Cambridge UP, 1990.
Clukey, Amy, and Jeremy Wells. "Introduction: Plantation Modernity." *Global South* 10.2 (2016): 1–10.
Clymer, Jeffory A. *Family Money: Property, Race, and Literature in the Nineteenth Century.* Oxford UP, 2012.
Coates, Ta-Nehisi. "The Black Family in the Age of Mass Incarceration." *Atlantic* (Oct. 2015).
——. "The Case for Reparations." *Atlantic* (June 2014).
Cohen, Hennig, and William B. Dillingham, eds. *Humor of the Old Southwest.* 1964. 3rd ed. U of Georgia P, 1994.
Comegna, Anthony. "'The Dupes of Hope Forever': The Loco-Foco or Equal Rights Movement, 1820s–1870s." Diss., U of Pittsburgh, 2016.
Cotterill, R. S. *The Old South: The Geographic, Economic, Social, Political, and Cultural Expansion, Institutions, and Nationalism of the Ante-bellum South.* Arthur H. Clark Co., 1936.
Cowan, William Tynes. *The Slave in the Swamp: Disrupting the Plantation Narrative.* Routledge, 2005.
Cowie, Alexander. Intro. *The Yemassee. A Romance of Carolina.* Edited by Alexander Cowie. 1835. American Book Co., 1937.
Crawford, Martin. "Old South/New Britain: Cotton, Capitalism, and Anglo-Southern Relations in the Civil War Era." *Transatlantic Exchanges.* Edited by Richard Gray and Waldemar Zacharasiewicz. Verlag der Österreichischen Akademie der Wissenschaften, 2007. 455–72.
Cunliffe, Marcus. *Chattel Slavery and Wage Slavery: The Anglo-American Context, 1830- 1860.* U of Georgia P, 1979.

Dance, Daryl. "Wit and Humor in the Slave Narrative." *Journal of Afro-American Issues* 5 (1977): 125–34.

Davidson, Cathy N. Intro. *The Coquette*. 1797. Oxford UP, 1986. vii–xx.

Davis, David Brion. *The Problem of Slavery in the Age of Revolution, 1770–1823*. 1975. *The Antislavery Debate: Capitalism and Abolitionism as a Problem in Historical Interpretation*. Edited by Thomas Bender. U of California P, 1992. 15–104.

Davis, Richard Beale. *A Colonial Southern Bookshelf: Reading in the Eighteenth Century*. U of Georgia P, 1979.

——. *Intellectual Life in the Colonial South, 1585–1763*. U of Tennessee P, 1978.

——. *Intellectual Life in Jefferson's Virginia, 1790–1830*. U of North Carolina P, 1964.

Dawson, Graham. *Soldier Heroes: British Adventure, Empire, and the Imagining of Masculinities*. Routledge, 1994.

Dekker, George. *The American Historical Romance*. Cambridge UP, 1987.

Denning, Michael. *Mechanic Accents: Dime Novels and Working-Class Culture in America*. Verso, 1987.

Donald, David. *Charles Sumner and the Coming of the Civil War*. Knopf, 1960.

——. "The Proslavery Argument Reconsidered." *Journal of Southern History* 37.1 (1971): 3–18.

Dorfman, Joseph. *The Economic Mind in American Civilization, 1606–1865*. Vol. 2. Viking P, 1946.

——. "George Tucker and Economic Growth." Intro. *The Theory of Money and Banks Investigated*. 1839. By George Tucker. Augustus M. Kelley, 1964. 5–22.

Duck, Leigh Anne. *The Nation's Region: Southern Modernism, Segregation, and U.S. Nationalism*. U of Georgia P, 2006.

Dudley, David L. *My Father's Shadow: Intergenerational Conflict in African American Men's Autobiography*. U of Pennsylvania P, 1991.

Duncan, Ian. *Modern Romance and Transformations of the Novel: The Gothic, Scott, Dickens*. Cambridge UP, 1992.

Durkheim, Émile. *The Division of Labor in Society*. 1896. Translated by George Simpson. Macmillan, 1933.

Eaton, Clement. *The Mind of the Old South*. Louisiana State UP, 1964.

Etcheson, Nicole. *Bleeding Kansas: Contested Liberty in the Civil War Era*. UP of Kansas, 2004.

Faber, Richard. *Young England*. Faber & Faber, 1987.

Fahs, Alice. *The Imagined Civil War: Popular Literature of the North and South, 1861–1865*. U of North Carolina P, 2001.

Faust, Drew Gilpin, ed. *The Ideology of Slavery: Proslavery Thought in the Antebellum South, 1830–1860.* Louisiana State UP, 1981.

——. *A Sacred Circle: The Dilemma of the Intellectual in the Old South, 1840–1860.* Johns Hopkins UP, 1977.

Fenton, Elizabeth. *Religious Liberties: Anti-Catholicism and Liberal Democracy in Nineteenth-Century U.S. Literature and Culture.* Oxford UP, 2011.

Fidler, William Perry. *Augusta Evans Wilson, 1835–1909: A Biography.* U of Alabama P, 1951.

Fogel, Robert. *Without Consent or Contract: The Rise and Fall of American Slavery.* Norton, 1989.

Fogel, Robert, and Stanley Engerman. *Time on the Cross.* Little, Brown, 1974.

Foner, Eric. "Abolitionism and the Labor Movement in Antebellum America." *Anti-Slavery, Religion, and Reform: Essays in Memory of Roger Anstey.* Edited by Christine Bolt and Seymour Drescher. Archon Books, 1980. 254–71.

——. *The Fiery Trial: Abraham Lincoln and American Slavery.* Norton, 2010.

——. *Free Soil, Free Labor, Free Men: The Ideology of the Republican Party before the Civil War.* Oxford UP, 1995.

Ford, Lacy K. *Deliver Us from Evil: The Slavery Question in the Old South.* Oxford UP, 2009.

Foster, Francis Smith. *Witnessing Slavery: The Development of Ante-bellum Slave Narratives.* Greenwood P, 1979.

Fox-Genovese, Elizabeth, and Eugene D. Genovese. *Fruits of Merchant Capital: Slavery and Bourgeois Property in the Rise and Expansion of Capitalism.* Oxford UP, 1983.

——. *The Mind of the Master Class: History and Faith in the Southern Slaveholders' Worldview.* Cambridge UP, 2005.

Freedgood, Elaine. "Banishing Panic: Harriet Martineau and the Popularization of Political Economy." *New Economic Criticism: Studies at the Intersection of Literature and Economics.* Edited by Martha Woodmansee and Mark Osteen. Routledge, 1999. 210–28.

Freehling, William W. *The Road to Disunion,* vol. 1: *Secessionists at Bay, 1776–1854.* Oxford UP, 1990.

——. *The Road to Disunion,* vol. 2: *Secessionists Triumphant, 1854–1861.* Oxford UP, 2007.

Frye, Northrop. *Anatomy of Criticism: Four Essays.* Princeton UP, 1957.

Gaines, Francis Pendleton. *The Southern Plantation: A Study in the Development and the Accuracy of a Tradition.* Columbia UP, 1925.

Gallagher, Catherine. *The Industrial Reformation of English Fiction: Social Discourse and Narrative Form, 1832–1867.* U of Chicago P, 1985.

Garcha, Amanpal. *From Sketch to Novel: The Development of Victorian Fiction.* Cambridge UP, 2009.

Genovese, Eugene. *The Slaveholders' Dilemma: Freedom and Progress in Southern Conservative Thought, 1820–1860.* U of South Carolina P, 1992.

Gervin, Cari Wade. "Protesters Have Wanted Forrest Bust Gone since Installation in 1978." *Nashville Scene,* 18 Aug. 2017.

Giles, Paul. *Atlantic Republic: The American Tradition in English Literature.* Oxford UP, 2006.

——. "Narrative Reversals and Power Exchanges: Frederick Douglass and British Culture." *American Literature* 73.4 (2001): 779–810.

——. "Transnationalism and Classic American Literature." *PMLA* 118.1 (2003): 62–77.

Gilroy, Paul. *The Black Atlantic: Modernity and Double Consciousness.* Harvard UP, 1993.

Glickstein, Jonathan A. *American Exceptionalism, American Anxiety: Wages, Competition, and Degraded Labor in the Antebellum United States.* UP of Virginia, 2002.

——. *Concepts of Free Labor in Antebellum America.* Yale UP, 1991.

Goodwyn Jones, Anne, and Susan V. Donaldson. *Haunted Bodies: Gender and Southern Texts.* UP of Virginia, 1997.

Gordon-Reed, Annette. *The Hemingses of Monticello: An American Family.* Norton, 2008.

——. *Thomas Jefferson and Sally Hemings: An American Controversy.* UP of Virginia, 1997.

Grammer, John M. *Pastoral and Politics in the Old South.* Louisiana State UP, 1996.

Gray, Richard, and Waldemar Zacharasiewicz, eds. *Transatlantic Exchanges: The American South in Europe—Europe in the American South.* Verlag der Österreichischen Akademie der Wissenschaften, 2007.

Green, Martin. *Dreams of Adventure, Deeds of Empire.* Basic Books, 1979.

Greeson, Jennifer Rae. "Expropriating *The Great South* and Exporting 'Local Color': Global and Hemispheric Imaginaries of the First Reconstruction." *American Literary History* 18.1 (2006): 496–520.

——. "The 'Mysteries and Miseries' of North Carolina: New York City, Urban Gothic Fiction, and *Incidents in the Life of a Slave Girl.*" *American Literature* 73.2 (2001): 271–309.

——. *Our South: Geographic Fantasy and the Rise of National Literature.* Harvard UP, 2010.

Grillo, Virgil. *Charles Dickens' "Sketches by Boz": End in the Beginning.* Colorado Associated UP, 1974.

Guilds, John Caldwell, ed. *"Long Years of Neglect": The Work and Reputation of William Gilmore Simms.* U of Arkansas P, 1988.

——. *Simms: A Literary Life.* U of Arkansas P, 1992.

Habermas, Jürgen. *The Structural Transformation of the Public Sphere: An Inquiry into a Category of Bourgeois Society.* 1962. MIT P, 1989.

Hack, Daniel. *Reaping Something New: African American Transformations of Victorian Literature.* Princeton UP, 2017.

Halttunen, Karen. *Confidence Men and Painted Women: A Study of Middle-Class Culture in America, 1830–1870.* Yale UP, 1982.

Hamilton, Phillip. *The Making and Unmaking of a Revolutionary Family: The Tuckers of Virginia, 1752–1830.* U of Virginia P, 2003.

Handley, George B. *Postslavery Literatures in the Americas: Family Portraits in Black and White.* UP of Virginia, 2000.

Hanlon, Christopher. *America's England: Antebellum Literature and Atlantic Sectionalism.* Oxford UP, 2013.

Hardin, Stephen. *Texian Iliad: A Military History of the Texas Revolution, 1835–1836.* U of Texas P, 1994.

Hardwig, Bill. *Upon Provincialism: Southern Literature and National Periodical Culture, 1870–1900.* U of Virginia P, 2013.

Hare, John L. *Will the Circle Be Unbroken? Family and Sectionalism in the Virginia Novels of Kennedy, Caruthers, and Tucker, 1830–1845.* Routledge, 2002.

Hartman, Saidiya. *Scenes of Subjection: Terror, Slavery, and Self-Making in Nineteenth-Century America.* Oxford UP, 1997.

Haskell, Thomas. "Capitalism and the Origins of Humanitarian Sensibility, Parts 1 & 2." 1985. *The Antislavery Debate: Capitalism and Abolitionism as a Problem in Historical Interpretation,* edited by Thomas Bender. U of California P, 1992. 105–60.

Haynes, Sam W., ed. *Contested Empire: Rethinking the Texas Revolution.* Texas A&M UP, 2015.

Hedin, Raymond. "The American Slave Narrative: The Justification of the Picaro." *American Literature* 53.4 (1982): 630–45.

Helderman, Leonard C. "A Social Scientist of the Old South." *Journal of Southern History* 2 (1936): 148–74.

Henry, Nancy, and Cannon Schmitt, eds. *Victorian Investments: New Perspectives on Finance and Culture.* Indiana UP, 2009.

Hobsbawm, Eric. "The Making of the Working Class, 1870–1914." *Workers: Worlds of Labor.* Pantheon Books, 1984.

——. *Workers: Worlds of Labor.* Pantheon Books, 1984.

Hoffheimer, Michael H. "Race and Terror in Joseph Baldwin's *The Flush Times of Alabama and Mississippi* (1853)." *Seton Hall Law Review* 39 (2009): 725–78.

Holman, C. Hugh. *The Roots of Southern Writing: Essays on the Literature of the American South.* U of Georgia P, 1972.

Homestead, Melissa. *American Women Authors and Literary Property, 1822–1869.* Cambridge UP, 2005.

Hoole, W. Stanley. *Alias Simon Suggs: The Life and Times of Johnson Jones Hooper.* U of Alabama P, 1952.

Horsman, Reginald. *Race and Manifest Destiny: The Origins of American Racial Anglo-Saxonism.* Harvard UP, 1981.

Howell, William Huntting. *Against Self-Reliance: The Arts of Dependence in the Early United States.* U of Pennsylvania P, 2015.

Hubbell, Jay B. *The South in American Literature, 1607–1900.* Duke UP, 1954.

Hughes, Helen. *The Historical Romance.* Routledge, 1993.

Huston, James L. "Theory's Failure: Malthusian Population Theory and the Projected Demise of Slavery." *Civil War History* 55.3 (2009): 354–81.

Hutchison, Coleman. *Apples and Ashes: Literature, Nationalism, and the Confederate States of America.* U of Georgia P, 2012.

Jameson, Frederic. *The Political Unconscious: Narrative as a Socially Symbolic Act.* Cornell UP, 1981.

Johanssen, Robert W. *To the Halls of the Montezumas: The Mexican War in the American Imagination.* Oxford UP, 1985.

Johnson, Walter. *River of Dark Dreams: Slavery and Empire in the Cotton Kingdom.* Harvard UP, 2013.

———. *Soul by Soul: Life inside the Antebellum Slave Market.* Harvard UP, 1999.

Jones, Paul C. *Unwelcome Voices: Subversive Fiction in the Antebellum South.* U of Tennessee P, 2005.

Jones, Suzanne W., and Richard Gray, eds. *South to a New Place: Region, Literature, Culture.* Louisiana State UP, 2002.

Jordan-Lake, Joy. *Whitewashing Uncle Tom's Cabin: Nineteenth-Century Women Novelists Respond to Stowe.* Vanderbilt UP, 2005.

Joshi, Priti. "*Michael Armstrong:* Rereading the Industrial Plot." *Frances Trollope and the Novel of Social Change.* Edited by Brenda Ayres. Greenwood P, 2002. 35–52.

Jusdanis, Gregory. *Belated Modernity and Aesthetic Culture: Inventing National Literature.* U of Minnesota P, 1991.

Justus, James H. *Fetching the Old Southwest: Humorous Writing from Longstreet to Twain.* U of Missouri P, 2004.

Kazanjian, David. "Mercantile Exchanges, Mercantilist Enclosures: Racial Capitalism in the Black Mariner Narratives of Venture Smith and John Jea." *CR: The New Centennial Review* 3.1 (2003): 147–78.

Kendi, Ibram X. *Stamped from the Beginning: The Definitive History of Racist Ideas in America.* Nation Books, 2016.

Kestner, Joseph. *Protest and Reform: The British Social Narrative by Women, 1827–1867.* U of Wisconsin P, 1985.

Kohl, Lawrence Frederick. *The Politics of Individualism: Parties and the American Character in the Jacksonian Era.* Oxford UP, 1989.

Kreyling, Michael. *Figures of the Hero in Southern Narrative.* Louisiana State UP, 1987.

——. *Inventing Southern Literature.* UP of Mississippi, 1998.

——. *The South That Wasn't There: Postsouthern Memory and History.* Louisiana State UP, 2010.

Kvach, John F. *De Bow's Review: The Antebellum Vision of a New South.* UP of Kentucky, 2013.

Ladd, Barbara. "Literary Studies: The Southern United States, 2005." *PMLA* 120.5 (2005): 1628–39.

——. *Nationalism and the Color Line in George Washington Cable, Mark Twain, and William Faulkner.* Louisiana State UP, 1996.

Lander, Ernest M., Jr. *Reluctant Imperialists: Calhoun, the South Carolinians, and the Mexican War.* Louisiana State UP, 1979.

Lang, Andrew F. "Memory, the Texas Revolution, and Secession: The Birth of Confederate Nationalism in the Lone Star State." *Southwestern Historical Quarterly* 114.1 (2010): 20–35.

——. "'Upon the Altar of Our Country': Confederate Identity, Nationalism, and Morale in Harrison County, Texas, 1860–1865." *Civil War History* 55.2 (2009): 278–306.

Lee, Julia Sun-Joo. *The American Slave Narrative and the Victorian Novel.* Oxford UP, 2010.

Lenz, William E. *Fast Talk and Flush Times: The Confidence Man as a Literary Convention.* U of Missouri P, 1985.

Lepler, Jessica. *The Many Panics of 1837: People, Politics, and the Creation of a Transatlantic Financial Crisis.* Cambridge UP, 2013.

Levander, Caroline. "Confederate Cuba." *American Literature* 78.4 (2006): 821–45.

Levecq, Christine. *Slavery and Sentiment: The Politics of Feeling in Black Atlantic Antislavery Writing, 1770–1850.* UP of New England, 2008.

Levine, Caroline. *Forms: Whole, Rhythm, Hierarchy, Network.* Princeton UP, 2015.

Levine, Robert S. *Race, Transnationalism, and Nineteenth-Century Literary Studies.* Cambridge UP, 2018.

Li, Stephanie. "Motherhood as Resistance in Harriet Jacobs's *Incidents in the Life of a Slave Girl*." *Legacy* 23.1 (2006): 14–29.

Limón, José E. *American Encounters: Greater Mexico, the United States, and the Erotics of Culture*. Beacon P, 1998.

Lowe, John Wharton. *Calypso Magnolia: The Crosscurrents of Caribbean and Southern Literature*. U of North Carolina P, 2016.

Lukács, Georg. *The Historical Novel*. 1937. Translated by Hannah and Stanley Mitchell. Beacon P, 1963.

Lynn, Kenneth S. *Mark Twain and Southwestern Humor*. Little, Brown, 1959.

MacKethan, Lucinda. Intro. *Swallow Barn; or, A Sojourn in the Old Dominion*. 1832. Louisiana State UP, 1986.

——. "Plantation Fiction, 1865–1900." *The History of Southern Literature*. Edited by Louis D. Rubin Jr. Louisiana State UP, 1985. 209–18.

Manning, Susan. "Did Mark Twain Bring Down the Temple on Scott's Shoulders?" *Special Relationships: Anglo-American Affinities and Antagonisms, 1854–1936*. Edited by Janet Beer and Bridget Bennett. Manchester UP, 2002. 8–27.

Martínez-Fernández, Luis. *Torn between Empires: Economy, Society, and Patterns of Political Thought in the Hispanic Caribbean, 1840–1878*. U of Georgia P, 1994.

Marx, Karl. *Economic and Philosophic Manuscripts of 1844*. Translated by Dirk J. Struik. International Publishers, 1964.

Marx, Karl, and Friedrich Engels. *The Communist Manifesto*. 1848. Edited by Frederic L. Bender. Norton, 1988.

May, Robert E. "Reconsidering Antebellum U.S. Women's History: Gender, Filibustering, and America's Quest for Empire." *American Quarterly* 57.4 (2005): 1155–88.

——. *The Southern Dream of a Caribbean Empire, 1854–1861*. 1973. 2nd ed. UP of Florida, 2002.

Mays, Kelly J. "Slaves in Heaven, Laborers in Hell: Chartist Poets' Ambivalent Identification with the (Black) Slave." *Victorian Poetry* 39.2 (2001): 137–63.

McColley, Robert. *Slavery and Jeffersonian Virginia*. 1964. 2nd ed. U of Illinois P, 1973.

McFeely, William S. *Frederick Douglass*. Norton, 1990.

McKee, Kathryn, and Annette Trefzer, eds. "Preface: Global Contexts, Local Literatures: The New Southern Studies." *American Literature* 78.4 (2006): 677–90.

McLean, Robert Colin. *George Tucker: Moral Philosopher and Man of Letters*. U of North Carolina P, 1961.

McPherson, Tara. *Reconstructing Dixie: Race, Gender, and Nostalgia in the Imagined South*. Duke UP, 2003.

Merish, Lori. *Archives of Labor: Working-Class Women and Literary Culture in the Antebellum United States*. Duke UP, 2017.

Merritt, Keri Leigh. *Masterless Men: Poor Whites and Slavery in the Antebellum South.* Cambridge UP, 2017.

Mesle, Sarah. "Sentimentalism's Nation: Maria J. McIntosh and the Antebellum Contexts of 'Southern' Fiction." *Studies in American Fiction* 40.2 (2013): 203–30.

Michaels, Walter Benn. *The Gold Standard and the Logic of Naturalism.* U of California P, 1987.

Moltke-Hansen, David. "Ordered Progress: The Historical Philosophy of William Gilmore Simms." *"Long Years of Neglect": The Work and Reputation of William Gilmore Simms.* Edited by John Caldwell Guilds. U of Arkansas P, 1988. 126–47.

Montgomery, David. *Citizen Worker: The Experience of Workers in the United States with Democracy and the Free Market during the Nineteenth Century.* Cambridge UP, 1993.

Moretti, Franco. *The Way of the World: The Bildungsroman in European Culture.* Verso, 1987.

Morris, Pam. *Imagining Inclusive Society in Nineteenth-Century Novels: The Code of Sincerity in the Public Sphere.* Johns Hopkins UP, 2004.

Morrison, Michael A. *Slavery and the American West: The Eclipse of Manifest Destiny and the Coming of the Civil War.* U of North Carolina P, 1997.

Morrison, Toni. *Playing in the Dark: Whiteness and the Literary Imagination.* Harvard UP, 1992.

Moss, Elizabeth. *Domestic Novelists in the Old South: Defenders of Southern Culture.* Louisiana State UP, 1992.

Noble, Donald R., Jr. Intro. *The Valley of Shenandoah; or, Memoirs of the Graysons.* By George Tucker. 1824. U of North Carolina P, 1970.

O'Brien, Michael. *Conjectures of Order: Intellectual Life and the American South, 1810–1860.* U of North Carolina P, 2004.

———. *Rethinking the South: Essays in Intellectual History.* Johns Hopkins UP, 1988.

Olney, James. "I Was Born: Slave Narratives, Their Status as Autobiography and as Literature." *Callaloo* 20.4 (1984): 46–83.

Onuf, Peter S. "Antebellum Southerners and the National Idea." *The Old South's Modern Worlds: Slavery, Region, and Nation in the Age of Progress.* Edited by L. Diane Barnes, Brian Schoen, and Frank Towers. Oxford UP, 2011. 25–46.

Osterweis, Rollin G. *Romanticism and Nationalism in the Old South.* Yale UP, 1949.

Ostrowski, Carl. "Slavery, Labor Reform, and Intertextuality in Antebellum Print Culture: The Slave Narrative and the City-Mysteries Novel." *African American Review* 40.3 (2006): 493–506.

Parks, Edd Winfield. *Ante-Bellum Southern Literary Critics.* U of Georgia P, 1962.

Patton, Robert L. *Charles Dickens and "Boz": The Birth of the Industrial-Age Author.* Cambridge UP, 2012.

Payne, David. *The Reenchantment of Nineteenth-Century Fiction: Dickens, Thackeray, George Eliot, and Serialization.* Palgrave Macmillan, 2005.

Peel, Robin, and Daniel Maudlin, eds. *Transatlantic Traffic and (Mis)Translations.* U of New Hampshire P, 2013.

Peip, Karsten H. "Liberal Visions of Reconstruction: Lydia Maria Child's *A Romance of the Republic* and George Washington Cable's *The Grandissimes.*" *Studies in American Fiction* 31.2 (2003): 165–91.

Pérez, Louis A., Jr. *Cuba in the American Imagination: Metaphor and the Imperial Ethos.* U of North Carolina P, 2008.

Peterson, Beverly. "Mrs. Hale on Mrs. Stowe and Slavery." *American Periodicals* 8 (1998): 30–44.

Phillips, Richard. *Mapping Men and Empire: A Geography of Adventure.* Routledge, 1997.

Poovey, Mary. *Genres of the Credit Economy: Mediating Value in Eighteenth- and Nineteenth-Century Britain.* U of Chicago P, 2008.

Popkin, Richard H. "George Tucker, an Early American Critic of Hume." *Journal of the History of Ideas* 13.3 (1952): 370–5.

Potter, David M. *The Impending Crisis, 1848–1861.* Harper & Row, 1976.

Reid-Pharr, Robert. *Conjugal Union: The Body, the House, and the Black American.* Oxford UP, 1999.

Reynolds, David S. *Beneath the American Renaissance: The Subversive Imagination in the Age of Emerson and Melville.* Knopf, 1988.

Rezek, Joseph. *London and the Making of Provincial Literature, 1800–1850.* U of Pennsylvania P, 2015.

Ridgely, J. V. *John Pendleton Kennedy.* Twayne, 1966.

——. *Nineteenth-Century Southern Literature.* UP of Kentucky, 1980.

——. *William Gilmore Simms.* Twayne, 1962.

Roberts, Alasdair. *America's First Great Depression: Economic Crisis and Political Disorder after the Panic of 1837.* Cornell UP, 2012.

Rodriguez, Jaime Javier. *The Literatures of the U.S.-Mexican War: Narrative, Time, and Identity.* U of Texas P, 2010.

Roediger, David R. *The Wages of Whiteness: Race and the Making of the American Working Class.* 1991. Verso, 2007.

Rohrbach, Augusta. "'Truth Stronger and Stranger than Fiction': Reexamining William Lloyd Garrison's *Liberator.*" *American Literature* 73.4 (2001): 727–55.

Romine, Scott. *The Narrative Forms of Southern Community.* Louisiana State UP, 1999.

——. *The Real South: Southern Narrative in the Age of Cultural Reproduction.* Louisiana State UP, 2008.

Rothman, Adam. *Slave Country: American Expansion and the Origins of the Deep South.* Harvard UP, 2005.

Rourke, Constance. *American Humor: A Study of the National Character.* Harcourt, Brace, 1931.

Rubin, Louis D., Jr. "The Division of the Heart: Cable's *The Grandissimes.*" *Southern Literary Journal* 1 (1969): 27–47. *Critical Essays on George Washington Cable.* Edited by Arlin Turner. G. K. Hall & Co., 1980. 195–208.

——. *The Edge of the Swamp: A Study in the Literature and Society of the Old South.* Louisiana State UP, 1989.

——. *George Washington Cable: The Life and Times of a Southern Heretic.* Pegasus, 1969.

——. *Southern Renascence: The Literature of the Modern South.* Johns Hopkins P, 1953.

Santamarina, Xiomara. *Belabored Professions: Narratives of African American Working Womanhood.* U of North Carolina P, 2005.

Schlesinger, Arthur M. *The Age of Jackson.* Little, Brown, 1945.

Sekora, John. "Black Message/White Envelope: Genre, Authenticity, and Authority in the Antebellum Slave Narrative." *Callaloo* 32 (1987): 482–515.

Sellers, Charles. *The Market Revolution: Jacksonian America, 1815–1846.* Oxford UP, 1991.

Shell, Marc. *Art and Money.* U of Chicago P, 1995.

——. *The Economy of Literature.* Johns Hopkins UP, 1978.

——. *Money, Language, and Thought: Literary and Philosophical Economies from the Medieval to the Modern Era.* U of California P, 1982.

Shields, Joanna Nichol. "A Sadder Simon Suggs: Freedom and Slavery in the Humor of Johnson Hooper." *Journal of Southern History* 56.4 (1990): 641–64.

——. "Writers in the Old Southwest and the Commercialization of American Letters." *Journal of the Early Republic* 27.3 (2007): 471–505.

Shillingsburg, Miriam J. "Simms's Failed Lecture Tour of 1856: The Mind of the North." *"Long Years of Neglect": The Work and Reputation of William Gilmore Simms.* Edited by John Caldwell Guilds. U of Arkansas P, 1988. 183–201.

Shore, Laurence. *Southern Capitalists: The Ideological Leadership of an Elite, 1832–1885.* U of North Carolina P, 1986.

Simpson, Lewis P. *The Dispossessed Garden: Pastoral and History in Southern Literature.* U of Georgia P, 1975.

Smith, Jon. *Finding Purple America: The South and the Future of American Cultural Studies.* U of Georgia P, 2013.

Smith, Jon, and Deborah Cohn, eds. *Look Away! The U.S. South in New World Studies.* Duke UP, 2004.

Smith, Laura. "'Don't Be Too Careful of Your Silks and Rags': Domesticity and Race in 19th-Century American Literature." *Literature Compass* 9.5 (2012): 343–56.

Smith, Valerie. *Self-Discovery and Authority in Afro-American Narrative.* Harvard UP, 1987.

Snavely, Tipton R. *George Tucker as Political Economist.* UP of Virginia, 1964.

Sperber, Jonathan. *The European Revolutions, 1848–1851.* 1994. Cambridge UP, 2005.

Stanley, Amy Dru. *From Bondage to Contract: Wage Labor, Marriage, and the Market in the Age of Slave Emancipation.* Cambridge UP, 1998.

Starling, Marion Wilson. *The Slave Narrative: Its Place in American History.* G. K. Hall, 1981.

Stecopoulos, Harilaos. *Reconstructing the World: Southern Fictions and U.S. Imperialisms, 1898–1976.* Cornell UP, 2008.

Stepto, Robert. *From behind the Veil: A Study of Afro-American Narrative.* U of Illinois P, 1979.

Stewart, Samuel Boyd. "Joseph Glover Baldwin." Diss. Vanderbilt U, 1941.

Stover, Johnnie M. *Rhetoric and Resistance in Black Women's Autobiography.* UP of Florida, 2003.

Straka, Gerald M. "The Spirit of Carlyle in the Old South." *Historian* 20 (1957): 39–57.

Streeby, Shelley. *American Sensations: Class, Empire, and the Production of Popular Culture.* U of California P, 2002.

Sydnor, Charles. *A History of the South: The Development of Southern Sectionalism, 1819–1948.* Vol. 5. Louisiana State UP, 1948.

Tamarkin, Elisa. *Anglophilia: Deference, Devotion, and Antebellum America.* U of Chicago P, 2008.

Tate, Adam L. *Conservatism and Southern Intellectuals, 1789–1861: Liberty, Tradition, and the Good Society.* U of Missouri P, 2005.

Taylor, Melanie Benson. *Disturbing Calculations: The Economics of Identity in Postcolonial Southern Literature, 1912–2002.* U of Georgia P, 2008.

Taylor, William R. *Cavalier and Yankee: The Old South and American National Character.* G. Braziller, 1961.

Templin, Mary. *Panic Fiction: Women and Antebellum Economic Crisis.* U of Alabama P, 2014.

Tennenhouse, Leonard. *The Importance of Feeling English: American Literature and the British Diaspora, 1750–1850.* Princeton UP, 2007.

Thomson, Rosemarie Garland. *Extraordinary Bodies: Figuring Physical Disability in American Culture and Literature.* Columbia UP, 1997.

Thorp, William. "Suggs and Sut in Modern Dress: The Latest Chapter in Southern Humor." *Mississippi Quarterly* 13 (1960): 169–75.

Tillotson, Kathleen. *Novels of the Eighteen-Forties.* Clarendon, 1954.

Tompkins, Jane. *Sensational Designs: The Cultural Work of American Fiction, 1790–1860.* Oxford UP, 1985.

Tracy, Susan J. *In the Master's Eye: Representations of Women, Blacks, and Poor Whites in Antebellum Southern Literature.* U of Massachusetts P, 1995.

Turner, Arlin. *George W. Cable: A Biography.* Duke UP, 1956.

———. "Seeds of Literary Revolt in the Humor of the Old Southwest." *Louisiana Historical Quarterly* 39 (1956): 143–51.

Vanden Bossche, Chris R. Intro. *Past and Present.* 1843. By Thomas Carlyle. U of California P, 2005. xix–lxix.

Voss, Kim. *The Making of American Exceptionalism: The Knights of Labor and Class Formation in the Nineteenth Century.* Cornell UP, 1993.

Wakelyn, Jon L. *The Politics of a Literary Man: William Gilmore Simms.* Greenwood P, 1973.

Walker, Juliet E. K. *Free Frank: A Black Pioneer on the Antebellum Frontier.* UP of Kentucky, 1983.

Walters, Ronald G. *The Antislavery Appeal: American Abolitionism after 1830.* Johns Hopkins UP, 1976.

Warren, Kenneth. *What Was African American Literature?* Harvard UP, 2011.

Watson, Charles S. *From Nationalism to Secessionism: The Changing Fiction of William Gilmore Simms.* Greenwood P, 1993.

Watson, Ritchie Devon, Jr. *The Cavalier in Virginia Fiction.* Louisiana State UP, 1985.

———. *Yeoman versus Cavalier: The Old Southwest's Fictional Road to Rebellion.* Louisiana State UP, 1993.

Watt, Ian. *The Rise of the Novel: Studies in Defoe, Richardson, and Fielding.* 1957. Chatto & Windus, 1960.

Weisbuch, Robert. *Atlantic Double-Cross: American Literature and British Influence in the Age of Emerson.* U of Chicago P, 1986.

Wells, Jeremy. *Romances of the White Man's Burden: Race, Empire, and the Plantation in American Literature, 1880–1936.* Vanderbilt UP, 2011.

Werner, Craig. "The Old South, 1815–1840." *The History of Southern Literature.* Edited by Louis D. Rubin Jr. Louisiana State UP, 1985. 81–91.

Wesling, Meg. *Empire's Proxy: American Literature and U.S. Imperialism in the Philippines.* New York UP, 2011.

Whalen, Terence. *Edgar Allan Poe and the Masses: The Political Economy of Literature in Antebellum America.* Princeton UP, 1999.

White, Hayden. *Metahistory: The Historical Imagination in Nineteenth-Century Europe.* Johns Hopkins UP, 1973.

Williams, Eric. *Capitalism and Slavery.* U of North Carolina P, 1944.

Wimsatt, Mary Ann. *The Major Fiction of William Gilmore Simms: Cultural Traditions and Literary Form.* Louisiana State UP, 1989.

Woodmansee, Martha, and Mark Osteen, eds. *The New Economic Criticism: Studies at the Intersection of Literature and Economics.* Routledge, 1999.

Woodward, C. Vann. *Origins of the New South, 1877–1913.* Louisiana State UP, 1951.

Woodworth, Steven E. *Manifest Destinies: America's Westward Expansion the Road to the Civil War.* Knopf, 2010.

Wright, Gavin. *The Political Economy of the Cotton South: Households, Markets, and Wealth in the Nineteenth Century.* Norton, 1978.

———. *Slavery and American Economic Development.* Louisiana State UP, 2006.

Wyatt-Brown, Bertram. *Southern Honor: Ethics and Behavior in the Old South.* 1982. Oxford UP, 2007.

Zimmerman, David A. *Panic! Markets, Crises, and Crowds in American Fiction.* U of North Carolina P, 2006.

INDEX